MAKING WOMEN COUNT

MARIAN SAWER is an Adjunct Professor in the School of Social Sciences, ANU, where she leads the Democratic Audit of Australia. She has published a number of books on gender, politics and public policy, including *The Ethical State? Social Liberalism in Australia* (MUP, 1990).

MAKING WOMEN COUNT

A history of the Women's Electoral Lobby in Australia

Marian Sawer
with Gail Radford

CAR
PP

A UNSW Press book

Published by
University of New South Wales Press Ltd
University of New South Wales
Sydney NSW 2052
AUSTRALIA
www.unswpress.com.au

© Marian Sawer 2008
First published 2008

National Library of Australia
Cataloguing-in-Publication entry
Author: Sawer, Marian, 1946-
Title: Making women count: a history of the Women's Electoral Lobby in Australia/
Marian Sawer.
Publisher: Sydney: University of New South Wales Press, 2008.
ISBN: 978 086840 943 6 (pbk.)
Notes: Includes index.
Subjects: Women's Electoral Lobby (Australia) – History.
        Women's rights – Australia – History.
        Women – Australia – Social conditions.
Dewey Number: 305.40994

Design Josephine Pajor-Markus
Front cover image photo of Kellie Nixon by Grant Neufeld
Printer Ligare

This book is printed on paper using fibre supplied from plantation or sustainably
managed forests.

CONTENTS

ABBREVIATIONS

ABC	Australian Broadcasting Commission/Corporation
ACT	Australian Capital Territory
ACTU	Australian Council of Trade Unions
AFWV	Australian Federation of Women Voters
AIRC	Australian Industrial Relations Commission
ALP	Australian Labor Party
ALRA	Abortion Law Reform Association
ANESBWA	Association of Non-English Speaking Background Women of Australia
ANU	Australian National University
ASIO	Australian Security Intelligence Organisation
AWEC	Australian Women's Education Coalition
AWHN	Australian Women's Health Network
BPW	Business and Professional Women (Australian Federation of)
CAPOW!	Coalition of Participating Organisations of Women
CEDAW	UN Convention on the Elimination of All Forms of Discrimination against Women (also UN Committee for the Elimination of Discrimination against Women)

CEP	Community Employment Program
CES	Commonwealth Employment Service
CSIRO	Commonwealth Scientific and Industrial Research Organisation
CWA	Country Women's Association
DLP	Democratic Labor Party
EDC	Employment Discrimination Committee
EEO	equal employment opportunity
EOWA	Equal Opportunities for Women Association
FLAG	Feminist Legal Action Group
GST	goods and services tax
IAW	International Alliance of Women
ILO	International Labour Organisation
IVF	in vitro fertilisation
IWD	International Women's Day
IWY	International Women's Year
MP	Member of Parliament
NEAT	National Employment and Training Scheme
NFAW	National Foundation for Australian Women
NGO	non government organisation
NOW	National Organization for Women (US)
NPEC	National Pay Equity Coalition
NSW	New South Wales
NWJC	National Women's Justice Coalition
NWMC	National Women's Media Centre
OSW	Office of the Status of Women
RCAGA	Royal Commission on Australian Government Administration
RTLV	Right to Life Victoria
SA	South Australia
SDA	Sex Discrimination Act
TAFE	Technical and Further Education
UAW	Union of Australian Women
UN	United Nations

US	United States
WA	Western Australia
WAA	Women's Action Alliance
WCTU	Woman's Christian Temperance Union
WEL	Women's Electoral Lobby
WIRE	Women's Information and Referral Exchange
WIS	Women's Information Switchboard
WSPU	Women's Social and Political Union
WWDA	Women with Disabilities Australia
WWWW	Women Who Want to be Women
YWCA	Young Women's Christian Association

ACKNOWLEDGMENTS

This history would not have been possible without the contributions of many people. First and foremost of these is Gail Radford, who volunteered to help with the project, little realising how many years it would take or the scale of the work involved. She co-ordinated the ambitious WEL history survey and was the key to it achieving such a good response rate. As the first convenor of WEL–ACT she had excellent networks, despite having been preoccupied for many years in reforming the employment practices of the Australian Public Service. She also co-ordinated and did much of the work in developing other databases generated by the project. These include the media database and the WEL submissions database. These searchable databases are an invaluable legacy. As well, Gail mapped the distribution of WEL groups, tracked down former co-ordinators, oversaw the accumulating archival materials and photographs, did pictorial research, obtained permission for quoting survey responses and read early drafts. She prepared the initial media report and charts analysing the patterns of WEL's media impact over time. Her reports can be found on the WEL history website at <http://wel.anu.edu.au>

Another volunteer and invaluable contributor to the project was social statistician Erica Fisher, who developed the final survey design, did the statistical analysis of the survey data and read early drafts. Other WEL members provided insightful responses to the survey, contributed to focus groups, answered queries and read drafts. Beatrice Faust, the founder of WEL, was one of those who answered our call, and the late Helen Leonard, who was WEL Executive Officer when the WEL history was conceived, was a major supporter. Juliet Richter was generous in sharing her unfinished MA thesis and Heather Gunn in sharing her work on rural WEL. Others who kindly checked sections of text include Joan Bielski, Kim Boyer, Marie Coleman, Dianne Davidson, Erica Lewis, Helen L'Orange, Winsome McCaughey, Deborah McCulloch, Val Marsden, Robyn Murphy, Chris Ronalds, Margaret Sing, Viv Szekeres, Margaret Thornton, Jo Wainer and Diana Wyndham. Gwendolyn Gray and Carol Johnson read chapters and provided useful comments, while Merrindahl Andrew, Sarah Maddison and James Jupp read the whole text and made invaluable suggestions, as did Elspeth Menzies and Sally Denmead of UNSW Press.

Research assistance and technical support was provided to the project over the years by Margot Harker, Megan Jones, Lee-Ann Monk, Sarah Morrison-Gardiner, P-J Aguilar, Gillian Evans, Robin Tennant-Wood, Peter Brent and Sonya Welykyj, while Darren Boyd and Philip Larkin scanned many pictures for us and Catherine Strong did an outstanding job in editing successive manifestations of the book. Staff at the Melbourne University Archives, the Mitchell Library, the Archives Office of Tasmania and the National Library of Australia were particularly helpful. The WEL history was funded by a three-year Australian Research Council Large Grant. Further financial assistance to support the publication of the history was provided by Eve and Frank Mahlab, Jan Harper, the Faculty of Arts at the Australian National University and the ANU's Publication Subsidy Scheme.

FOREWORD

There's something peculiarly discomfiting about reading the history of an organisation of which you were a founding member. It's not just that it situates you in the past, an uncomfortable country at the best of times, but it also challenges the way you read your own story; some of the passions and disagreements that seemed so pressing then, now look trivial, even quaint, while problems that have evolved into grave challenges today barely rated a mention then.

There can be no doubt, however, of the enthusiasm of the group of young women (of whom I was one) who met in Beatrice Faust's living room to form the Women's Electoral Lobby (WEL); we were already caught up in a global push to redesign the roles of women, no longer content to tread our preordained paths. Even the most cautious among us really did believe that we could make our mark on the political landscape in Australia; we thought the times were right to force a re-examination of women's roles and to challenge the many barriers to our full participation in Australian life. Some of us certainly harboured more radical aspirations, but were prepared at least to contemplate working for more pragmatic and tangible, short-term objectives.

As the women's liberation movement was growing in influence in the sixties, little attention was paid to translating the agenda into politically attainable demands. Indeed, some women regarded the formal political system as part of the problem. WEL, on the other hand, was formed with the explicit purpose of persuading candidates for the 1972 election to commit to policies which would improve the position of women in Australian society. We hoped to be able to define women as a distinctive constituency and to persuade politicians that progressive women's votes could determine their success or failure.

Our first major action was to conduct a survey of all the candidates for the election to gauge their knowledge, attitudes toward and proposed action on a range of issues which affected women's lives. Results would be publicised in the form of a guide to electors. The survey also provided us with a vehicle to recruit members and to debate and agree on policy in areas which needed attention: family planning, child care, women in education and the workforce, social welfare, marriage and divorce, and general areas of discrimination. While the first meeting deliberately drew on similar, successful campaigns devised by American feminists, most of us were, at first, largely unconscious of the many women who had gone before us in the Australian battle for women's equality. With the self-absorption and unflinching certainty of the young, we were confident that what we were doing was ingenious and novel. We were trailblazers – at least we thought so.

The fact that WEL enjoyed the amazing early success that this history documents made it clear that we were not alone in our eagerness for change. Women from all over the country flocked to join and to play their part in this new political phenomenon; women lobbying for policies to benefit women. For many of them, as Marian Sawer observes, this meant that 'their ways of thinking about themselves and about the world shifted irrevocably'. It was also the first time they had shared their frustrations about the limitations imposed on them and the first time they had sought to do something about it, growing in confidence and competence as they did so.

We were young, educated and impatient with the world of our mothers. We saw that the society we lived in was riddled with inequality and discrimination and stifled by conservatism and complacency. And we did not accept that this was inevitable. We had seen our mothers corralled into hearth and home, encouraged to be content with raising children and caring for their husbands while burying their own desires and talents in suburban conformity.

We argued that women were constrained by attitudes and expectations which belittled their intellectual capacity and restricted their choices and that it didn't have to be so. The general expectation, which we rejected, was that women should exclusively embrace the roles of wife and mother, leaving work and participation in public life to the men. Lest the conservative commentariat shriek – again – that we belittled motherhood and decried relationships with men, let me be clear that the prevailing view among the women I met was one of cherishing their children and wanting genuine partnership with their husbands and partners. We were neither men-haters nor po-faced apparatchiks intent on forcing others to live as we dictated. We simply wanted our country to really embrace equality and to give us a chance to live full lives.

Wherever we looked, we saw much that needed to change if we were to achieve that objective; keeping the policy agenda to a manageable size was one of the more difficult early tasks of WEL members, but we were able to agree on what mattered most. For one thing, we were no longer prepared to comply with the social expectation that we should move seamlessly from the role of daughter to wife, from one family to another, barely experiencing true independence between these life stages. Nor did we accept that every marriage should survive, no matter what the costs, or that divorce should be so frowned upon and so difficult, painful and costly to obtain. Opening up women's choices and reforming the divorce laws were critical to our project.

We saw too that while there had been a welcome improvement in the number of women completing school and going on to further study, they were still in a minority. Young girls were not encouraged to study science or maths and they were often pressured to limit their academic interests and select subjects consistent with traditional roles. It was common for WEL recruits to regale one another with stories of being coerced into leaving school early or having few options for areas of study but those deemed 'suitable' for young women. Social commentator Rosalie Stephenson remembers being told by a spiteful schoolmate that her mother was unimpressed with Rosalie's prizes because she would have 'hard work to get a husband'. Her own mother predicted spinsterhood. These experiences were repeated daily around the country. As a result, girls' underachievement was commonplace and they often left school prematurely. Improving women's education was embraced by us as a priority.

While the number of women in full-time work was rising, it was evident that women's employment was still seen as problematic, especially if they were married and had children. In fact, for women, paid work was often portrayed as simply incompatible with marriage and motherhood. Images of the 'career woman' incorporated the idea that she was in some respects de-sexed, unattractive to men and lacking in 'feminine' qualities. Rosalie observed that 'disapproval of married women working is still widespread and is based on the belief that a wife who is employed outside the home inevitably neglects her family and household duties'. Such either/or choices rankled.

Many of the women who joined WEL had tertiary qualifications and were dismayed at the blatant discrimination they encountered when they entered – or tried to enter – the workforce. In my own university it was still a requirement into the 1970s that a staff member get the permission of her head of department to marry if she wished to retain permanency. All over the country, women teachers were routinely denied permanency if they married and were required to repay their bonds. Very few women reached senior positions in any field of work since they were denied opportunities for promotion. In surveying the need for change, we were aware that in neither the public nor the private sector did women receive equal pay, and that there were no provisions for affordable child care for those mothers who did work. Both issues became strong rallying points for WEL campaigns.

When WEL was founded, women were still unable to fully control their own reproduction. Although the pill had made better fertility control possible, it was still extremely difficult and risky to have a pregnancy terminated, no matter what a woman's circumstances.

Sexual assault and violence toward women were still taboo subjects and under-reported, and women were often portrayed as contributing to their own abuse. There was little in the way of appropriate support or refuge. All of these issues engaged WEL women, either in policy development or in action to support those in need.

It's fair to say that many of the tasks placed on the initial WEL agenda and pursued with such energy over the ensuing decades are still unfinished. It is also obvious that discrimination, especially in education and employment, has been significantly reduced and that women's life choices and chances have improved. Some of the issues we campaigned on have been transformed, although not necessarily in ways we would have wished. For example, responsibility for providing child care was assumed by the federal government and there are many centres now in operation, but places, although subsidised, are increasingly unafford-able in a largely private and unregulated market. Equal pay is a legal right, but there is still a substantial pay gap stemming in part from the preponderance of women trying to balance their work and family lives by working in low-paid part-time and casual jobs that under-utilise their skills. There is also a continuing pay gap for full-time workers, reflecting in part the traditional undervaluing of women's work and the low pay of jobs in community services. There has also been relatively little success in recasting men's and women's roles and responsibilities, and violence against women remains sadly commonplace.

While our right to fully participate in society is now taken for granted, it is not always fully realised. The depiction of women in the media and entertainment is as stereotyped and superficial as it ever was. Indeed, there are reasons to think the situation may have worsened, with the unashamed sexualisation of very young girls; the image of eight-year-olds dressed by their mothers to look like hookers is deeply disturbing. And there are deeper, nagging doubts about just how much women's (and men's) lives have really improved. Does it really improve the quality of our lives to spend endless hours at work, depriving ourselves of precious time with friends and family; of time for leisure and creativity?

These caveats aside, the story of WEL deserves to be told, not least because it is a story of purpose and collaboration, of women working together to improve their lives and their society. This is not the story of individual achievement: there were no leaders and no stars. But perhaps the most remarkable characteristic of WEL was the enormous amount of energy and enthusiasm people threw into pressing for change. And the seriousness. And the impatience. And the intelligence. And the affection. And the sheer excitement of it all.

– The Hon. Carmen Lawrence

INTRODUCTION

The 'second wave' of the women's movement rolled through the Western world at the end of the 1960s as a new generation of women took up the slogan 'sisterhood is powerful'. These were women radicalised by the civil rights, anti-war and student movements but dissatisfied with their subordinate status within these so-called liberation movements: 'Only the chains have changed'. The new social movements had reproduced the old expectations that men would lead and women would follow, that men would take the microphone while women made the tea or typed the minutes. But now women began to share with each other their experiences of oppression and explore the connections between their second-hand status and the nature of their private lives.

The personal became the political. Being dissatisfied was no longer a mark of personal inadequacy but rather an indictment of society and its political arrangements – a society that, in the words of Di Graham, overlooked and wasted the skills and talents of women, marooned them in the suburbs, expected them to spend the most productive part of their lives in housework, and then discounted their views as simply those of 'housewives'.

New frames for viewing the world revealed the political nature of women's subordination and opened up the possibility of changing that subordination through political action. While some of the new women's movement groups pinned their hopes on revolutionary social transformation, others emerged to press for legislative and policy change. In the United States, Betty Friedan founded the National Organization for Women in 1966 to put pressure on the Equal Employment Opportunity Commission to take up its mandate on sex discrimination. In Canada, the umbrella National Action Committee on the Status of Women was launched in April 1972 to press for the implementation of the recommendations of the Royal Commission on the Status of Women, which had reported two years before.

In Australia, the Women's Electoral Lobby (WEL) became another of the new organisations springing up across the globe to take to government the demands of newly mobilised women. WEL's forms of action were initially borrowed from elsewhere but were successfully adapted for local purposes. The young women who founded the new second-wave organisations here were aware of what other new social movements were doing, and of what women were doing in the United States, but they knew relatively little about what women had already done over generations of feminist advocacy in this country. This historical amnesia reflected the biases of those who had previously been writing the history books but also, sometimes, a rejection of the 'politeness' of the immediately preceding generation.

One clear example of the reinvention of repertoire long practised by the women's movement was the rating of politicians on their attitudes to issues of particular concern to women. This repertoire dated back to campaigns for suffrage and social reform in the 1890s and was still being used in the 1960s in Australia and other countries. Yet when it was reinvented at the beginning of the 1970s and given a new professional gloss, it captured the imagination of the media and brought many recruits to the women's movement, most of them totally unaware of the century of feminist rating of political candidates that had preceded them. One new factor was that the influx of women into higher education meant that social science and even the computer could now be brought to bear in surveying male politicians.

In the United States, at the end of 1971, high-profile feminist speaker and activist Gloria Steinem used all her renowned powers of persuasion to conduct an experiment – a professionally-produced women's magazine (rather than a roneoed newsletter) to be run by feminists. A preview edition of *Ms.* magazine was published as a 'one-shot' sample insert in *New York* magazine. It carried the article on the rating of US presidential candidates which sparked off a series of similar initiatives in other countries. While the *Ms.* survey involved a wide-ranging questionnaire and follow-up interviews, the ratings were presented in a popular style with symbols to indicate the categories 'taking women seriously', 'making waves' and the 'machismo factor'. Pictures and profiles of candidates were included, with their attitudes towards various social policy and women's rights issues. Ted Kennedy, for example, relied on his 'boiler room girls', who kept the Kennedy machine going but were 'rewarded with parties not promotions'.[1]

In Australia the *Ms.* ratings of candidates certainly inspired Beatrice Faust, the founder of WEL. As we shall see in this history, she had observed Women's Liberation in Melbourne but was tired of talk and wanted action. In February 1972 she brought a hand-picked group of women together, including journalists, to see if they could replicate the American exercise. This was the beginning of WEL. In Canada the *Ms.* ratings also inspired Doris Anderson, the editor of the largest-circulation Canadian women's magazine, *Chatelaine*. In May 1972 she ran a cover report on a survey, conducted by registered letter, of all members of parliament, and interviews organised with a smaller number, including Liberal Cabinet ministers. The topics ranged from equal pay, retraining and child care to abortion and pensions for housewives. She provided tabulated results as well as vignettes from the interviews, such as the Progressive Conservative MP who had no time for Women's Liberation but liked women to be 'soft, gentle, kind and feminine'. Anderson advised readers to take a long look at the man or woman they were going to vote for.[2] This was very similar to the form-guide WEL issued later in the year.

Like women's organisations in North America, WEL followed up its candidate surveys with public meetings where candidates and party leaders were 'grilled' on their attitudes to women's issues. Politicians were shown up as rank amateurs in terms of their knowledge of matters of vital importance to women, such as child care. At the same time as this very public repertoire was grabbing attention, WEL was also developing policy skills and impressing at least one professor of political science, who wrote in the *Australian* that WEL 'has managed to get down to detailed and well researched submissions and to clearly impress politicians with the importance of feminism to such an extent that they run after it, not WEL after them'.[3] There were to be some 900 of these submissions by the time of writing the WEL History. As Senator Pat Giles observed in 1989, when giving the inaugural Pamela Denoon Lecture, the word 'submission' took on a new meaning for women.

WEL was born under unusually favourable circumstances, with 23 years of conservative federal government about to end and with a reform-minded government about to be elected. But WEL did not just inherit favourable political opportunities; it helped create them. The new federal Labor government might have been bent on reform, but the Australian Labor Party did not even have a women's policy in its platform when it was elected. In the 1972 campaign it was WEL that put women's issues near the top of the electoral agenda for the first time and extracted commitments from all parties. Even the conservative Prime Minister, William McMahon, agreed to a Royal Commission into the Status of Women. The Labor Party committed to immediate action on equal pay and removal of the luxury tax on the pill, as well as responding positively to a host of other WEL demands. Such was WEL's impact that, for the next thirty years, no major party would go to an election without a women's policy.

But WEL was not only shaping the political agenda, it was also transforming its members' lives. Discovering how little politicians knew about things that mattered was empowering as well as enraging. The increased confidence and skills that came from WEL membership flowed through into new careers and new directions for women who had been marooned in the suburbs with their Bex headache powders.

They discovered sisterhood and the power of an idea whose time has come which propelled them into government and into new services designed to take women seriously. They would never look back with nostalgia to those pre-feminist days when decision-making was left to men who thanked their wives for packing their bags but left them and their needs behind.

A note on sources

From the very beginning, WEL members showed awareness of the fact that they were participating in the making of women's history and the reshaping of the political world. Some were too busy making history to pay much attention to recording it – and all were extraordinarily busy in those early years, balancing families, second-chance education, jobs and WEL lobbying. In the early years WEL members were also heavily involved in providing information to women in the community on health, family law and other matters, a function performed by all WEL groups before they succeeded in getting publicly-funded women's information services established. They were also establishing child-care centres and women's services such as refuges, and rostering themselves as volunteer workers until funding finally came through from government.

However, some members were very conscious of the need to preserve good records, most notably Katy Richmond of WEL–Victoria. In August 1973 she was already pleading with WEL groups to keep their material for future historians. She talked of being inundated by students doing theses on WEL as a pressure group. WEL–Victoria led the way, with a librarian sorting and filing material prior to archiving at the University of Melbourne archives.[4] In Sydney a similar problem was being experienced in terms of pressure from students. One member commented, 'as an informal organisation we seem increasingly to be regarded as a curiosity to be researched and recorded in some detail by a variety of students before we disintegrate into oblivion as have other women's pressure groups'.[5]

In fact, the records of WEL's activities over 35 years are voluminous, held in libraries and archives across Australia as well as in members' garages. By 1974–75 there were 52 groups in regional and rural Australia, quite apart from the metropolitan and suburban groups. They were prolific publishers of newsletters, position papers, election questionnaires and briefing kits, quite apart from conference papers, correspondence, policy submissions and media monitoring. The very bulk of this material has posed a barrier to a full-scale history, despite a number of valuable theses and small-scale histories.[6]

WEL groups not only surveyed political candidates, they also surveyed themselves: data on membership characteristics and attitudes exists almost from the beginning. Supplementing this data are the autobiographical accounts of the organisation's impact on the lives of its members. These accounts appear in collections such as those edited by Jocelynne Scutt, herself a WEL activist. Some early leaders have published autobiographies, including Susan Ryan, Wendy McCarthy and, most recently, Margaret Reynolds.

Over the years 2001–07 the WEL history project trawled through all this material, reading the records of the groups around Australia, their newsletters, submissions and organisational histories, as well as the theses and personal accounts. In addition, the project has generated new data, firstly from a large-scale membership survey conducted in 2002–03. This employed 42 questions seeking information about membership characteristics and attitudes as well as providing space for memories of WEL. There were 550 responses, which have been analysed in terms of four cohorts, corresponding to changes in federal government. The cohorts consist of members who joined in the McMahon/Whitlam period; the Fraser period; the Hawke/Keating period and the Howard period. Focus groups were also conducted with members from these different cohorts to follow up some of the hints from the survey data concerning changing organisational dynamics. Detailed reports on the survey data can be found on the WEL history website at <http://wel.anu.edu.au>

The history project has also prepared several large searchable databases that indicate the range of the policy interests of different WEL groups over time, and WEL's media impact. The media database has some 4200 items and is also searchable by subject, date and media type. There is a bias towards the print media in the database and towards metropolitan rather than regional or suburban newspapers. In addition, the online newspaper databases available from the mid-1980s provide more comprehensive coverage than the earlier clippings services. The WEL history used Parliamentary Library and other clippings files for the early period and Factiva and ParlInfo for the later years. Federal parliamentary debate is available in searchable digital format only from 1981. Mentions of WEL before 1981 eluded the Hansard index and had to be painstakingly extracted from the printed debates.

The submissions database covers some 900 submissions prepared over thirty years and can be searched by subject, date and WEL group responsible. Other new data provided by the project includes mapping the distribution of WEL groups in regional and rural Australia in the 1970s. These maps are available on the history website, as is a selection of the many photographs generously provided by members, together with WEL posters.

The history of WEL is an ongoing project and this book does not pretend to be the final word on the subject. But we trust that these beginnings will prompt others to amplify the record and use the resources that we have accumulated.

1

THE BIRTH OF WEL

'The girl from WEL', read the story in the *Sun*, which featured a slim young WEL member striding toward the camera with her tote-bag of WEL T-shirts for sale. 'Hubbies hold the baby', read the story on the next page. It was January 1973 and WEL's first national conference was being held in Canberra. There was an all-male staff of nine working on the conference desk and there would have been more men at the conference, a spokeswoman assured a reporter, if they hadn't been at home baby-sitting. Attractive young women and husbands holding the babies were the main story. But if readers persevered to page 32, there was a whole page on WEL's demands for things such as an equal opportunity commission and an enquiry into discrimination in hiring apprentices.[1]

The mixed messages found in the media were part of the heady world of the early days of WEL. Could women be young and attractive and still want equal opportunity? What about men – could they support the challenge to gender roles and the redistribution of domestic work that seemed to be required? Would women abandon the home?

The conference was held less than two months after the first Australian election in which 'women's issues' had become an important campaign theme. In 1972, the auspices were particularly promising for those seeking change. The conservative Coalition government, in power for 23 years, had clearly grown old in office and was out of step with the times. It was being challenged by a modernising Labor Party, reaching out to the young and to the new social movements. Labor was extending the language of equal opportunity beyond its traditional class-based boundaries to encompass women, migrants and Aboriginal Australians. The economy was buoyant, there were more educated women than ever before, and in general the political opportunity structure could not have been more favourable for a new push by the women's movement.

WEL's effect on the political agenda made its conference a major news story. More than 350 women had 'untied their apron strings, shoved aside typewriters and hung up their professional gowns and white coats' to come to Canberra.[2] There was excitement at being part of history and of historic social change. For those used to political conferences there had never been a gathering like it. 'Women were serious, warm, happy. No evidence of fanaticism, factionalism, bigotry, purity or mania.'[3] While other families were holidaying at the coast, WEL members were sitting in the heat in a tent, listening to lawyer Mary Gaudron. In its first week in office the Whitlam government had asked her to reopen the equal pay case. Two days later came the decision that one and a half million working women would now be eligible for full pay. Fourteen years later she became the first woman on the High Court.

Frances MacGillycuddy, 'The girl from WEL', WEL's first national conference. *The Sun,* 22 January 1973, p. 7. *Courtesy The Herald and Weekly Times Pty Ltd.*

Time to move beyond talk

Although the opportunities were local, the new ways of looking at the world had largely come from overseas. Women active in the anti-Vietnam War movement seized upon the roneoed Women's Liberation material brought back from the United States. American sisters opened their eyes to their lack of equality in this supposedly radical movement. As the first Australian Women's Liberation leaflet said: 'Only the Chains Have Changed'.[4] In 1968 small groups of women in Chicago and New York had adopted a new mode of political action that came to be known as consciousness-raising. It drew on the way that black activists in the civil rights movement had testified about their personal experiences of oppression and also on Mao's slogan, 'Speak pain to recall pain'. Consciousness-raising involved women speaking in turn from their life experiences within a supportive group. They learned from the similarities of their stories that their problems were political rather than just personal. In fact the personal *was* political. This became the characteristic mode of action of the loosely organised groups known as Women's Liberation, first set up in Australia in 1969–70.

Women's Liberation arrived in Melbourne but WEL founder Beatrice Faust quickly became convinced it was time for the women's movement to move beyond talk. Again the inspiration was from the United States – an article in the preview issue of Gloria Steinem's *Ms.* magazine about how feminists had been rating presidential candidates.[5] With a federal election looming in Australia, it seemed a perfect time to try something similar.

In February 1972, Faust called a meeting of ten women in her own house in Carlton (Melbourne) and WEL was born. The ten included journalists Iola Hack (Mathews) and Sally White, psychologist Carmen Lawrence and sociologist Jan Harper. The first public meeting, advertised in *The Age* and *Nation Review*, took place in April. The initial plan was to survey Victorian candidates through a mail-out questionnaire on their attitudes to issues such as equal pay and equal opportunity, child care, abortion and family planning. Faust had already been getting medical students from Monash University to write to members of parliament (MPs) asking about their views on abortion, using the name 'Parliamentary Abortion Lobby', the prototype for 'Women's Electoral Lobby'.

The name 'Women's Electoral Lobby' (WEL) caught on from the start and lent itself to slogans such as 'Think WEL before you vote'. The women whom Faust summoned all had professional skills of some kind or another, and this was to be a hallmark of the new organisation. Women journalists played a crucial role in the media impact of WEL in its first year and hence on further recruitment of members, while the young social scientists worked on survey design and professional credibility. These were exciting days as women discovered the power of collective action and sharing of new skills. In the words of one member:

> Never one to do anything by halves, I flung myself into the activities of Women's Electoral Lobby, soon being on the co-ordinating committee, editing the Broadsheet, interviewing politicians, appearing on television and radio, helping to write submissions, visiting Canberra. They were heady days. Groups of us would sit up all night, planning and writing. The subject was new, so the impact of our findings was great. We found supportive women of all ages in every profession, in every suburb, in the country, in other states. We realised what could be achieved by working together. We discovered we had power.[6]

There were some initial hiccups, and few responses to the initial mail-out version of the survey. It was decided it must be face to face, with two women present at each interview, one to conduct the interview and one to scribe. And it had to be national. The group in Melbourne would need assistance from women all around Australia. Faust set off to other capital cities to talk to women about founding WEL groups. WEL had to come into being on a national scale to make an impact in the election.

The survey turned out to be an ideal exercise for mobilising women, many of whom had no previous contact with the women's movement and had not previously been involved in politics. Many read about the WEL survey in newspaper articles and were attracted by the idea of 'doing something practical'. Others were drafted to interview candidates in far-flung electorates. They 'hunted in pairs' and became famous for their persistence in pursuit of reluctant candidates.

The interviews were a revelation as women found out how little the male candidates, of whom they had often been in awe, knew about the issues of concern to women. A not untypical reaction was: 'What does this peanut think he's doing standing for parliament?' One interviewer found that she was repeating like a cockatoo, 'That's nice, that's nice', as candidates kept telling her, 'My wife is quite happy to stay at home with the children'.[7] Another wrote:

> I'll never forget my interview with the experienced and powerful member of parliament who fumbled and stuttered when asked about sex discrimination, mumbling something about sexuality and people's freedom, trying to figure out what he was supposed to think about sex.[8]

Young social scientists helped devise the 45-item candidate questionnaire, not without some strong disagreements that threatened to derail the whole process. In Melbourne, psychologists Carmen Lawrence and Pat Strong and sociologist Helen Glezer favoured a format that would help educate the candidates and commit them to action, as well as obtaining information on attitudes. In Sydney, WEL members led by Eva Cox favoured a simpler market research-type tick-a-box model.

The questions were designed to probe candidates' knowledge of existing facilities for child care, family planning and retraining for women re-entering the workforce; their attitudes on issues such as sex education in schools or discrimination against working women; and their willingness to commit to action on issues such as removing the ban on the advertising and display of contraceptives or introducing anti-discrimination legislation.[9] The survey epitomised WEL's belief in 'evidence-based change', serving to educate both the candidates and the women doing the interviews.

There were over 600 federal candidates to be interviewed. While WEL tried to have women from the relevant electorate interview candidates, some candidates were interviewed in airports and Canberra WEL members interviewed those who were sitting MPs at Parliament House. The least co-operative were the mainly Catholic Democratic Labor Party (DLP) candidates. A WEL member in Bennelong reported that a Catholic candidate 'threatened to throw us out of his office if we mentioned the word sex again'.[10]

The impact of the survey on the political agenda was remarkable. Women journalists helped sell its academic credentials to editors and it was given wide coverage in broadsheets and tabloids throughout Australia. As a result of the media coverage, there was a very high survey response rate: 77 per cent rising to 94 per cent if the DLP were excluded. *The Age* printed the form guide for Victorian candidates as a particularly successful lift-out Green Guide.[11] *Age* journalists Sally White and Iola Hack (Mathews) had persuaded the editor, Creighton Burns, that the survey results were academically respectable and should be given a run. The *National Times* described WEL on its front page as the 'rising new force in Australian politics', while Nancy Dexter wrote in *The Age*: 'The 1972 federal election must go down in history as the first in which the average woman is really interested. Much of this interest is due to WEL ...' Robert Turnbull, in the *New York Times*, described WEL as 'an organized and formidable factor' in the election campaign.[12] No other non-party organisation was so successful at promoting its issues during a federal election until the Tasmanian Wilderness Society/Australian Conservation Foundation combination in the 1983 campaign.

The ALP had gone into the 1972 election without a women's policy[13], but its shadow ministers tended to be distinctly more responsive to the issues WEL was raising than Coalition ministers, foreshadowing some dramatic improvements for women if the ALP won government. While Prime Minister William McMahon gave his WEL interviewers half an hour, the Foreign Minister, Nigel Bowen, could spare them only thirteen minutes and doubted there was anybody in Australia who didn't know about birth control. The Minister for the

Environment, Aborigines and the Arts, Peter Howson, was 'unaware of any areas of discrimination against women' while the Minister for Education, Malcolm Fraser, thought that to allow the advertising or display of contraceptives would be offensive.[14]

In South Australia, a complaint was lodged with the Electoral Office by a sitting member, Sir John McLeay, about failure to place an authorisation at the bottom of leaflets carrying the detailed WEL ratings. WEL–SA withdrew 3500 leaflets and arranged to have them overprinted with authorisation and the printer's name. When it was realised that whoever provided the authorisation was likely to be charged with an electoral offence, Karla Tan volunteered, because as a 'housewife' she would be least affected by a conviction. In fact she became interested in the law as a result of her involvement in WEL and had to disclose the conviction when admitted to the bar. The young printer was so upset by the Federal Police inquiry that he sold his printing press.[15]

The question of how much information to provide on the performance of parties rather than individual candidates was controversial, given fears of being accused of partisanship. WEL in Brisbane telegrammed its intention 'to resign en masse with [a] blaze of publicity' if any party breakdown was provided, and South Australia was similarly disaffected.[16] The WEL media action group, on the other hand, was conscious that this was the information journalists wanted and could, in any case, extract from the data on individual candidates.

Despite these hiccups, the overall effect of WEL's intervention in the 1972 federal campaign was such that political parties no longer felt comfortable going into election campaigns without a women's policy. As we shall see, this was to remain true for more than thirty years.

WEL–Victoria meeting, Mary Owen leaning forward in the centre. 'The Women Voters' Guide', *The Age*, 20 November 1972. *The Age Archives, courtesy The Age.*

Recruiting

To turn the survey into a national exercise and to spread WEL beyond Melbourne, Faust sent out letters to her existing abortion law reform and Women's Liberation networks. The Abortion Law Reform Association (ALRA) preceded the arrival of the new wave of the women's movement and provided many of its early members. A survey conducted at the national WEL conference in January 1973 found almost a fifth of those present had an ALRA background.[17]

Faust anticipated resistance from Women's Liberation because of its rejection of reformist action. Her letter to a Women's Liberation contact in Canberra said: 'If you believe the democratic process is useless, perhaps you could pass this on to someone who still has hopes of it'.[18] The letter was passed on to Gail Wilenski, who with others had already created a Women's Liberation action workshop. Wilenski responded positively, saying that the workshop would establish a subcommittee of WEL. Faust travelled to Sydney and Brisbane to talk to women about starting WEL groups and would have come to Canberra but missed the plane – so WEL had to begin in Canberra without her.

In Sydney, a meeting was organised at the house of Julia Freebury, an ALRA activist. Those attending were only mildly enthusiastic, feel-

Table 1.1   Founding of metropolitan WEL groups

1972	February	WEL–VIC
	May	WEL–NSW
	May	WEL–ACT
	June	WEL–QLD
	July	WEL–TAS
	July	WEL–SA
	August	WEL–NT
1973	March	WEL–WA
1975	March	WEL–NZ

ing that Faust was too critical of Germaine Greer and Women's Liberation, but Caroline Graham accepted the role of convenor and Wendy McCarthy and June Surtees (later Williams) became the deputy convenors of the new organisation. In 1972 it wasn't always easy to find WEL in Sydney – one woman was said to have waited in a carpark beside a car with a WEL sticker until the owner returned so she could join.

In Brisbane, the meeting was organised at the house of Barbara Wertheim or, rather, in a shallow, drained swimming pool in her garden that was used as a conversation pit. Thirty years later, women had memories of feminist campaigner Merle Thornton collecting cane toads from the floor of the pool during this meeting, as her young son sold toads to the university laboratories to supplement his pocket money. Thornton decided not to join WEL because she mistakenly saw it as a women-only organisation, but not long afterwards she was an inspiring guest speaker at a weekend workshop organised by WEL–Darwin.

Further south, WEL was also spreading to Adelaide and Hobart. In Adelaide WEL started with thirteen members and had its first public meeting in late July; by September, it had more than 100 members and soon claimed 1000, inspired by an idea whose time had come – that women deserved a better deal from politicians.[19] Around Australia, many members joined after reading about the WEL survey and the need for more volunteers. The enormous publicity generated by Germaine Greer, touring Australia to promote the paperback edition of her book *The Female Eunuch*, also helped. Her book, 'which was everywhere', was a turning point for many women who joined WEL and were hungry for action.

These founding meetings aroused the suspicion of the Australian Security Intelligence Organisation (ASIO), for whom women's rights were part of a communist agenda. The flyers advertising the first WEL meetings were collected and 'inquiries' made of those involved.[20] Sharing premises with Women's Liberation and anti-war groups or, in Hobart, with the Committee for Democracy in Chile, fuelled these suspicions.

WEL took a little longer to reach Western Australia. A few WA

WEL–Darwin members modelling T-shirts, 1974. L to R, Lucille Kidney, Leith Cameron, Lenore Coltheart and Maureen McDonald (Cleary). *Lenore Coltheart.*

activists, including Pat Giles from Women's Liberation, had managed to join WEL and travelled to Canberra for the first national conference. On their return they set up WEL in Perth and held a packed first meeting in March 1973 in the Nursing Federation Hall. Pat Giles, later to have an illustrious political career, became the inaugural convenor.

WEL was spreading not only in Australia but also over the Tasman. In March 1975 the desire to move beyond talk to action brought into being WEL–New Zealand. Marijke Robinson described the catalyst as a party held at Victoria University in Wellington to honour visiting socialist feminist writer, Juliet Mitchell, at which Mitchell said that if women really wanted to bring about change they would have to develop a theory. Robinson, then doing sociology honours, had not been able to find any theory that satisfactorily explained women's oppression. She got up at question time and expressed her impatience with the idea that action would have to wait on theory:

> It's all very well to say we have to know what we are doing,
> and to have a theory, but in the meantime we are being
> oppressed and those men on the Hill, in Parliament, are doing
> whatever they like while we're not getting anywhere. I say,
> let's just do something about that, as women, as a pressure
> group. I have just heard about WEL in Australia. Let's do
> something like that![21]

In recalling this moment, Robinson added: 'This was the first time I had ever spoken in public, and I remember I had a glass of sherry in my hand when I rose to speak. When I sat down I had absolutely no sherry left in my glass – it had all shaken out.' Judy Zavos, just returned from Australia where she had been impressed by WEL's successes, came up to Robinson afterwards and the planning of WEL–New Zealand began.

The foundation story of WEL–New Zealand shows clearly the role of emotions in political mobilisation. It was indignation at injustice and the desire to do something practical about it that propelled women into action, not the calculation of interests nor the light of theory. One of the founders of WEL in Coffs Harbour, New South Wales, was amazed at the level of anger expressed at the first meeting there: 'The intensity of the anger staggered me. Every story told of discrimination in the work place and repressive sexist attitudes'.[22] This story of pent-up rage over discrimination is one that is often told and is a key to the energy women poured into WEL in its early years.

From the beginning, the under-employment of tertiary-educated women was often seen as the impulse behind WEL.[23] Women's participation in higher education had been expanding fast in the 1960s but the barriers to careers, particularly for married women, were still firmly in place. Of WEL members who joined in 1972–75, just over half had at least a bachelor degree; this proportion rose to around three quarters in later years, with the removal of tertiary fees. Of those in paid employment, the most common profession was teaching. The contrast with the broader population was very marked, with the 1971 census showing only 1 per cent of women having a university degree. An early survey of Victorian WEL members concluded that they were a 'homogeneous group of young well-educated women [who were] characteristically married to liberal, professional or "white-collar" husbands'.[24]

While university qualifications were stressed in establishing the credibility of the election survey, when seeking to establish the representative credentials of WEL other characteristics were emphasised. In South Australia, for example, WEL's publicity officer stressed that 'WEL is not a top-heavy, intellectual organisation. Its followers come from the ranks of housewives (who make up 47 per cent of the membership), shop assistants, typists and dressmakers, as well as professional and career women'.[25]

Nonetheless, in all cities around Australia there was a pool of educated women who seemed to have been waiting for WEL. Marriage bars, lack of child care and plain discrimination were preventing many from using their qualifications in paid employment. They were often stranded in new suburbs with their children, with little in the way of support services or intellectual companionship. 'The woman isolated in the home' was a frequent topic at early WEL conferences, and one such woman later wrote:

> In the 1970s, I was one of the women in the new housing
> developments around Adelaide who suffered a special kind
> of isolation … with a working-studying husband and three
> young children, domesticity engulfed me and I felt starved
> intellectually. Salvation arrived unexpectedly. At a school
> Mother's Club meeting, a letter was tabled from a new group
> called Women's Electoral Lobby. I joined immediately …
> I was swept along with the excitement and energy of this
> lobby group and my sense of isolation diminished … Acts
> of Parliament, Hansard, statistics and official submissions
> became part of my daily life when I joined the Australia-wide
> team lobbying for the abolition of succession duties between
> spouses.[26]

Around three quarters of the first cohort of WEL members were married and had children when they joined. In fact, 38 per cent had children under school age. Early surveys of membership, such as one conducted

WEL members marching with their children, Sydney, International Women's Day 1975. *WEL–NSW Office.*

in Western Australia in 1974, confirm the WEL history's finding that the statistically average member at that period was aged between 26 and 35, was married and had between one and three children.[27] The organisations in which WEL members were most likely to have been active before joining WEL were Parents and Citizens Associations or their equivalents. Marjorie Luck described how a guest speaker at the Taroona Primary School Mothers Club shocked her into joining WEL–Tasmania in 1972: 'Women who sell men's shoes get paid less than men who sell men's shoes. Women who sell women's shoes get paid even less'.[28]

Motherhood meant women were more likely to be out of the paid workforce, to be available for WEL activities and to have a keen interest in child care. WEL was seen as a comfortable place for women with young children. Conversely, it was possible for single women to feel WEL did not sufficiently cater for them. In 1973, Anne Summers told a journalist that she was not a member of WEL because it was too much occupied with child care in which, as a childless woman, she was not greatly interested.[29] Ironically, one of Summers' great coups when she first went into government as head of the Office of Status of Women was to get the Hawke government to commit to 20 000 new child-care places for the 1984 election policy.

Perhaps linked to their higher levels of education, WEL members also differed from the general population of women in terms of religion. WEL members were more secular than the norm, with 80 per cent later claiming they had no religious affiliation when they joined. By contrast, only 5 per cent of all women in the 1971 census admitted to having no religious denomination. Twice as many WEL members had grown up as Anglicans (30 per cent) than as Catholics (14 per cent), contrary to some later mythologies. A large proportion (28 per cent) also came from 'other denominations', perhaps reflecting the traditional links between dissenting protestant churches and the women's movement.

The history survey reveals that the characteristics of WEL members changed quite dramatically over thirty years, with the later cohorts reflecting general social changes. For example, while three quarters of the first WEL members were married, by the time of those joining in the Howard era only one third were married. The proportion of those with children went down from 72 per cent to around 50 per cent while the proportion of those in paid employment rose significantly.

Unlike Women's Liberation, WEL always had a few men among its membership, usually supportive husbands or partners. Indeed, in 1975 Georgette and Howard Whitton took a turn as joint editors of the WEL–ACT Newsletter. From time to time questions were raised concerning men's participation in specific events, but on the whole support was gratefully received.

From the start WEL was raising Aboriginal issues, including in the initial mail-out survey. In Canberra, Aboriginal woman Pat Eatock and her baby lived for some time in the Bremer Street Women's House attending WEL and Women's Liberation meetings. She had to stay until the end of all the meetings as they were held in the room where she slept.[30] She stood in the 1972 federal elections as a Black Liberation

candidate and topped WEL's ratings for the ACT with all the knowledge she had gained. However, despite supporting Aboriginal issues,
WEL was not successful in attracting more than a handful of Aboriginal
members.

Not enough ashtrays

Did WEL members in the 1970s conform to our image of how middle-
class reformers behave? Witness the letter sent by WEL to the Tasmanian
Teachers' Federation in May 1974:

> Dear Miss Backhouse,
>
> I have been instructed by the Women's Electoral lobby to
> write to you on the matter raised in your letter of May 8th.
> We are sorry that your cleaners have been put to such an
> effort cleaning after our public meeting and regret that those
> attending should have ground out their cigarette butts into the
> cork floor. Unfortunately there were not enough ashtrays to
> give each of our 300 participants one each; perhaps the problem
> will be solved in future by the provision of No Smoking signs
> in the hall.[31]

In Canberra, Maureen Worsley, soon to be elected to the Legislative
Assembly for the Australia Party, was dissatisfied not only with the
lack of voting procedures at WEL meetings but also with 'sitting in an
overcrowded room on six square inches of carpet with a matchbox for
an ashtray and being exhorted to empty my ashtray, "clear up your
shit sister" etc'.[32] While WEL members might eschew fashion items
such as high-heeled shoes that were 'harmful to the body', like other
social movement activists of the period they smoked a lot, and drank
more wine than would today be considered good for them. They were
caught up in the heady business of changing the world, a process that
might require sitting around a cask of white wine on the floor until late
at night or 'drilling ourselves like a military operation' for meetings
with federal ministers. In the early years WEL meetings sometimes
went on until three in the morning:

there were the long nights of submission writing, of sitting
together at someone's house with wine or coffee and a plate
of raw vegetables and dip or cake and biscuits, talking over
the issues … Slowly, over nights of discussion, our submission
would emerge, combining our insights and the facts we would
gather between meetings … After presentation to a WEL
general meeting for endorsement, the submission was sent off
and a strategy enacted for getting it heard. We might make
visits to key people, or give radio interviews, or organise a
mailing of copies to everyone that came to mind.[33]

While much of this repertoire was not too different from that of older
women's organisations such as the Australian Federation of Women
Voters, the style was definitely different. WEL women tended to be
forthright on matters of sex and access to contraception and abortion,
in a manner sometimes shocking to older women's rights campaigners, who had pressed for the abolition of the double standard through
'purity for men' rather than sexual freedom for women.

WEL women had high energy levels and were incredibly busy – they
wanted to change the world and there were a lot of half-open doors
waiting to be pushed. Every opportunity had to be taken, regardless of
timing. In South Australia, one of the WEL members giving evidence
to a parliamentary inquiry into sex discrimination had contractions
throughout the hearing and gave birth at 6 o'clock that evening. In
Western Australia, Yvonne Henderson had to feed her newborn baby
in the State Arbitration Commission while presenting WEL's equal pay
submission. In Sydney, Wendy McCarthy was delivering press releases
around town during the day with the children in the back seat, going
to meetings at night and returning home exhilarated.[34]

Government agencies and public institutions still practised many
overt as well as covert forms of discrimination against women, as did
private companies. WEL members developed a 'nose for discrimination'. They sent off letters to Ministers and chief executives, as well
as to employment discrimination committees, to show 'Big Sister' was
watching. Long-time labour activist Edna Ryan, who was 68 when she
retired to devote her time to WEL, wrote: 'WEL is flourishing – happen-

ing after happening. We are as enchanted as the flower power people. Telephone trees, WEL badges for sale, husbands helping produce the newsletter, child care survey ... Child care kit outlines, seminar on disarmament, survey on abortion ...'[35]

Yet the communications equipment available to WEL members was primitive in the extreme, from the perspective of thirty years on. There were no computers, laser-printing, email, websites, fax machines or conference calls. Neither were photocopiers generally available. Instead, there were typewriters and carbon copies, the Gestetner for duplicating, the post, the telephone, the telegram and silk-screen printing. Urgent messages which might lead to a telegram to the prime minister had to be circulated by means of telephone trees, with the membership divided into groups and messages passed on in an agreed order. Telephone trees didn't always work: 'some stroppy woman would start arguing, "Well, I can't agree with that!" and I'd have to ring backwards down the tree'.[36]

The cost of long-distance phone calls contributed to frequent communication breakdowns between different WEL groups, for example, between Melbourne and Sydney. They could also be a cause of family friction, when family budgets had to be readjusted. As late as 1985, there was still reliance on telephone trees for purposes such as the campaign to persuade the prime minister to proceed with federal affirmative action legislation (some women had to ring up to 45 other women each).

Newsletters were typed, pasted up, run off on duplicating machines and then collated, with these tasks rotating around the membership. Changing the world started with learning how to make stencils and use the Gestetner. A 1973 letter by a member of WEL–Brisbane gives some idea both of the busyness and of the equipment that underpinned it:

> WEL is so busy ... We are working on child care and hope to
> undertake a comprehensive survey of all centres in Brisbane
> and are working to establish centres in the suburbs – this
> means mostly demonstrating the need and then persuading the
> councils to take up the available subsidies. Unfortunately most

councils don't want to do anything at all. Battered babies also come into this – apparently one of the needs is somewhere for the mothers to leave their children for a few weeks to relieve the pressures. We are also about to work on a submission on discrimination to a Status of Women Enquiry in Queensland – which gave us precisely 28 days in which to prepare it!! I am also typing half the newsletter each month and we are supposed to be teaching everyone how to use the duplicating machine and make stencils etc.[37]

Like other women's centres in capital cities, the Canberra Women's House obtained a new Gestetner machine out of an International Women's Year grant in 1975. It also ran a screen-printing workshop where WEL made T-shirts, posters and car stickers for their own use and for other WEL groups. It was flat out in 1975:

It was the time of Sue Ryan's campaign to be elected as Senate Rep. WEL was giving her as much support as we could. There was a screen-printing workshop to print 'A Woman's Place is in

 Junior–WEL at Joyce Nicholson's house, Gestetner machine in background, Melbourne, 1975. *Jan Harper.*

the Senate' on hundreds of T-shirts for sale. Two women artists
ran it, to teach us novices how to do it. At the end of the day
you couldn't find any arms or legs or faces or clothing or hands
or hair that weren't covered in this terrible ink-dye stuff, and to
add insult to injury, we were so committed, we bought all the
'smudgy' ones with blurred writing that hadn't worked out and
took them home with us.[38]

The commitment that led novices to buy up their own screen-printing
failures arose from the nature of the issues that WEL members were
trying to get onto the agenda and into parliament.

Policy the first priority

When WEL was founded there were no women in the House of Representatives, no women in any Cabinet in Australia and very few on
boards. In NSW, where there were over sixty boards in the health and
education portfolios, the vast majority had no women members.[39] Similarly, three quarters of federal advisory bodies contained no women.
However, contrary to what political scientists have sometimes claimed,
WEL was not formed to put women into parliament – it was policy
that was the first priority. WEL wanted to raise issues of concern to
women and get candidates and parties committed to doing something
about them. Its aims were 'to influence governments and politicians to
make laws and change laws so that women can have equal opportunity and economic independence, as well as the services they need to
achieve these'.[40]

It was not until the cohort of members joining in the 1990s that
women's participation in politics ranked with policy issues relating to
employment, education and health. That was when the issue of women
and public decision making (and electoral quotas) became prominent on
both national and international policy agendas. Earlier on, the priority
of policy was true both of Australia and of WEL–New Zealand, where
the initial aims were to inform women about discrimination; to work
for the introduction and enactment of legislation to benefit women;

and to secure the appointment and election of persons and policies that advanced the rights of women.[41]

At the time WEL was founded, a particularly urgent issue was a woman's right to control her own fertility. Many of the first cohort of WEL members were already active in abortion law reform and for them the issues of abortion, family planning and sexual health were the most important, followed by general discrimination against women, discrimination in workplace employment, equal pay and child care (see Table 1.2).

As a founding member wrote in 1972:

> The impetus for WEL's work is in the circumstances under which the vast majority of ordinary Australian (and migrant) women exist – with insufficient sex education, sparse family planning clinics, unnecessarily expensive contraceptives, inadequate child care centres and poor chances, compared with men, for good education, good jobs and good pay.[42]

Victorian WEL members were soon seen on television marching on Parliament with condoms on sticks to protest against the statutory ban on advertising contraceptives. In 1974, WEL–Victoria carried out

Table 1.2   Issues for founding WEL members (1972–75)

Issue	%
Abortion, family planning, sexual health	29
General discrimination against women	24
Discrimination in workplace/employment	24
Equal pay	23
Child care	21
Women's issues, rights and equality	19
Education issues	13
Women in politics and government	7

SOURCE WEL history survey 2002–03.

a detailed survey of women's experiences of contraception. Over half the respondents had difficulty getting adequate advice from doctors, including advice about alternative methods and possible side-effects, and more than half said they had suffered from fear of pregnancy at some stage of their lives. As one respondent, who had had two children in less than two years, said: 'Fear of pregnancy dominated my life for the first ten years of my marriage'.[43]

A survey conducted at the 1975 national conference in Sydney resulted in a somewhat different ordering of issues (see Appendix A1), but women in politics still ranked at the bottom. Education had moved up and abortion and contraception had moved down. The survey's author commented somewhat over-optimistically that the relegation of family planning issues was 'probably because the battle is now virtually won'.[44] While WEL achieved major breakthroughs on the funding of family planning services and the advertising of contraceptives (except in Tasmania where the display and advertising of contraceptives was banned until 1987), the battle over abortion was far from won.

Discrimination in employment was so overt it was an easy target for the articulate and increasingly confident WEL women. For example, the federal secretariat of the Liberal Party of Australia was not shy in stating that a male graduate would be preferred when it advertised for a research officer in late 1972.[45] At the time, it was standard in the *Sydney Morning Herald* for the many pages of classified job advertisements to be divided between those for men and boys and those for women and girls and, needless to say, the pay packets and career opportunities were very different. The separate advertising of male and female jobs did not disappear until it was made unlawful by the passage of the long-awaited federal *Sex Discrimination Act* in 1984. In the 1970s it was regarded as normal for organisations, including universities, to restrict positions such as laboratory or technical staff to men, while of the dozens of different apprenticeships normally only hairdressing was available for women. At the beginning of 1973, WEL was pursuing the Government Printer in Canberra for refusing to allow a woman an apprenticeship.[46]

Discrimination against married women was still rife, despite the lifting of the marriage bar in the Commonwealth Public Service in 1966. A member of WEL in Brisbane commented on the paradox that while marriage was regarded an honourable estate, those who entered it were treated punitively, at least if they were women:

> Even the most permissive of the permissive society do not hold the marriage state in such contempt as to suggest that entering into matrimony is a serious misdemeanour warranting the deprivation of one's livelihood, as apparently held by banks, assurance offices, city councils and hospitals, at least when the guilty party is a woman. Her partner in guilt escapes without penalty.[47]

One of the founding members of WEL in Victoria, Helen Glezer, had been refused a job in the public service because she was married. An honours graduate, she had assumed that because the marriage bar was shortly to be removed, it would not matter if she married. Instead, the job was given to a man who had only a pass degree and, naturally, was paid more than she would have been.[48] Victorian membership records from the 1990s showed equal opportunity to be still by far the most important issue for WEL members.

In Canberra, a national delegation led by Edna Ryan met with a sympathetic Minister for Labour, seeking paid maternity leave for all women in the workforce and training places for women. WEL was also seeking the ratification of the ILO convention on equal pay and the extension of the minimum wage to women.[49] In New South Wales, the WEL Discrimination Group and Joan Bielski were hunting down the discrimination rife in every nook and cranny of public sector employment and large corporations, where women were largely confined to typing pools and process work:

> The Departments like the Railways and the Electricity Commission do not offer apprenticeships to girls ... An Electricity Commission personnel officer stated that, in power stations, electricians often had to be big and burly to lift large motors. When I asked if they would reject a weedy male with

a good school record, he replied that he liked women to remain
feminine. The conversation ended on a somewhat acrimonious
note.[50]

When it was the fire service's turn to be lobbied, it reacted by writing
to the wives of firemen asking them what they thought of the idea of
women being employed.

One issue that spanned both industrial relations and social security was that of female poverty. The WEL–NSW submission to the
Henderson Poverty Inquiry in 1973 received so much media coverage
and was so much in demand that the stencils wore out and had to be
retyped. Despite women being more at risk of being poor, the WEL
survey found a frightening lack of information about the social services
to which they were entitled. For example, only about one in five knew
where to go in the event of a husband's death or desertion. The general
discrimination against women by banks and financial institutions was
given added poignancy when a bank refused credit to a widow for her
husband's funeral without a male guarantor.

Another major issue which WEL campaigned on for the next three
decades was that of the poverty trap arising from the clawing back of
pension dollars the minute a woman earned over a tiny sum, together
with the lack of affordable child care. A related issue was the level of
surveillance over women on welfare and the fear that children would
be taken away if a man stayed 'after television is finished'. Sole parents
had only achieved a real opportunity to keep their babies with the
introduction of the Supporting Mothers' Benefit in 1973. Unmarried
mothers had previously been pressured into adoption, but after the
introduction of the benefit adoptions fell away dramatically. Yet when
Sydney WEL members surveyed party leaders and frontbenchers before
the 1973 State election they found that quite a few believed the new
Supporting Mothers' Benefit encouraged 'immorality'.[51]

While WEL encountered resistance to change, it experienced little
in the way of organised opposition until Right to Life organisations
mobilised against the 1973 attempt at abortion law reform discussed
below. It was on this issue that WEL met its match in the shape of

the organising ability of the Catholic Church and of lobbyists such as Margaret Tighe, who was to conduct Right to Life Victoria (RTLV) electoral campaigns for many years. Borrowing from WEL's repertoire, RTLV conducted candidate surveys and published pro-life form guides for candidates. This formidable opposition meant that policy change in the abortion area required strenuous and exhausting campaigns, still being fought in the late 1990s and the early years of the new century.

Reform and revolution

As mentioned earlier, many founding WEL members had originally belonged to Women's Liberation groups. While Women's Liberation members saw themselves as engaged in revolution and were critical of reformism, in practice there was much overlap, particularly in Canberra.[52] Gail Wilenski had already been taking Women's Liberation down the path of submission writing, with a submission to a Senate inquiry into divorce in June 1972. At the same time in Melbourne, Women's Liberation was preparing its submission for the 1972 equal pay case in the Commonwealth Arbitration Commission. Yet it was consciousness-raising rather than submission-writing for which Women's Liberation was known. Women's Liberation was also hungry for ideas that would provide a systematic explanation of the world and rival masculine grand theories. In some ways WEL was a reaction to this search for grand theory. This is not to suggest that WEL members were necessarily hostile to theory, just that they were anxious to set about remedying the wrongs already visible to them. Prominent Women's Liberation members, such as Helen Garner and Anne Summers, criticised this 'jumping on the Labor bandwagon' to press for piecemeal reforms.

Nonetheless, WEL and Women's Liberation worked together in the capital cities to establish women's services and women's centres, they marched in the same International Women's Day marches and in Canberra they played cricket against each other. Major joint actions included the historic Women's Commission in Sydney in

 WEL–Diamond Valley marching with Women's Liberation, Melbourne, early 1970s. *Sandy Turnbull (Kilpatrick)*.

1973 – where some 150 women testified about their experience as mothers, workers, wives, sex objects and medical patients, in the presence of hundreds more. Another notable joint action was the 'Women's Embassy' outside Parliament House in Canberra in May 1973, emulating the Aboriginal Tent Embassy of the previous year.[53] The Women's Embassy was organised in support of the McKenzie-Lamb Bill, an attempt by Labor backbenchers to legalise first trimester abortions in the ACT. As there were no women members of the House of Representatives, women had to have an embassy outside instead. Although no woman was able to contribute directly to the parliamentary debate, the Bill's mover, David McKenzie MP, quoted a WEL survey of 2000 women.[54] Outside, Right to Life arrived in force on the day the vote was to be taken. The Right to Life marquee 'towered' over the Women's Embassy and supporters of the Bill were greatly outnumbered, despite the WEL loudspeaker broadcasting

'I Am Woman, Hear Me Roar' over and over again.[55] The Bill was defeated.

But despite overlapping membership and joint activities, WEL groups tended to be conscious of the barriers the media images of Women's Liberation posed to policy influence. It was thought that to recruit a broader range of women, 'the respectability of WEL's image is very important, especially in some States and country areas'.[56] WEL iconography was less threatening than that of Women's Liberation. When producing buttons for the Women's Liberation demonstration against the 1968 Miss America contest in Atlantic City, Robin Morgan had placed the clenched fist of male radicalism within the women's symbol, a visual jolt. She had used the radical colour of red on a white background, calling the colour 'menstrual red' to deter lipstick manufacturers from appropriating it. Instead of the fist, WEL placed its acronym within the women's symbol, and used a variety of colours. Purple, green and white were not popularised as women's movement colours until 1975.[57]

Spokeswomen stressed that WEL stood for 'obvious reforms', like equal pay, and did not threaten the home. It appealed to women who found the personal journey Women's Liberation offered too frightening, but were interested in working with other women on particular issues. At a large Canberra meeting on the topic of the relationship between WEL and Women's Liberation some of the new WEL recruits appeared shocked by the more confrontational style of the 'women's libbers'.[58]

A subtext of some of the media coverage of Women's Liberation and contributing to its bad press was the issue of lesbianism. Women's Liberation had become identified in some eyes with political lesbianism, the idea that 'sleeping with the enemy' led to unacceptable compromises with patriarchy. Although WEL founder Beatrice Faust had taken on a role, characteristic of the times, of heterosexual public relations officer for the Australasian Lesbian Movement, WEL was accused of being pusillanimous on the issue. The lesbian critique was that WEL was too concerned with erasing any impression that they were 'just a bunch of lesbians' and gave priority to being taken seriously by the media and by government. They thought that if WEL was serious about sex role stereotyping it should give as much support to homosexual law reform as it had given to abortion law reform.[59]

Despite differences of opinion, the 1974 WEL national conference adopted four resolutions relating to homosexuality, including law reform, discrimination in public service recruitment and issues of child custody. There was no equivalent to the drama in the United States where the founder of the National Organization for Women, Betty Friedan, was convinced that the 'lavender menace' would do irreparable damage to the women's movement.[60]

While seeking to change the way policymakers understood the world, WEL was doing so through the language of equal opportunity rather than a language of revolution, making it easier for policymakers to pick up its demands. In its lobbying styles, WEL also set out to allay the fears aroused by confrontational styles of dress and demeanour. Its delegations were well-dressed, well-spoken and armed with facts. They acknowledged the strategic advantages of having a more radical group to the Left of them:

> Some prickliness existed between WEL and Women's Lib in the early years but generally it was an effective partnership in that Women's Lib presented far more radically than WEL so, by comparison, our demands seemed more 'reasonable'. A bit tough on the activists! They were very committed though and didn't seem to mind, just thinking we were too faint-hearted.[61]

Direct action

While WEL was honing its skills as a lobby group engaging with the policy process, it was also displaying its social movement origins in various forms of direct action, from street demonstrations, to 'WEL on the trams', to vigils and pickets. The social movements of the 1960s had, for the first time, brought large numbers of the university-educated onto the streets to participate in protest actions. For the first time, in 1972 middle-class women swelled the ranks of those marching on International Women's Day. WEL affirmed its movement identity and solidarity through participating in expressive events such as International Women's Day and Reclaim the Night marches, as well as engaging in more instrumental forms of collective action.

In Victoria, the advertising of the entrance examination for the administrative division of the Victorian Public Service for 'males only' was grist to the mill of the new organisation. Beatrice Faust collected application forms and, with other WEL and Women's Liberation members, drummed up applications, getting seventy young women to apply. Two slipped through, Beata Parker and Hilary Erwin, receiving letters headed 'Dear Sir' that gave them exam numbers. WEL then organised television and press coverage and picketed the Exhibition Building in Melbourne on 24 June 1972 to make sure they were allowed to go in. ASIO was watching these plans carefully and filed the map showing where to picket the building. The picket was attended by 'one very senior police officer, several lesser ranks, two policewomen and two paddy wagons' as WEL Secretary, Pamela Thornley, noted in a letter to *The Age*.[62]

The women were admitted and despite doing very well in the examination failed the medical test on the grounds they were female. WEL pursued the matter with Premier Rupert Hamer, and by September received a letter promising that in future women would be able to enter the Administrative Division on the same terms as men. This meant that women for the first time could share the public service career structure rather than hitting the ceiling at Clerk Grade 2.[63]

The following year, seeking a less 'middle-class' issue than entrance to administrative positions, WEL–Victoria organised a 'WEL on the trams' day. About fifty WEL members boarded trams, asking passengers if they thought women should be able to be drivers. Although women had been allowed to drive trams during World War II, the communist-led Tramways Union had subsequently been successful in excluding them. Women were not allowed to progress beyond the position of conductor and hence were ineligible for promotion. In May 1973, the union threatened to hold stop work meetings if women were allowed to become trainee tram drivers, on the grounds that 'if women were allowed to drive trams a number of positions as ticket examiner, depot-starter and inspector would be open to them'.[64] Exactly.

The demonstration received good press coverage, which continued in 1974 when Hilary Freeman (McPhee) and Di Gribble conducted interviews on the issue of peak-hour trains and trams being cancelled for lack of drivers and guards. The Tramways Board was still refusing to have a confrontation with the union over women being allowed to train for the positions.[65] The breakthrough was finally achieved late in 1975.

Lobbying

At the same time as taking direct action such as the picket of the public service exam or a shopping-trolley protest against superfluous packaging in Canberra, WEL was embarking on a different kind of action, the preparation of submissions to government. A tariff inquiry in mid-1972 provided an opportunity to enter this previously all-male domain and raise the issue of the duty imposed on contraceptives. At this time, not only were there ubiquitous State and Territory laws banning the advertising of contraceptives, there was also a range of imposts, from sales tax to tariff duties, that made them unnecessarily expensive. As WEL pointed out, the sales tax of 27 per cent on the pill was the same as that for mink coats.

WEL was assisted by a professional Canberra lobbyist, Peter Cullen, in drawing up an impressive submission calling for the general tariff on contraceptives to be reduced to the British preferential rate. This first incursion into professional lobbying received good press coverage, including an editorial in *The Age* and a long article in the *Australian Financial Review*. The Canberra Women's Liberation Newsletter was somewhat more sceptical: 'It's all called "learning how to play the male chauvinist pigs' game" – so you can beat them at it'.[66]

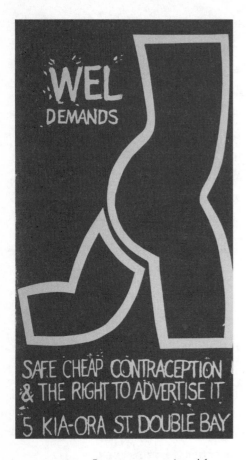

WEL
DEMANDS

SAFE CHEAP CONTRACEPTION
& THE RIGHT TO ADVERTISE IT

5 KIA-ORA ST. DOUBLE BAY

Poster screen-printed for
WEL–NSW, Canberra,
September 1972.
Design: Carol Ambrus.

WEL's intervention in the Tariff Board inquiry helped ensure that family planning issues were high on the agenda of the federal Labor Party, poised to win the forthcoming election. Within a week, the shadow minister for health, Bill Hayden, told *The Age* that a Labor government would not only remove the sales tax on contraceptives but would make them free on prescription and support the development of a network of family planning clinics. In December, the newly elected Whitlam government acted to remove the sales tax on contraceptives, repeal the ban on advertising contraceptives in the ACT, add the pill to the Pharmaceutical Benefits Scheme and provide funding for international family planning programs.

The Tariff Board submissions were the harbinger of a major strand of WEL activity over the next thirty years – the preparation of well-researched submissions to public inquiries on issues ranging from economic policy through to industrial relations, education and training, paid maternity leave, child care and social security. Some 900 submissions over these years are a testament to WEL's record of sustained policy engagement. As we have seen, the word 'submission' now meant something completely different for women.

But while WEL is often seen as a lobby group primarily targeting government, it was not only politicians who were being lobbied. WEL–Tasmania recommended its members buy small parcels of shares so they could speak out at shareholder meetings. In New South Wales, 'even in the early seventies we knew we had to lobby some of corporate

Australia: Nestlé on infant formula, Drake Personnel on employment practices, Mark Foys on window displays'.[67] WEL was also encouraging the development of new women's groups in unions and having considerable impact in public service and teacher unions.

Repertoires old and new

Social movement theorist Charles Tilly has developed the useful concept of 'repertoires of contention' to refer to the combination of forms of political action used by social movements to present their claims.[68] Repertoires may be inherited from the past, borrowed or adapted from other social movements, or involve innovation on the basis of existing and available forms of action. In seeking to draw attention to issues and to get them on the public agenda, WEL drew on existing models of collective action but also innovated within them.

Some of its activity, particularly in its early years, drew directly on recent social movement and Women's Liberation repertoires. This meant action in the streets, such as the march on Parliament with condoms on sticks, the picket of the Victorian public service exams, the Women's Embassy in Canberra and the symbolic action on Melbourne trams. But WEL also inherited older repertoires, stretching back to the suffrage era.

The rating of political candidates, for example, had a long history in the women's movement. What was new in this case was the professionalism of the WEL approach. Journalists were impressed by the social science credentials of those who designed the questionnaire and that the results were 'to be put through a computer' at Melbourne University.[69] The processing of results by computer was seen as giving them a scientific objectivity. The media skills of WEL members, some of whom were journalists while others were quick learners, also helped raise the profile of what was quite a traditional advocacy technique.

The candidate survey was for a time used by WEL groups everywhere, from Hobart to Darwin to Perth, and in local government as well as in State and federal elections. Increasingly, there was a big effort to educate candidates in advance of actually administering the candidate survey. For example, in the run up to the 1974 federal election Canberra WEL members helped co-ordinate and write a five-page background brief on education, workforce and child-care issues. Illustrating their 'insider' resources, they stole a march by hand-delivering copies to sitting Senators and Members at the very instant of the double dissolution of Parliament. Similar briefing was distributed to candidates in the WA State election in the same year.

Another snap federal election in 1975 meant further demands but candidate surveys still received good coverage, as did the award of the wooden spoon for ignorance of women's affairs to a Liberal candidate for a blue-ribbon Melbourne seat.[70] The WEL survey in the 1974 Queensland State election found candidates generally still deplored the need for child-care centres.[71] As the candidate survey and form guide lost its novelty value, however, WEL concentrated on surveys of party election policies, something it sustained over decades. The format and presentation varied over time, seeking to attract the fickle attention of a media focused on the 'horse-race' aspects of elections rather than policy issues. Candidate education continued in other forms, such as the 'Survival Kit for WEL–Informed Candidates' used in the 1980 federal election. It provided handy statistics to assist politicians, said to be often still five to ten years behind voters in their attitudes.[72] In the 1990 federal election, Victorian candidates were given briefing papers together with purple and green WEL highlighter pens.

A new performance element introduced in 1972 was the 'Meet the Candidates' meetings, at which WEL members and others would cross-examine candidates on issues of concern to women. This struck some seasoned activists as a novel format for election meetings, bringing candidates of different parties together on the same platform.[73] Gender roles were being reversed, with women performing as experts and testing the knowledge and attitudes of often nervous male candidates. As we shall see in chapter 4, media stories frequently used terms such as 'women grilling the candidates' or even 'candidates under fire from women'. The first such meeting was held at the time of a by-election for the NSW State seat of Mosman.[74] About 200 people attended to hear the candidates answer questions on survey issues such as equal pay, maternity leave, abortion law reform, the sales tax on contraceptives, and child care. The DLP candidate, Neil Mackerras, brother of psephologist Malcolm Mackerras and conductor Charles Mackerras, said that in his experience women were more interested in getting married than having a career.

Other well-attended meetings held during the 1972 federal election included those in the federal electorates of Angas, Bass, Bennelong, Berowra, Bonython, Boothby, Brisbane, Chisholm, Canberra, Hawker, Kingston, New England, Northern Territory, Petrie, Riverina, Sturt and Sydney. In Boothby, Labor candidate Anne Levy enjoyed the occasion immensely as the sitting member, Sir John McLeay, was 'obviously flustered and antagonising his audience with every word he uttered'.[75] Levy was later the first woman in Australia to be a parliamentary presiding officer. The candidate meetings generally attracted audiences of several hundred and received good media coverage. They could be organised more readily than full candidate surveys and became a standard part of the WEL repertoire for elections at all levels of government.

One variation was leaders' meetings that brought together party leaders in a public forum and another was women candidates' meetings. WEL–ACT, for example, began regular breakfasts for Territory elections with women candidates being given a few minutes to present policies and then to respond to questions from the floor. An even harder test was to have candidates answer questions drawn from a hat on the gender impact of policies.

WEL members also attended many election meetings held by the parties. At a Liberal Party meeting in the seat of Flinders in 1972 those at the front heard someone say, 'Ask the woman at the back, she's not with that group'. The woman at the back proceeded to ask why only $5 million had been budgeted for child-care centres. Then came the instruction, 'No more questions from women'.[76] At another meeting that was being televised, Di Gribble 'wasted' precious television seconds by responding 'I'm no lady' when addressed as 'the lady up the back'.

Other social movements soon borrowed the 'Meet the Candidates' device as part of their own repertoires. The environment movement and conservation councils started to organise election meetings at which candidates could defend their party's environmental credentials. Councils of Social Service began doing likewise to scrutinise social policy credentials.

The quest for sex discrimination legislation

Things happened quickly after Labor won government in December 1972. On his second day in office, Prime Minister Gough Whitlam authorised the reopening of the equal pay case, which the previous government had opposed, and gave Mary Gaudron the government brief. On the third day, he announced the lifting of the sales tax on the contraceptive pill and on the sixth day, a substantial contribution to the UN Fund for Population Activities. Soon ILO Convention 111 on discrimination in employment and occupation was ratified, and paid maternity leave and even a week's paternity leave were introduced into the Australian Public Service. Funding was found for child care and for the Supporting Mothers' Benefit. The new women's services received support, including women's refuges, rape crisis centres and women's health centres. The adult minimum wage was extended to women.

WEL had been lobbying for all of these Whitlam government initiatives, but was less successful in an area it became particularly identified with: the achievement of sex discrimination legislation. In November 1972, WEL–ACT had achieved a commitment from Senator Lionel Murphy, soon to be Attorney-General, that legislation to prohibit discrimination against women would be an early priority in government.[77] 'The need to remove discrimination against women is obvious,' he said, but the new government was quicker to move on race than on sex discrimination.

The Whitlam government introduced the Racial Discrimination Bill into parliament in 1973, relying on the UN Convention on the Elimination of All Forms of Racial Discrimination to provide Consti-

 The invitation said lounge suit, WEL members arrived 'suitably attired'. L to R Meredith Hinchliffe, Mary Sexton, Elizabeth Kentwell, Kay Vernon, Kirsty McEwin, Jenni Neary, Gail Radford Wilenski (Radford). Reception for the Women and Politics Conference, Canberra. *The Daily Telegraph*, 1 September 1975, p.1. *Newspix/News Ltd*.

tutional authority. This was controversial, as the use of the external affairs power to enable the Commonwealth government to move into the human rights area was as yet untested. WEL demanded, unsuccessfully, that the Bill be amended to include sex along with race in each of its clauses. WEL welcomed the Human Rights Bill of 1974, which relied on the International Covenant on Civil and Political Rights, and would have provided some redress for sex discrimination. This Bill lapsed with the 1974 double dissolution of the federal parliament and in any case was on somewhat shaky ground, as the covenant had not yet entered into force.

It was not until late in the life of the beleaguered government that the office of the Attorney-General circulated a memorandum on a 'Proposed Bill to Prohibit Discrimination against Persons by Reason of their Sex or Marital Status'. It was to be one of many pieces of the reform agenda that were postponed indefinitely by the dismissal in November.

In South Australia WEL was more fortunate, with the passage of the first sex discrimination act in Australia in 1975. In New South Wales, lobbying was also under way for the *Anti-Discrimination Act* that would be passed two years later. Nor were efforts abandoned at the Commonwealth level: after 1975 a campaign for federal legislation gradually built up momentum despite persistent blocking by the National Party at Cabinet level, a story told in chapter 5.

Setting up the wheel of women's affairs

Another major public policy change associated with WEL was the setting up of women's policy machinery in government. Even Prime Minister McMahon, whose government had recently opposed equal pay, announced in his 1972 election policy speech that his government would set up a Royal Commission into the Status of Women. Such commissions had been established in the United States and Canada, and WEL had suggested Australia follow suit. Labor front-bencher Clyde Cameron, on the other hand, was dismissive: 'We shouldn't have to wait two or three years for a Royal Commission dominated by men to discover the many self-evident examples of discrimination against women.'[78]

The idea of a Royal Commission was quickly superseded by the pace of change under the Whitlam government. Not only did Cameron, as Minister of Labour, respond favourably to WEL's call for his Women's Bureau to be upgraded[79], but action was also taken to appoint a Women's Adviser to the Prime Minister, an idea originating with Gail Wilenski. The appointment of Elizabeth Reid in 1973 became an important step in the evolution of government machinery for women. When the *Sydney Morning Herald* asked women's organisations what women wanted from the new Women's Adviser, only

WEL mentioned the need for additional staff.[80] By 1974, a section to provide support for Reid had been established in the Department of Prime Minister and Cabinet.

WEL's concern with such machinery of government issues marked it out from women's organisations elsewhere and said much about its founding members and the political opportunities opening up for them. Feminists like Sara Dowse were being recruited into ministerial offices as press secretaries and research officers.[81] The use of the Royal Commission on Australian Government Administration to develop and promote WEL's ideas on the design of women's policy machinery is described in chapter 5. The wheel model of women's policy machinery devised by WEL, with its focus on policy monitoring rather than program delivery, was to become a good practice model disseminated by the United Nations and a forerunner of the 'gender mainstreaming' approach to women's policy adopted internationally at the Beijing Conference in 1995.

Closer to home, the wheel model was what WEL successfully lobbied for across Australia. WEL members migrated into government to head these new units or to re-energise older units, such as the Women's Bureau in the Department of Labour. In particular, WEL women such as Kim Boyer in Tasmania, Deborah McCulloch and later Carol Treloar in South Australia, and Carmel Niland and later Helen L'Orange in New South Wales, played pioneering roles in establishing women's policy machinery at the State level.[82]

Meanwhile, another initiative promoted by WEL (and by the overlapping group, Women in Australian Government Employment) was also taking off. This was the creation of equal employment opportunity (EEO) structures in the public service. Much care was taken to distinguish EEO programs from women's policy machinery. While women's policy units were concerned with the effects of policies on women in the community, EEO was concerned with employment issues only. WEL was able to convert not only the government but also the opposition to the cause of EEO: in 1974 Liberal frontbencher Malcolm Fraser visited WEL in Melbourne and stressed his party's commitment to an EEO section in the Public Service Board, so that the public service could become a pacesetter. WEL expressed its delight: 'In 1972 would anyone have thought seriously that the Liberal Party would have consulted WEL before drafting its policy? Or that Mr Fraser would have missed a session of the House to attend a meeting with WEL?'[83]

Meanwhile, Gail Wilenski had been gaining expertise in EEO on the national committee overseeing ILO Convention 111, and in 1975 was appointed to head the new section in the Public Service Board. Wilenski's appointment was attacked as an example of 'jobs for the girls' because of her husband's prominence in the Whitlam government. The attack was badly timed, coming as it did while the International Women's Year Women and Politics Conference was being held in Canberra. Carmel Niland read on air a telegram from 400 women protesting over the Opposition's treatment of the appointment. Wilenski reverted to her professional name of Gail Radford soon after joining the public service and her EEO reputation was built under that name.

Another initiative of the Whitlam government was the Royal Commission on Human Relationships, a peace offering after the defeat of the McKenzie-Lamb attempt at abortion law reform. Justice Elizabeth Evatt headed the Commission and WEL members Joan Bielski and Alison Ziller joined it as research officers. Its recommendations, delivered under the Fraser government, became benchmarks for policy in areas such as family planning and sex education, the treatment of rape and domestic violence, the rights of adoptive children and relinquishing mothers, anti-discrimination legislation and equal opportunity programs, work/family issues and retraining programs for sole parents.

Another landmark was the release of the Schools Commission report *Girls, School & Society* in 1975, to which many WEL members had contributed. Its analysis of the ways in which schools had limited girls' opportunities and its recommendations for curriculum and organisational change set the agenda for reform for the next twenty years.[84] Serious advances were also being made in the child-care area. The

WEL–ACT members Carmel Niland and Rosa Walden being interviewed by Claudia Wright at 2CA, 4 September 1975.
Ann Graham (Keira Lockyer)

Whitlam government had been elected with a commitment to a year's free preschool but no child-care commitment. Preschools were organised on a sessional basis and so were unsuitable when both parents were in the workforce. WEL plunged into a battle to redirect funds to long day care, competing with the strongly organised and experienced kindergarten lobby that had a close ally in the Education Minister. As part of its commitment to more participatory processes, the Whitlam government allowed community groups to have direct access to Cabinet committees, and the first time that such groups were able to present their case directly to Cabinet ministers was in relation to child care. Soon after her appointment, Elizabeth Reid arranged for

Prime Minister Gough Whitlam with child-care delegation of WEL members. L to R, Pamela Gorring, Suzanne Dixon (Wills), Alma Morton, Winsome McCaughey, Michelle Grieve (Renshaw), Helen Molony (McConaghy). *The Age*, 10 May 1973, *Home News*, p. 3. *The Age Archives, courtesy The Age.*

the 'United Women's Action Group' (WEL women from four States and the ACT) to see the Prime Minister and members of the Cabinet Committee on Social Welfare. They were under-prepared for such an early high-level intervention and argued with each other in front of Cabinet, according to a highly critical account by Anne Summers.[85] According to participants, there was no such disagreement, although Alma Morton was ticked off afterwards by other WEL members for contradicting the Prime Minister when he confused kindergartens with child care. Morton put the incident down to the middle-classness of WEL.

NSW Labor women succeeded in having a serious commitment to child care put into the ALP platform before the 1974 election, but only a few months later WEL had to undertake a major national campaign to hold Labor to its election promises. The campaign put child care firmly on the policy agenda and WEL women soon became expert in writing funding submissions. They were involved in setting up many community-based centres and in persuading local government to enter the field. In South Australia, two WEL members wrote the new TAFE course for child-care trainees in 1973–74 and then got the jobs teaching it.

Over the years, WEL retained a watching brief over the women's policy and EEO machinery it had helped create in the heady period of the 1970s. Although it was to be joined by more specialised advocacy groups on specific policy issues affecting women, WEL was the only women's organisation that could consistently be relied on over the next thirty years to go public whenever restructuring, relocation or Budget cuts threatened the continuing existence or effectiveness of women's units in government.

2

SHIFTING FRAMES

In its early years WEL was hard at work trying to shift the way policy issues were viewed, so that women came into focus. It was also taking advantage of the equal opportunity themes that dominated the early 1970s to ensure that gender as well as class became a legitimate object of government concern. But, like any political actor, it was itself being framed in a range of different ways. In the early days WEL was sometimes dismissed as hopelessly reformist and middle class. Over the next thirty years, however, those once regarded as being in the reformist mainstream came to be seen as 'hairy-legged Stalinists' with an old-fashioned reliance on state action. An emerging men's rights movement blamed WEL for policy and legislation allegedly persecuting men and a new generation of feminist scholars described 1970s feminists as achieving sisterhood through the silencing of other voices.

Liberal reformers?

Conflicting images of WEL have been produced by bodies of knowledge such as Australian political science and women's history. In women's studies textbooks, WEL is often chosen to illustrate liberal reformism, particularly in contrast with socialist feminism or radical feminism. WEL had indeed inherited the social liberal view that equal opportunity is the hallmark of liberalism and requires an active role by the state in regulating the labour market, mitigating inequalities and providing social infrastructure to enable all to participate in the life of the community. When such understandings of equal opportunity were in the ascendancy it was relatively easy for WEL to be heard. It was a time when the Labor Party was responding to the new social movements by broadening its own view of equal opportunity. Historically, equal opportunity had been understood to address working class disadvantage – now it was being extended to cover different forms of disadvantage, whether arising from gender, race, ethnicity or disability. These new understandings were important not only for the Labor Party, but also for the Australian Democrats and for small 'l' liberals in the Liberal Party, as reflected in the 1974 Liberal campaign document *The Way Ahead.*

Textbook treatments sometimes confuse the forms of liberalism that shaped Australasia with the earlier forms of liberalism influential in the United States, which focused on freedom of contract, and negative rather than positive liberty.[1] There is also a tendency to exaggerate the differences between the radical feminism of Women's Liberation and the liberal reformism of WEL. In fact they worked together in the establishment of women's services, and members of both groups went into government to work at the policy end of such service provision.

While WEL spoke the language of equal opportunity, it also said repeatedly that it was not enough to participate equally in male structures – women must transform them. Some WEL members warned that while Women's Liberation might become cut off from other women through its emphasis on theory, without theory WEL risked co-option.[2] Some members saw WEL as a halfway house that could attract suburban women with its action program and give them the confidence to explore more challenging feminist ideas.

On the other hand, WEL and Women's Liberation were competing entities that for organisational reasons sometimes had to exaggerate their differences. Women's Liberation members might exaggerate the reformist limitations of WEL, while WEL members might exaggerate the talk-bound character of Women's Liberation. Moreover, the degree

WEL marching with Women's Liberation, International Women's Day, Pitt Street, Sydney, 1980. *Search Foundation-Tribune, Mitchell Library, State Library of NSW.*

of overlap in membership was highly variable. In Sydney, where tensions were often higher than in Canberra or Perth, for example, it was said that 'the W.L. woman attending a WEL event is more likely to be there as a critical observer than a helpful participant'.[3]

While there were organisational imperatives to differentiate WEL as the reformist wing of the women's movement, there was also disillusionment with 'reform' on the part of some members. This disenchantment was well expressed by Jan Mercer in her book *The Other Half*, itself a wonderful evocation of a lost ethos. A number of future professors and even a future vice-chancellor wrote for this collection, but their articles did not appear under their names. Mercer explained it was not relevant to 'indicate the academic status of individual writers because these have been allocated in terms of a male-dominated and defined system of rewards'.[4]

Mercer wrote of her experience in WEL: 'Had I allowed myself to be manipulated into thinking that submissions to the Government on child care would radically change the oppressive nature of the family?'[5] She came to the conclusion that the year she had spent researching and writing submissions and dealing with reporters had been misspent, and that such activities were part of the illusion that women could change society through the ballot box and political reform: 'WEL was asked to make formal submissions on child care, women in the workforce, equal pay, the Budget and a minimum wage, and so, eased quietly into the bureaucracy of government, it was no longer a threat'.[6]

While those seeking radical social change might be disillusioned with WEL's reformism, conservatives continued to regard it as a radical and dangerous element. In Queensland, it was denounced in Parliament as one of the groups responsible for women's refuges in Brisbane and Townsville being hotbeds of Marxist propaganda and lesbianism.[7] According to *News Weekly*, 'Radical feminists run Canberra' – because an active WEL member was leading the Labor team for the House of Assembly election, and an ACT Senator, Susan Ryan, was a founding member.[8]

In the 1990s new versions of feminism appeared that were also critical of WEL's liberal reformism, but from the perspective of cultural critique and the generation wars. Spokeswomen for young WEL groups in Sydney and Melbourne responded heatedly to Anne Summers' suggestion in her 'Letter to the Next Generation' that the inactivity of young women was jeopardising the gains of the women's movement. They declared themselves insulted by the failure to recognise the political work that active young women such as themselves were engaged in. Young WEL members were in turn criticised for privileging political activism and 'liberal spaces' over the more diverse cultural spaces where feminism was now being performed.[9] This was at the time that geekgirls, cyber chix and Riot Grrrls were distancing themselves from the 'no fun, no frocks feminism' they associated with the 1980s.

The cultural critics were also dubious about the policy outcomes brought about by feminist reformers, blaming them for women's movement into the paid workforce. WEL was emblematic of the liberal reformers who had encouraged women to believe they could 'have it all', both briefcases and babies, and were responsible for the 'work/family' collision experienced by a new generation of women.

> The plastic figurine for this memory of feminism is the briefcase-and-baby career woman ... Her thought balloon, carefully scribed by the Daughters of Feminism, reads: 'I can't juggle this briefcase and baby any more, the load is unmanageable, to my anguish and everlasting despair I'm going to drop one'.[10]

So while WEL members continued to pursue policy issues such as paid maternity leave, family-friendly work design, accessible child care and recognition of the value of household work, they were being blamed, sometimes by armchair critics, for being insufficiently successful in terms of policy outcomes. Such 'blaming feminism' approaches took little account of the difficulty of promoting work/family policy reform in a deregulatory policy environment, particularly during the Howard era.

Who is WEL speaking for?

While liberal reformism was a frame initially applied to WEL by Women's Liberation, critics described the members of both organisations as coming from privileged backgrounds with little insight into the problems of other women. WEL was often depicted in the media as part of a broader phenomenon of middle-class radicalism – ranging from resident action groups to the Campaign Against Moral Persecution (Camp Inc). This middle-class image was seen by participants in the 1975 WEL national conference as one of the 'bad things about WEL'.[11]

Some WEL members such as Joan Bielski reacted vigorously to

the attempt to frame feminism as middle class. She pointed out that all social movements had been led by middle-class reformers with the time and resources to take up causes. Being middle class didn't make people 'wrong' – it depended on what values they were espousing. When WEL was castigated as 'elitist, reformist and middle class', this often simply meant 'educated, articulate and with sufficient economic muscle to pursue reforms'. The reforms themselves – adequate and equal wages, equal job opportunities and the restructuring of working conditions – were essential if 'women were to deal with society and family from a position of strength'.[12] Edna Ryan, a veteran of working-class politics, reacted similarly to the 'middle-class' tag, which she felt ignored the industrial and other policy objectives of WEL: 'The tag apparently refers to professional competency, which is associated with the middle class, but ignores the content of our aims'.[13]

Early members in Victoria expressed similar views when interviewed in 1981. They agreed that WEL was a middle-class organisation, but believed that only the middle classes had the time, money and energy to push on behalf of all women. They believed that what women had in common, in terms of child-bearing, child-rearing and responsibility for the emotional wellbeing of families, was significantly greater than the class labels that divided them.[14] Those from working-class families were themselves sometimes convinced that middle-class women could better make themselves heard. According to 'Val', 'only the middle class have the ability to write submissions; they know how to talk to people; they speak the language of politics'. 'Dulcie' felt that:

> the 'establishment' and Parliament listen to the middle-class
> women. Both middle-class and working-class women are
> equally affected by discrimination, but the middle class get
> their ideas over better.[15]

In Queensland, when the Justice Minister established a Status of Women Inquiry in 1973, WEL presented nineteen submissions covering different areas of discrimination, often on behalf of less articulate women:

> WEL served as a rallying point for women in the community
> who felt they had a case to plead but lacked the skill to prepare
> a submission. These were often the normally inarticulate
> women who experienced the worst discrimination and their
> submissions were probably the most valuable of all.[16]

Education made it easier to feel at home in WEL, and this was regardless of ethnic or other background. Iraqi-born Elsa Atkin, with her triple matriculation in English, French and Arabic, said 'That I was not Australian-born was irrelevant', and felt that women had united to change society's unjust attitudes to women, 'regardless of nationality'.[17] Elizabeth Sloniec, a second-generation Polish Australian, had experienced culture conflict in an Australian suburban setting where married women 'appeared to disappear into a quick-sand of numbing domesticity. Enormous energy was needed to struggle out and WEL provided the means to do so'.[18]

The high levels of education of WEL members and their personal confidence could intimidate working-class women. One said of the academic and professional members: 'They made me feel quite inadequate; I don't suppose they meant to, but I used to feel quite put down at times'.[19] A number of speakers at WEL's 1973 national conference warned about pushing for reforms that would only help middle-class women and wanted to end the determining of life chances by competitive exam outcomes.[20] On the other hand, one member who had left school at 14 in Ipswich found that WEL prepared her well for the various social science disciplines she later studied at university. In South Australia, Denise Tzumli thought that without WEL's lobbying against discrimination, particularly in access to money, she, as a working-class single parent, would never have been able to buy her own house. Senator Rosemary Crowley commented that when her Women, Sport and the Media inquiry thought they had covered the area very comprehensively, it was a WEL member who asked what they were recommending for sport and recreation for women in prison.[21]

WEL's strategies were sometimes designed to deflect the label of being 'middle-class' as with the 'WEL on the trams' day in Melbourne.

Bringing small children along when meeting with politicians, bureaucrats or journalists was another way to underline that WEL members were 'ordinary women'. Children could be borrowed if necessary and if they misbehaved at meetings members were advised to apologise and to use the opportunity to stress the lack of adequate child care. In Sydney, Elsa Atkin remembered getting calls with instructions to go to certain places with her own and any other children she was minding to demonstrate or lobby for child-care grants, women's refuges or crisis centres – 'I did so willingly, and so did many others'.[22]

Although WEL spoke in the name of women when lobbying for equal opportunity, it did not claim to be representative of all women. WEL–NSW placards proclaimed 'WEL Stands for Women' but they had the subtext 'who are concerned about equal pay, fertility choice, child care, safeguarding women's rights'. Such distinctions were often lost in the hurly-burly of policy interventions, where WEL positioned itself and was portrayed as a 'voice for women'. WEL itself was conscious of the fact that its policy influence depended on being seen as broadly representative of women, not just those with middle-class qualifications or those in the workforce (see below).

WEL's representative claims came under challenge not only from Women's Liberation and conservative critics, but also from the new academic discipline of 'gender studies'. New postmodern perspectives framed 1970s feminism as ignoring 'difference'. Sisterhood had allegedly been achieved by the 'systematic silencing' of other voices and the mobilising of solidarity around a unitary notion of 'woman'.[23] It became received wisdom that second-wave feminists had been guilty of 'essentialising' women as a homogeneous group. Some of this framing of the deficiencies of 1970s feminism and its supposed suppression of diversity seems remote from the political activism of the time, however. WEL's action groups of that period do not seem to have been guilty of ignoring difference. They were energetic in the pursuit of a greater voice for diverse groups of women, setting up action groups to focus on, among others, Aboriginal women, women in the home and migrant women. When WEL women went into government they initiated consultations and advisory bodies focusing on the special needs of these groups and the need for seed funding for new advocacy organisations. As a result of such activism, in 1988 the National Women's Consultative Council became the first Commonwealth body outside the immigration portfolio where Australians from non-English speaking backgrounds had representation proportional to their presence in the population.

There were always challenges. Aboriginal activist Pat O'Shane was often quoted for her statement that the major issue for Aboriginal women was racism rather than sexism and that Aboriginal women might be more interested in stopping forced sterilisation than in the right to abortion.[24] WEL was criticised for assuming that because Aboriginal women suffered from sexism, they would ignore history and accept the idea of a shared sisterhood. While often disappointed in its attempts to reach out to Aboriginal women, WEL remained persistent. In 1974, WEL–Townsville was trying to initiate research and action on the disproportionate number of Aboriginal women in prison while the Port Augusta group was pushing for self-management in Aboriginal affairs.[25]

At the WEL national conference in Perth in 1976, some of the questions directed to Aboriginal speakers were described as 'patronising', but the first conference resolution was about the housing needs of Aboriginal women and the second called on WEL to draw in more Aboriginal women and 'take action with them in areas which they see to be matters of priority'.[26] When planning a demonstration in Perth against the injustices suffered by Aboriginal women in the legal system WEL declared: 'Their struggle is our struggle, their liberation is our liberation'.[27] The following year, when the national conference was in Brisbane, two Aboriginal women gave an address on the double discrimination experienced in north Queensland, while WEL–Darwin successfully lobbied for Aboriginal cleaners in settlements to receive equal pay rates.

In Canberra long-time WEL member Mary Sexton was centrally involved in the protracted but eventually successful attempt to set up the first national policy consultation with Aboriginal women in the early 1980s (Women's Business) and also undertook the outreach to Aboriginal women over the National Agenda for Women in 1986. WEL was commissioned to organise the main consultative conference and ensured that the large number of Aboriginal participants had a pre-conference day for caucusing. However, not all WEL interventions on Aboriginal issues were successful. In the mid-1990s, for example, Adelaide WEL members were part of an unsuccessful campaign in support of Ngarrindjeri women, with Betty Fisher drawing on 30-year old interview notebooks to support 'women's business' claims concerning Hindmarsh Island. After the early years of trying to draw in Aboriginal women, WEL adopted more modest goals of supporting Aboriginal women in their efforts to form their own advocacy bodies and have a greater role in policy-making.

WEL also took up the cause of South Sea Islander women, inspired by member Faith Bandler who addressed the 1975 national conference in Sydney. The second of the resolutions passed by the conference (after one calling for women to be allowed to return to Darwin after Cyclone Tracy) was a demand that the Australian Government amend legislation so that Australians of South Sea Islander descent were eligible for the same benefits as Aborigines and Torres Strait Islanders. Bandler argued that while South Sea Islanders had also been discriminated against they should not have to forswear their identity and sign themselves as Aborigines in order to receive benefits.

From its early days WEL had pursued issues concerning migrant women. In Melbourne, WEL prepared a multilingual (English, Italian and Greek) brochure and 10 000 copies were printed for distribution in factories. A submission prepared for a Whitlam government task force foreshadowed many of the issues later pursued by immigrant women's organisations – which included cultural diversity training for those in the human services, the provision of a general interpreter service for medical and other purposes, bilingual social workers, English classes in factories and culturally appropriate child care. Olga Lippman, an immigrant from Poland and part of the team that prepared the WEL submission, emphasised the effects on women of the lack of interpreters to assist with gynaecological and obstetric consultations and with cross-cultural awareness in maternity wards. The same team wrote asking the Prime Minister for fair compensation for the women in the clothing industry who would lose their jobs because of the 1973 tariff cuts.[28] Married women were generally ineligible for unemployment benefits, despite their families' dependence on two incomes.

In Sydney, Greek-born Dorothy Buckland Fuller founded the Australian Migrant Women's Association and received a small IWY grant for a program bringing together migrant women and WEL members. Eva Cox, herself a Jewish refugee from Vienna who had come to Australia as a 10-year-old child, obtained Regional Employment Development money to ascertain the needs of migrant women in the Marrickville and South Sydney area. At the State WEL conference in 1976 there was a big push on the shortfall in child care for newly-arrived migrant communities. Fifty per cent of migrant

Multilingual brochure produced by WEL–Victoria for distribution in factories. *Courtesy University of Melbourne Archives.*

families with pre-school-aged children had been found to have both parents in the workforce. The *Sydney Morning Herald* editorialised on the subject, calling for WEL to be supported in any attempt to improve the situation.[29]

In the 1980s groups such as migrant women and women with disabilities became organised at the national level with some assistance from the Office of the Status of Women. The new groups included the Association of Non-English-Speaking Women of Australia (ANESBWA) and Women with Disabilities Australia (WWDA). They promoted perspectives they felt were inadequately recognised or represented by either male-dominated organisations such as the Federation of Ethnic Communities Councils of Australia or Disabled People International (Australia) – or by women's movement organisations such as WEL.

In the case of WWDA (or rather the National Network that preceded it) there was a particular grievance with WEL over failure to reimburse the costs of representatives who participated in a National Agenda for Women conference in Canberra in 1986. WEL had a small amount of money to disburse to assist women to participate in this conference, but much of it went to assist Indigenous women to come from remote communities. The issue rankled with WWDA members: 'I don't think any of us renewed membership with WEL for at least a decade or so, if at all'.[30]

WEL in the countryside

WEL is usually thought of as an organisation of urban reformers, but it also had a significant impact in regional towns, where Women's Liberation had barely penetrated. Women in country towns were often drafted into WEL to help administer the 1972 candidate survey, for finding recruits in federal electorates across the country was a mammoth exercise. A WEL–NSW newsletter reported the hunt for interviewers for candidates in Condobolin, Coonabarabran, Coonamble, Narrabri, Dubbo, Lismore, Narromine and many other places far afield.[31]

In Victoria two WEL members travelled more than 1000 miles

around rural districts interviewing candidates, getting publicity for WEL in country papers and starting local groups. Women from groups in the Latrobe Valley, Ballarat, Bendigo, Shepparton, Wangaratta and Wodonga were among those at the first country conference the following year, starting to plan the survey of country candidates in the State election.[32]

WEL members were certainly more representative of Australian women as a whole than were members of Women's Liberation. By 1974–75 there were 52 WEL groups in rural and regional Australia, something often overlooked. It is the metropolitan and suburban groups that have received more attention than the presence and characteristics of WEL in the countryside. Some of these groups were quite large, as with the 147 members of Border–WEL in Albury-Wodonga, while others relied on a few dedicated individuals. As in the cities, participation in the candidate survey was itself a dramatic consciousness-raising exercise as women found out how little male candidates knew about their issues. An account from the Gold Coast would be true of many other non-metropolitan groups:

> Our first few members were educated into WEL ways in a hurry. Almost as soon as they had handed over their subs they were out interviewing candidates for the State Government elections. Candidates who at first had never heard of WEL were inclined to treat the questionnaire as a bit of a joke. After the public meeting ... they began to do some homework. When the Country Party candidate was defeated he put most of the blame on WEL. We had arrived.[33]

These women were sometimes anxious not to be confused with Women's Liberation: 'As a member of Women's Electoral Lobby you can be as womanly as you please and still work for the improvement of conditions important to women'.[34] The country women also had different perspectives from their city sisters on how to organise, being less influenced by the collectivism of Women's Liberation. Nevertheless they were quite determined that women should have a political say and candidate meetings in country towns such as Wagga or Cooma were run with great efficiency.

WEL–Cooma 'Meet the Candidates', 1976 NSW State election. L to R, Tom Barry (Country Party), WEL timekeeper, Wilga Pruden (Chair), Hope Marland (Liberal Party) and John Akister (ALP). *Courtesy Cooma-Monaro Express.*

One study of WEL members in the Victorian country towns of Ballarat and Shepparton found that most were 'outsiders', being city born and usually with university education[35], who had moved to the country, sometimes as teachers or, in one case, as a Methodist minister. They had read books such as Germaine Greer's *The Female Eunuch* or Betty Friedan's *The Feminine Mystique*. One Shepparton member was at home with two young children and had been strongly discouraged by her husband from obtaining paid work. She felt 'isolated and useless' and working for WEL was one outlet for her frustration.[36] In both towns WEL groups lobbied for Council to provide child-care services and to use the Regional Employment Development Scheme to provide employment for women. In Ballarat they won a battle for women Council employees to retain their jobs when they became pregnant. In both towns they gave up on the topics of abortion and sex education, given repressive social attitudes.

Setting up WEL branches in conservative rural towns intolerant of dissenters often required considerable courage. The convenor in one Victorian country town complained that while the group was quite large, she was the only member willing to be identified with WEL in the local newspaper. Organisations with deep roots in the countryside, such as the Country Party, were deeply antagonistic to any challenge to traditional gender roles inside or outside the family, and were likely to identify such challenges as communist-influenced. The husband of one woman refused to allow her to chair a meeting, because he had heard that WEL was 'run by a pack of communists'.[37] The Country Women's Association (CWA), founded to improve the welfare and conditions of women in the country, not to seek equality, reflected many of the same conservative attitudes. The CWA was most visible through the restrooms it established in country towns, and it was the CWA hall that might provide the venue for the founding meeting of a rural WEL group and even for its regular meetings. During the 1970s some WEL members joined the CWA with the intention of changing it from within, but 'always in a ladylike way', a member of WEL–Coffs Harbour said.[38]

While most rural WEL members lived in country towns, one who lived on a farm in mid-west Western Australia has described what WEL membership meant to her in the 1980s:

> For the first 14 years of my WEL membership I was in the country and treasured my monthly newsletter. It opened me up to another world – of women who cared enough about women to spend their free time meeting, writing submissions, thinking women were important enough to work hard for. It inspired me and encouraged me to extend myself, to try and be more assertive, more independent.[39]

Pam Casey, on a cattle property in south-west New South Wales, wrote in the first WEL journal of spending the summer of 1972–73 fighting a bushfire and hand-feeding cattle in temperatures over 100° F. As a result she was too exhausted to talk at the first WEL national conference but made up for it by writing about the plight of rural women for the *WEL*

Papers. The policy issues she had wanted to raise included the hardy perennial of the cost of telecommunications in rural areas.[40]

WEL members in the country were often responsible for setting up the first women's services in their region, including women's health centres and refuges as well as child-care and family planning services and non-sexist resource centres for local schools. WEL groups conducted surveys on unmet needs, which could then be presented to Council. In Alice Springs, for example, a door-to-door survey on child-care needs was the first action taken by the new WEL group. In Wagga, WEL successfully lobbied Council for a full-time social worker, for police-women and for a women's refuge. The lack of family planning services in Wagga hit the headlines in 1977, but it was WEL members who demanded a feminist women's health centre like those established in Sydney, rather than something that would follow a hierarchical medical model.[41]

The pattern of WEL-initiated services was repeated in many places and was reported on at WEL regional conferences. From Port Pirie to Portland to Hervey Bay, WEL was responsible for establishing family planning clinics, child-care centres and women's refuges. This often involved more than needs surveys and advocacy. For example, when a weekly family planning clinic was achieved in Alice Springs, WEL members were rostered on for secretarial duties. When WEL held a regional conference in Echuca, a participant spoke of the importance of such services in ensuring WEL's work was continued into the future.[42]

Betty McLean in Wodonga described the experience of setting up a women's refuge:

> Some of us went to a WEL conference in Sydney and we visited a refuge a group of women had set up. Memory says that they had taken over some houses on Anglican Church land, we returned all agog to get a refuge – no luck. My husband and I had moved to Wodonga from the (Army) Camp at Bandiana. My husband (a wonderful support) converted a double garage into a flat and we set up the first refuge.
> Finally the Albury Wodonga Development Corporation gave us the use of a vacant house on Sydney road. We had a

Ruth Schnukal (WEL–Victoria) at Portland regional conference, 1982. *Kerry Lovering.*

> Rent-a-loo out the back. We had no funding so appealed for
> furniture etc. We were given so much, many saying 'I wish
> there had been a place like this when I was young', the surplus
> we stored in the wool store.[43]

Thirty years later the refuge had a sign outside the front: 'Betty's Place'.

In Cairns, women responding to an IWY speech by Margaret Reynolds overflowed the house where they met to found a WEL group. They took up issues such as DDT in breast milk, flammable nightwear for children and conditions for women prisoners in the watch-house, including a young Aboriginal woman charged with the murder of her violent partner. Domestic violence became a huge issue in Cairns. In the early years WEL members opened their houses to women escaping violence, some of them 'referred' by a local doctor.[44] Federal funding for a refuge was achieved after *Cairnsweek* ran a helpful article about how a mother fleeing violence with her children was forced to sleep in a bus shelter overnight.[45] WEL still had to run lamington drives to make up the shortfall in the purchase price of the house and later a successful second-hand bookshop supplemented operational funding. As elsewhere, the creation of the first women's service quickly revealed the need for more. Because the refuge workers were spending so much time on phone counselling WEL began a women's information service, which later also obtained federal funding. The Cairns Women's Information and Referral Centre was opened in the 1980s by Margaret Reynolds, by now a senator.

At its founding meeting in Coffs Harbour, WEL developed a program of action that was to guide it for the next ten years:

> It included child care, child minding centres and pre-school education, a family planning clinic, interest in local government and attendance at Council meetings, better education for girls, end to financial discrimination against women, part-time work for women, town planning, conservation and parking facilities and civil liberties![46]

The teachers who founded WEL in Coffs Harbour were amazed at the conservatism of some of the responses – such as the parish priest who made them remove a copy of Virginia Woolf's *A Room of One's Own* from a WEL information stall at the church hall. In Bowral, Council members got cold feet over the explicit nature of diagrams in material advertising cancer-detection clinics for women and WEL members had to turn up in camouflage (tweeds and pearls) to see if they were allowed to continue using Council premises. Nonetheless, WEL groups successfully sought allies and persuaded the community of the need for services such as a women's refuge, a women's resource centre, a family planning unit and eventually a women's health centre. They also worked to expand the subject choices available to girls in schools, where they had previously been excluded from technical subjects.[47]

Despite these flurries of activity in lobbying councils and getting services established, most of WEL's rural groups went into decline after a few years. This may well have been because they were the initiative of 'outsiders' rather than those with deeper roots in the land. The next big mobilisation of rural women did not come until a decade later, when State Labor governments initiated Rural Women's Networks, followed by the appearance of specialised organisations such as Australian Women in Agriculture and the Foundation for Australian Agricultural Women.

A Labor Party front?

From the time of the first election survey, there were accusations that WEL was a front for the Labor Party. These particularly came from the Democratic Labor Party (DLP), whose predominantly Catholic candidates received poor ratings when they participated at all. WEL responded by pointing out that it did not see tagging behind one of the existing political parties as an effective method of exerting political pressure.[48] Closely associated with the DLP was the Melbourne-based National Civic Council, which went further in accusing WEL of being a Communist Party front. Its mixed bag of evidence included advertisements that had appeared in a WEL newsletter for a forum on political cartooning to be held at the Communist Party headquarters, and the fact that WEL's Canberra office shared an address with the newly established Lesbian Line.[49]

Despite attempts to paint it as a Labor or Communist Party front, from the beginning WEL treasured its non-party status, making sure that convenors and co-ordinators were not identified with a political party, and always seeking representatives of all parties to speak at forums and conferences. The first NSW State conference was attended by the future Liberal leader Peter Coleman, and WEL newsletters carried statements from all parties and ads for events such as National Liberal Women's Conferences.[50]

In the 1972 federal election a member of the co-ordinating committee of WEL–Victoria was careful to resign her position before accepting Australia Party nomination for the seat of Kooyong. By contrast, Pam Gorring of WEL–Brisbane was happy to reveal in conservative Queensland that she was a card-carrying member of the Country Party, particularly when asking politicians their views on lifting bans on the advertising and display of contraceptives.[51] In Western Australia, WEL asked members who belonged to a political party not to make use of information acquired through WEL for partisan purposes. In 1995 members of WEL in Sydney were debating whether their long-standing prohibition on paid convenors having a public role in a political party contravened anti-discrimination law.

Despite such niceties, WEL groups including WEL–NSW were accused from time to time of becoming 'an instrument of the Labor Party'. In fact there was never a cosy relationship between WEL and the ALP, even when the Whitlam government in its first weeks in power seemed to be implementing a WEL agenda. During the election WEL had incurred ALP wrath by campaigning for Independent Black Liberation candidate Pat Eatock. Moreover, WEL was highly critical of the Whitlam government over the defeat of the attempt at abortion law reform and the stumbles over child care. WEL's expectations were very high. In 1973 it was 'not satisfied' with a promise of equal pay if the prices and incomes referendum were passed, and demanded by telegram an assurance from the Prime Minister of sex discrimination legislation.[52]

When under siege by the Opposition-dominated Senate, the Whitlam government did sometimes seek help from women's groups. In October 1975 the Labor Attorney-General asked for pressure to be brought on Opposition senators to pass the Legal Aid Bill, given the importance of legal aid for family law matters. If the Bill did not survive its passage through the Senate the government would not be able to fulfil its commitment to outposting legal aid officers in the Hunter Region Working Women's Centre and the Brisbane Women's Centre.[53]

Late 1975 was a tumultuous period. WEL's Australia-wide protests against the Labor government in October over the Women's Adviser position were followed in November by great anxiety over whether a conservative government would maintain the child care and other equal opportunity initiatives of the Whitlam government. While some members were so distressed by the dismissal of the Prime Minister that they thought WEL should come out in support of Labor at the 1975 federal election, others successfully argued that WEL must maintain its non-partisan and non-aligned stance.

The election of a conservative government saw a general reduction, although not an elimination, of NGO influence on government. There began a pattern, repeated by WEL in subsequent decades, of using the Opposition and minor parties (particularly the Democrats from 1977) where direct access to government failed. An early example was the disappearance of the ACT Consultative Committee on Children's Services, an avenue for community groups to have input into the funding and range of children's services. It was only reinstated after WEL organised for members of Parliament to ask questions in the House of Representatives.[54]

While more open to NGOs, the ALP was frequently impatient of criticism from advocacy groups, believing they should be suitably grateful for 'half loaves' rather than continuing to argue for the whole one. In or out of government, the ALP was unappreciative of critics such as Mary Owen, co-ordinator of the Working Women's Centre in Melbourne from 1975–85 and a long-time WEL advocate on industrial relations matters. Owen was a persistent critic of the influence of the Shop, Distributive & Allied Employees Association, which opposed equal opportunity legislation. She wrote in *Labor Essays* that politically aware women might find the Liberal Party more progressive than the ALP, because of the structural equality of women in the party organisation in Victoria and because of Fraser government policies such as setting up the National Women's Advisory Council.[55]

In Tasmania, it was a Liberal Opposition Leader who took up WEL's concerns about discriminatory advertising of public service jobs such as clerks, cadets, technical officers and technicians, and obtained a commitment from the Labor government that such discrimination would cease.[56] Nonetheless, another Tasmanian Liberal politician fell out with WEL, with serious consequences later on. Jocelyn Newman described herself as a founding member of WEL in Launceston, who had become disillusioned when her local branch passed a motion condemning the dismissal of Prime Minister Whitlam by the Governor-General.[57]

A struggle ensued over the Launceston women's refuge. A Hobart women's refuge had already been initiated by WEL but when WEL–Launceston made a successful application, Newman was responsible for a conservative takeover. The refuge committee acquired a male president who declared he had no intention of it becoming a collective on the model of mainland refuges.[58] WEL members were refused voting rights on the grounds their membership applications (and payment of subscriptions) had not been approved by the committee. After she became Minister Assisting the Prime Minister for the Status of Women in 1996, Senator Newman was responsible for abolishing WEL's operational funding in 1999.

The move of the Liberal Party to the right under the Howard leadership took the party in policy directions that WEL believed to be inimical to women's interests, particularly in the areas of tax and industrial relations. Howard had long made clear his conservative social agenda and his desire to change the tax system in ways that would have a detrimental effect on secondary earners. This agenda was commented on by WEL–Victoria in 1985: 'Howard reveals his true colours (and they are certainly not green and purple)'. Howard's declaration on Sydney radio in the mid-1980s that his government would look to abolish paid maternity leave for federal public servants was taken as indicative of his attitude.[59]

Women within the Liberal Party attempted to resist these new directions. For example, the federal Women's Committee objected to women in the workforce being described as 'economic conscripts', and Senator Amanda Vanstone was interviewed for *WEL–Informed*.[60] But the drift continued and it became increasingly difficult for WEL to work with the Coalition, just as in the United States it was becoming increasingly difficult for the National Organization for Women to work with the Republican Party. While at first non-partisan feminist advocacy made inroads into all sides of politics, shifts to the Right reframed feminist advocacy as a tool of the Left.

During the time of the Hawke and Keating governments a number of WEL policies were achieved. However, WEL was still very critical over Keating's proposal to introduce a broad-based consumption tax in 1985 and the introduction of the enterprise bargaining principle in 1991. WEL's position on indirect taxation and decentralised wage-bargaining was consistent regardless of the political party promoting such policies. WEL provided visible support for the Hawke government's *Sex Discrimination Act* in 1984 but it also provided visible support to the Howard government over gun control in 1996.

Even when the ALP was most responsive to the WEL agenda, as at the time of the Whitlam government, there were no illusions:

> The ALP made a much better showing in the form guide than the LCP, but it is riddled with male chauvinists who believe that women's place is in the home. If we fail to keep up the pressure they will let women's issues gather dust on obscure shelves.[61]

If we look at the ratings of candidates and party policies published by WEL between 1972 and 2004 we find that it is generally minor parties such as the Australia Party, and later the Australian Democrats and Greens, who came out on top. This is not surprising when, for example, the Australian Democrats were making the running on paid maternity leave but the ALP sometimes expected greater support than it received. In South Australia, Labor politician Anne Levy had less to do with WEL in the 1980s and 1990s as she believed it had become a 'nest of Democrats' who denigrated equally the Liberal and Labor parties. She still asked questions in parliament, however, whenever WEL wanted her to.

Party affiliations

But what of WEL members themselves? Was the non-party character of the organisation subverted by the partisan loyalties (or disloyalties) of its members? Among those who joined WEL in the first three years,

22 per cent of those responding to the WEL history survey said they were active in a political party at the time of joining: 20 per cent in the ALP and two per cent in the Australia Party. A survey of WEL membership in Western Australia in 1974 also found that of those who identified with a political party more identified with the ALP (41 per cent) than with any other party, while significant minorities also identified with the Liberal Party (24 per cent) and the Australia Party (26 per cent).[62] The survey of participants in the 1975 WEL national conference in Sydney found about 28 per cent belonged to a political party (19 per cent ALP, 6 per cent Australia Party, 2 per cent Liberals and 1 per cent others).[63]

A 1981 survey of Melbourne WEL members who joined in 1972 and were still members in 1975 found that they tended to be small 'l' liberals who were active in both Labor and Liberal parties.[64] One wrote in her application for membership that her husband had been president of the Camberwell branch of the Liberal Party, that she was involved with the Family Planning Clinic and the Brotherhood of St Laurence, but had time to spare and thought WEL a wonderful concept.[65] In the mid-1970s WEL–Victoria's office manager, Jan Plummer, was a Liberal Party member and Councillor on Nunawading Council.

Liberal Party members with a long-standing involvement with WEL included lawyer and businesswoman Eve Mahlab in Victoria (Businesswoman of the Year in 1982). Mahlab and others such as Julie Macphee and Prue Sibree MP created the Liberal Feminist Network within the Victorian Division of the Liberal Party. The Liberal Feminist Network produced a discussion paper in 1982 strongly opposing views being expressed by the Liberal Minister for Social Security, Senator Fred Chaney, on the family as an alternative to publicly-funded community services. WEL also worked closely with federal Liberal frontbencher Ian Macphee on discrimination matters during the Fraser and Hawke governments. Ian Macphee was a popular speaker at the Victorian State conference in 1977 and Dame Beryl Beaurepaire was another highly effective ally during the Fraser period.

In New South Wales in the 1970s Helen Coonan, later a Senator and Cabinet Minister in the Howard government, was a prominent participant in WEL lobbying for divorce law reform, prostitution law reform and the NSW *Anti-Discrimination Act*. In the 1990s she was active in saving the Sex Discrimination position, under threat from her own government and unfilled for over a year. Virginia Chadwick, later a Liberal State Cabinet Minister, was also a member of WEL–NSW. In South Australia Liberals Jennifer Cashmore and Joan Hall, who both became State Cabinet members, were WEL members, while SA Democrat Senator Janine Haines also was close to WEL while party leader.

Evidence from the WEL history survey confirms, however, that although most WEL members were not active in party politics, those who were active were more likely to support 'left of centre' parties. From early on WEL encouraged its members to become active within

Helen Coonan, Julia Freebury and Joan Bielski at WEL–NSW meeting, 1970s. *Joan Bielski.*

political parties to influence party policies in a feminist direction. After joining WEL the proportion of early members who were active in political parties rose from 22 to 49 per cent. There were some high-profile Liberal Party members with long-standing involvement with WEL, but as the Liberal Party moved to the Right in the 1990s, identification with feminism became increasingly difficult and a distinct career liability. This widening rift may be responsible for the under-representation of Liberal Party members in the WEL history survey of 2002–03, much more so than in surveys of WEL membership conducted in the 1970s.

The link between WEL membership and careers in the Labor Party was perhaps most obvious at the federal level, where all six ministers who had responsibility for the status of women under the Hawke and Keating governments had been WEL members. But a background in WEL did not guarantee an easy relationship with it in government. As we will see further on, Senator Susan Ryan, a founding member of WEL–ACT, was furious over WEL describing the *Affirmative Action Act* as a 'toothless tiger' because of its lack of sanctions for non-compliance. Senator Jocelyn Newman was similarly outraged by criticism of Howard government cuts to women's agencies and programs. So a minister's prior WEL membership did not necessarily make for smooth relations between WEL and government. On the other hand, ministers who had taken WEL values into government often ended up in conflict with government priorities.

Moreover, if we look at the two most recent cohorts of respondents to the WEL history survey we can see there is a changing pattern of partisan loyalties over time. The proportion active in the Greens after joining WEL has risen, with a corresponding decline in the proportion of ALP activists. If WEL members are liberal reformers, then it is the Greens who are increasingly attracting liberal reformers.

Practitioner perspectives

Over the years there have always been political women who have distanced themselves from the need for institutionalised feminist lobbying. They have expressed confidence in their own ability to enter mainstream political institutions and achieve the things they want without the support of feminist pressure from outside. Internationally, such attitudes were commonly expressed in the period just before the arrival of second-wave feminism, when feminist organisations had come to be seen as old-fashioned and out of date. This was a period marked by the closing down of many women's organisations within political parties, on the grounds they were holding women back. Soon afterwards such bodies were revived and re-energised to form a political base for affirmative action and other feminist demands.[66]

Here is an example of distancing from feminist advocacy by a conservative woman MP: 'I take issue with Women's Electoral Lobby, because the very name connotes that's all they are, that they go cap in hand to some man, the minister, asking for what they want. But I want to be the Minister.'[67] A very similar sentiment was expressed by a Labor Minister: 'Why join a women's group to lobby government ministers when you can become a Minister yourself?'[68]

On the other hand, separate institution-building creates public space in which women are central and women-centred perspectives can be crystallised. Such institutions provide a collective voice for women as well as organisational leverage. Moreover, international research suggests that the existence of separate institutions, mandated to focus on issues of gender equality, greatly strengthens the capacity and propensity of women parliamentarians and ministers to raise such issues themselves. Institutions of this kind may include women's caucuses within parliamentary parties or within Parliament, or women's movement organisations outside. Association with and membership of such organisations greatly increases the likelihood that women parliamentarians will act as advocates for gender equality issues.[69]

Janine Haines, the first woman leader of the Australian Democrats, captured this thought when paying tribute to the importance of WEL in helping her raise issues in Parliament of concern to women:

> By late 1974 I had begun to realise that women needed to take some positive steps to change their lot in life. Joining a lobby

group was one option. Becoming a politician was another.
In the end I chose both and although I was more active as a
member of parliament than as a member of WEL, I was also
more effective as a member of parliament because of the
presence and actions of members of WEL.[70]

Jennifer Cashmore, a South Australian Liberal Cabinet Minister,
agreed:

> Belonging to the Women's Electoral Lobby has always seemed
> to me to be mandatory for women politicians, whatever their
> political affiliation. There has been a political energy about
> WEL which enables members to tap into both long-standing
> and emerging issues which are of concern to women.[71]

WEL joins the 'new class'

WEL had inherited the social liberalism that had been an important
element in Australian history and in the history of the women's movement, looking to government to secure equal opportunity and the
public good. This orientation came into collision with the upsurge in
the English-speaking world of a populist form of market liberalism,
hostile to all forms of state provision and social welfare.[72] This 'market
populism' suggested that out of the social movements of the 1960s
and 1970s had emerged a new class which had a vested interest in the
expansion of the public sector.

Although its gendered nature was rarely spelled out, the core
members of this supposedly privileged 'new class', defined by concern
over issues such as the environment and human rights, were the well-
educated but underpaid members of feminised professions such as
social work, teaching and librarianship. WEL members were framed as
archetypal members of this new class. Their values were dismissed as
'political correctness' but also, and importantly, as expressing contempt
for the values of ordinary people.

The notion of a well-educated new class with a vested interest
in the public sector was reinforced by public choice theory, promoted

by free-market think tanks such as the Centre for Independent Studies in Sydney and the Institute of Public Affairs in Melbourne. This theory depicted all public interest groups as essentially rent-seeking 'special interests' attempting to gain a better return through the state than they could obtain through the market. Women's advocacy groups were debunked as trying to obtain returns for women that were well above those they could obtain through the market (or marriage).

Some leading Labor identities found such discourse quite appealing and joined in denouncing new-class 'elites' and 'special interests'. Feminists were identified as responsible for the alienation of blue-collar voters from the Labor Party through their insistence on elite concerns such as equal opportunity and child care. In 1987 Labor Finance Minister Peter Walsh suggested that campaigns for equal opportunity were achieving little other than giving 'jobs to hairy-legged Stalinists from Women's Electoral Lobby'.[73] According to Walsh, feminists were like other members of the new class in that they worked in the non-market sector, earned above-median incomes and advocated publicly-provided services such as child care because they provided sinecures for the new class.[74] Later, Labor leader Mark Latham agreed that WEL was part of a symbolic class that supported redistribution at the expense of working-class taxpayers and constructed women as victims.[75]

The men's rights groups that arose during the last decades of the 20th century as part of a backlash against reforms to family law also claimed that WEL was responsible for victimising working-class men. One of these groups wrote in a submission to a review of the *Affirmative Action Act*:

> There is no doubt, no doubt whatsoever, that the AA Act 1986 legislation was feminist-inspired and designed to replace men in our workforce by women … The main architect of this feminist-inspired legislation has been Women's Electoral Lobby (WEL) whose members have infiltrated the decision-making processes of Federal and State governments, assisted by the numerous women's departments and offices using the millions of taxpayers' dollars available.[76]

The tactic of portraying WEL as powerful 'man-haters' added an extra element to new-class discourse and the attribution of contempt for others. But, as we shall see, this idea of contempt was at its most powerful when it was seen as being directed at other women.

Having contempt for ordinary women?

Those promoting the new discourses in Australia suggested that feminists were an intrinsic part of a new class that would do well out of the promotion of equality. Given that the new public discourse was based on assumptions about the universality of self-interest, this was not sufficient in itself to discredit equal opportunity projects. Elites also had to be depicted as sneering at the values of ordinary people. Hence, despite feminist ideology being directed at the revaluation of women and the validation of their choices, feminists were now depicted as having contempt for other women. In 1998 Liberal Prime Minister John Howard spoke of the 'stridency of ultra-feminist groups in the community who sneer at and look down on women who choose to provide full-time care for their children'.[77] *Radio transcript*

Women outside the paid workforce became the alleged victims of feminist contempt, but were also portrayed as heroes because they were assumed to make few demands on the state, were content to be economically dependent on husbands and to provide community services on an unpaid basis rather than demanding equal pay. New groups such as REAL Women in Canada and Women Who Want to be Women (now Endeavour Forum) in Australia highlighted through their names an implied contrast with equality-seekers, who were not 'real' women. Women Who Want to be Women (WWWW) was a small but vociferous group founded by Babette Francis in 1979 to oppose feminist influence on government. WWWW not only campaigned against anti-discrimination and equal opportunity legislation but even lent its support to events such as beauty pageants. Such groups were welcome within free-market circles because their claims were seen as compatible with cheap government in a way that the claims of feminist equality-seekers, wanting paid community services, were not.

Increasingly, any measures to provide equal opportunity to women in the paid workforce, such as paid maternity leave, subsidised child care or re-entry allowances and training programs, were framed as a form of discrimination against women who had chosen to be home-makers, in addition to being wasteful public expenditure. The retention of the individual as the unit of account in the tax system was also seen as discriminating against single-income families; rather, family unit taxation that would impose high rates of tax on second earners was favoured. Anti-discrimination legislation was opposed on the ground that private employers with the incentive of the profit motive would make wiser choices than 'equal opportunity bureaucrats whose salaries are paid by taxpayers'.[78]

WEL constantly had to reiterate that it was a lobby for women in the home as well as women in the workforce and was not trying to force women into work at gunpoint or to crèche their children. It was society that had downgraded the status of women as homemakers, creating the 'just a housewife' syndrome, not equality-seekers. WEL–Tasmania, for example, wrote to the *Mercury* pointing out that WEL's pre-Budget submission calling for a shift from child endowment to an allowance paid to mothers would be recognition of the worth of this role and remove some of the economic pressure influencing women's choices.[79] In 1979 Mary Owen wrote to *The Age* to remind readers that half of WEL's members were full-time homemakers and that WEL was not hell-bent on getting all women into the workforce.[80] WEL's success in promoting feminist policy demands to government called forth the counter-attempt to undermine its representative claims and to create divisions between women at home and women in the paid workforce.

'Women in the Home' groups were formed within WEL in Melbourne and Sydney in the 1970s, highlighting the theme that women should have the choice to stay at home and not feel pressured to join the paid workforce. WEL emphasised that women might choose to stay at home for many reasons: because they wanted more

time with growing children; because they found satisfaction in working in the community, including in WEL; because they could not or did
not want to go back to jobs for which they had originally trained; or
because they were setting up a business at home. The newly formed
groups aimed to combat the problems experienced by women at home,
including economic dependence, lack of status, loss of self-identity and
lack of the stimulation of the adult world. They wanted to link women
at home with education, retraining, child care, feminist discussion and
information.

The convenor of the Melbourne Women in the Home group first
approached WEL in 1973, saying she was an 'ordinary housewife but
perhaps I could help with licking stamps or something'. She was greatly
encouraged by the response she received:

> Ordinary housewives are just what we want in WEL and
> the more the better – it is one of the main purposes of our
> existence and don't forget what you call an ordinary housewife
> is what we regard as a VIP. Goodness knows what talent each
> one has – interest alone will bring out whatever there is to help
> us get somewhere.[81]

The group, located in Maroondah in the outer suburbs, held a successful forum on the topic 'Who cares about the housewife?', provided
speakers to schools and mothers' clubs and submissions to government. The Sydney group found health to be a major issue, including
loneliness, depression, the attitudes of doctors and family, lack of self-
esteem and loss of confidence.[82] Meanwhile the Brisbane convenor of
WEL presented evidence to a Status of Women Inquiry that women at
home needed educational courses and better daytime radio and television to prevent the common resort to barbiturates: 'I know – I used to
do the same thing,' she said.[83] The support provided to women in the
home was often so successful it helped propel them out of the home:
'The only trouble was that they enthused each other to go to work,
or to study and, suddenly, Women in the Home, Maroondah region,
didn't exist any more'.[84]

A perennial question for women's movements in the 20th century was whether to promote the independence of women through payment for their household work. The economic dependence of women encouraged despotic attitudes within the family (then referred to as the 'Turk complex') and rendered women vulnerable to poverty on the loss of a male breadwinner. In the 1920s there was much interest in the concept of maternal and child endowment as a way of addressing the issue.[85] Such a strategy did involve risks, including the exclusion of married women from the paid workforce and the improbability that maternal endowment would be at an adequate level to secure financial independence. Later, it was also seen as an impediment to men sharing household work more equally. In the 1970s 'wages for housework' campaigns re-emerged in the United Kingdom and a number of other countries, and the issue was debated extensively within WEL. The 1974 national conference resolved, however, that the only conditions under which WEL would consider a 'mother's wage' would be under a proper work-value study and industrial determination, including margins for skill.[86] WEL did, however, support proper compensation and rehabilitation for women injured in the home.

Although WEL distanced itself from wages for housework campaigns, its 1984 national policy declared:

> That period of a person's life spent working full or part-time at home with children and other dependants should be regarded as socially productive to the community. WEL believes that responsibilities in the home – child-rearing, household management and finance – need to be equitably shared among the adults in the household. The child-caring parent needs to have the opportunity to participate in the life of the community in ways of his or her own choosing, including employment, education, professional, civic and industrial organisations, sports, arts and crafts.[87]

An example of WEL's commitment to women in the home was the big campaign in the 1970s for the reform of probate and the removal of death duties where property was passing to a surviving spouse

 NSW planning meeting, 1970s. Di Graham crouching.
Joan Bielski.

or common-law wife. This was a major concern for women without an independent source of income. Many women were left as at
least 'temporary paupers' on their husband's death, without access
to his estate from the day of his death until the granting of probate.
Despite having served as 'unpaid housekeepers' for perhaps forty
years they might well have to sell the family home to pay the death
duties on it, unless they could prove they had paid for at least half
from their own income. The campaign was initiated by WEL members
on the Gold Coast, where there were many retired people, and was
endorsed nationally in 1974. In Sydney Di Graham became convenor
of the probate action group. Graham's work for probate law reform,
as well as for equal rights to marital assets and rape law reform, was
recognised in 1997 through the award of an honorary doctorate by
Macquarie University.

WEL pointed out that women who had been discriminated against by being forced to leave paid employment on marriage were again discriminated against by death duties that did not acknowledge their enforced economic dependence. While members of parliament eulogised the family, they did nothing to prevent widows who had dutifully stayed home from being pauperised. The campaign had some successes, with State governments introducing exemptions for property passing to spouses, but it was soon rendered irrelevant by the abolition of death duties, beginning with the Queensland government in 1977. By 1981 all jurisdictions had abolished death duties.[88] The overall abolition of death duties, as contrasted with their removal from transfers of estates to surviving spouses, was not WEL policy. WEL supported the proper nature of death duties as an inter-generational rather than intra-generational tax and indeed suggested that any shortfall in revenue from abolition of death duties on spouse transfers could be made up by a small increase in other death duties. The abolition of death taxes removed an equitable source of revenue for the kinds of social expenditure in which WEL was interested and contributed to the increased reliance of State governments on regressive sources of revenue such as gambling taxes (and hence the fostering of gambling industries).

Marital property was another area where WEL persistently championed the claims of homemakers, in 1974 raising the issue in its submissions on the Family Law Bill, when a delegation, including Eve Mahlab from Melbourne and Desley Deacon from Canberra, spent 75 minutes with the Attorney-General, Lionel Murphy.[89] As a result the Bill was amended to allow women's contribution as homemakers to be taken into consideration in property settlements, and not simply the financial contributions a wife might have made. The Attorney-General did not accept WEL's suggestion of community of property, but went some way towards the recognition of the non-cash contribution of homemakers to the acquisition of property during a marriage.

The family law action group in Sydney, led by Jocelynne Scutt and Di Graham, found, however, that bias against homemakers was persisting in the new Family Law Court. Family law settlements still did not reflect women's in-kind contribution to marital property. A parliamentary review of the operation of the Act provided the opportunity for Scutt to write a 40-page submission on how it could be improved. Next, WEL distributed a discussion paper on community of property to Family Law Court judges, politicians, women's organisations, lawyers and law schools.[90] To broaden the discussion, Scutt and Graham published the book *For Richer, For Poorer* (Penguin 1984). Meanwhile, sharp divisions had arisen within the organisation over the concept of community of property, with some members believing it entrenched older views of marriage as a meal ticket.

A related concern was divorced women's lack of access to their husband's superannuation, despite their indirect contributions as home-makers.[91] Under the *Family Law Act* superannuation was not regarded as current property available to be divided, but the Family Court was able to adjust other assets to make up for loss of future superannuation rights. Although Prime Minister Fraser was said to be impressed by WEL's arguments concerning women's indirect contribution to super-annuation[92], it was to be more than twenty years before the Howard government gave the Court the power to divide superannuation bene-fits with a presumption of a 50:50 split. This again was controversial because the division of superannuation was associated with division of rights in the matrimonial home and hence its sale, where once there would have been a presumption in favour of the mother keeping the house.

In general, WEL supported the right of all women to have 'free choice in their decision to remain at home or enter the workforce' but it consistently opposed tax measures that were tied to women's non-participation in the workforce. Such measures were seen as militating against free choice by raising the effective marginal tax rates for second earners.[93] Tax benefits for the primary earner should be redirected into increased family allowances paid to the primary carer, in order 'to increase the economic independence of the woman in the home and gain social recognition of the productivity of domestic labour and the cost of child care'.[94] While some gains were made in this area, adequate recognition of women's unpaid work remained an intractable problem in policy terms.

The nature of WEL's policy advocacy on issues such as women in the home, however, had little to do with the way WEL was framed in the discourse of right-wing columnists, talk-back radio hosts and some political leaders. The political tide was running in the opposite direction to WEL's belief in the role of the public sector in underpinning equal opportunity. The desire to discredit a proactive role for government led to the portrayal of feminism as an elite agenda displaying contempt for ordinary women. This was an effective populist strategy, but extremely galling for those engaged in the long struggle to empower women.

WEL in political science

Traditionally, Australian political science had little time for women. However, in 1958 the Social Science Research Council (now the Academy of Social Sciences) took the radical step of sponsoring research on the role of women in Australian society. They commissioned assistant editor of the *New Statesman*, Norman MacKenzie, to come from London to undertake the project. When asked by a journalist to explain why a man had to be brought from overseas to undertake this research, MacKenzie explained it needed to be done by someone who was not a woman and not an Australian in order to be objective. The resulting book, *Women in Australia*, was a useful overview, but patronising rather than objective. The author was very dismissive of the 'sex antagonism' he saw as underlying women's organisations – the idea that women might have interests distinct from those of men or in conflict with them. He saw women's organisations as offering a 'cut-price version of sex equality', providing a protected environment for women unwilling to enter the masculine world on its own terms. Academic reviewers endorsed his critical attitude, one of them declaring that Australian women's organisations were themselves 'mainly responsible for Australian women's position as second-class citizens'. The book was updated in 1974 in time to warn a second wave of feminist activists against 'sterile forms of man-hatred'.[95]

Political science textbooks sometimes forgot to mention women at all – for example, there was no index entry for women in J.D.B. Miller's *Australian Government and Politics*, which was reprinted many times between 1954 and 1971. On the other hand, when WEL became a major political phenomenon some political scientists were over-inclined to provide advice or even a well-intentioned seal of approval for the organisation's survey technique. A new approach, neither patronising nor forgetful, was urgently needed to allow feminist activists to speak for themselves. This was the approach taken by Henry Mayer, the first professor of political science in Australia to take the new social movements seriously. In his book on the 1972 federal election, *Labor to Power*, Mayer included a section called 'Women in politics' that had six groundbreaking articles by WEL members on different aspects of the WEL campaign. Around the same time, in the process of encouraging Anne Summers to publish *Damned Whores and God's Police*, he realised that he should wash the dishes, which according to his wife he did from then on.[96]

WEL has long been the women's organisation most often named in textbooks on Australian politics or on websites devoted to the subject. The oldest of these websites is <http://www.Australianpolitics.com>, established in 1995 and oriented to providing resources for Year 12 school students doing politics in Victoria. When accessed in January 2007 the section on pressure groups contained information only on WEL and the Australian Medical Association, with the WEL entry highlighting activity on abortion and women's health. Similarly, when members of the Women's Caucus of the Australasian Political Studies Association surveyed first-year political science textbooks in 1996 they found that WEL was named in six of the nine most commonly used.[97]

In an authoritative article in one of these textbooks, political scientist John Warhurst identified WEL as the first single-issue group in modern times to 'directly threaten the political parties by intensively promoting a political issue across party lines'. He acknowledged that the term 'single-issue group' was a misnomer in that single issues might be 'views of the world potentially as broad as those on which our major parties are based'.[98] While this is correct at one level, there are problems in WEL being depicted simply as a pressure group, ignoring its social movement side. Social movement organisations are usually characterised not by the pursuit of pre-given interests but by the process of mobilising identities and reshaping norms. Pressure groups are also seen as somehow less legitimate than political parties because parties take responsibility for 'aggregating' policy demands, even if such aggregation is at the expense of women. The label 'single-issue group' may also lend support to the view that public interest groups are inevitably 'special interest groups' that seek to extend the role of the public sector for their own benefit and at the expense of business and ordinary taxpayers.

In Canada, feminist political scientists have contested the categorising of women's organisations as 'interest groups' and emphasised the expressive rather than instrumental functions of women's movement organisations. This process is well captured by Carleton University's Susan Phillips when she says, 'The politics of identity are reflexive and require a person to name herself, not simply to articulate an interest'.[99] So although much progress has been made in the recognition of women as political actors, the work of groups such as WEL is still not always being represented as clearly as it could be.

One mistake that a number of political scientists have made is to suggest that WEL was founded to get more women into politics. It was described in an authoritative journal as 'a non-partisan interest group formed in 1972 to secure the election of more women candidates [that] broadened its role in the late 1970s to promote women's issues in general'.[100] As we have already seen, WEL was founded to get women's issues onto politicians' radars rather than to get women into parliament. WEL–Sydney provided a succinct statement of its aims: 'We identify sexism in society, expose it and lobby against it.'[101]

Even when working most directly to encourage women candidates, as during the 1970s with Melbourne's local government kit, the encouragement of women candidates came only fourth in the listing of WEL aims and objectives. First was the education of candidates and councillors on feminist issues, then informing the voting public, then ascertaining the views of candidates and councillors and committing them to action, and only then the encouragement and support of women candidates. The issues of greatest concern at local government level were candidates' support for child-care centres, family planning clinics and other community services. Neither in Victoria nor in other States and Territories did women candidates necessarily rate highly in WEL surveys, and this was even the case when they ran under a 'women's' label.[102] Understanding and commitment were more important.

3

ORGANISATIONAL DILEMMAS

As a daughter of Women's Liberation, WEL was opposed to hierarchy – the masculine principle that had been imposed on women and had so stifled their creativity. Instead, every woman was to count equally and all decisions were to be taken collectively. All positions such as chairing meetings, convening action groups or editing newsletters were to rotate, so that hierarchy did not re-emerge. As the old joke has it: 'How many feminists does it take to change a light bulb?' Answer: 'Only one, but the chair has to rotate.'

Typically, journalists trying to write an International Women's Day story used to complain that the problem with communicating with both Women's Liberation and WEL was that they didn't believe in office-bearers or spokeswomen and 'even get upset if they are labelled leaders'.[1] Like Women's Liberation, WEL was committed to avoiding the features of male political institutions. This flew in the face of received wisdom about how pressure groups should behave, which included mirroring the institutions they were trying to influence. WEL had to deal with the dilemmas arising from being part of a social movement dedicated to empowering women through distributed leadership, while at the same time seeking to influence the policy decisions of political elites.

These dilemmas extended into the structures WEL was helping set up in government, where feminist organisational philosophy collided

International Women's Day march, Adelaide, 1970s. *Search Foundation-Tribune, Mitchell Library, State Library of NSW.*

with bureaucratic demands for managerial accountability. For example, in Western Australia WEL played a major role in the creation of a women's information service (WIRE) by the Burke Labor government in the 1980s. Its mandate was to empower women through the democratic provision of information and non-hierarchical collective decision-making. In one famous incident the government was embarrassed by a mailout for the Cockburn Sound Peace Camp going out through the Premier's Department. The Premier tried to reach the WIRE coordinator and when told she was away asked to speak to whoever was in charge. When told no one was 'in charge', he shouted 'You are all fired!'[2]

When government imposed a formal hierarchical structure on WIRE in 1990–91 and restricted the role of volunteers, WEL protested that the bureaucratisation of the service meant a loss of capacity to achieve its aims and a breaking of accountability to the women's movement.[3]

While WEL was opposed to hierarchy, this did not mean opposition to structure. Roneoed copies of 'The Tyranny of Structurelessness', an article by American Jo Freeman, were circulated widely. Freeman argued that the idea of 'structurelessness' had become a goddess in its own right in the Women's Liberation movement but was just as deceptive a notion as an 'objective' news story, 'value-free' social science or a 'free' economy.[4] Groups always gave rise to structures, whether formal or informal, and the idea of structurelessness served as a smokescreen for dominance by some. For everyone to participate on a more equal basis, the structures needed to be explicit and the rules available to everyone. Her answer to the 'tyranny of structurelessness' was a series of principles for democratic structuring, including distribution of authority for specified purposes and rotation of tasks.

WEL founder Beatrice Faust was influenced by Freeman as well as by feminist critiques of hierarchy. She believed a minimalist constitution was necessary and sought a structure with no president but with a secretary, treasurer and spokespersons to deal with the media. The idea of a constitution was controversial and some women walked out in protest. Faust blamed such collectivist philosophy for the failure of WEL's initial mailout survey in 1972. Politicians were alarmed by a communication that was not signed by an office-holder or indeed by anyone.[5]

In general WEL prided itself on giving women the confidence to become political actors; what was the organisational design appropriate to this goal? A founding member of WEL–Perth has written about the decision to have procedures that would liberate and empower as many women as possible:

> We would have rotating chairpersons and convenors so that
> a maximum number of women would gain experience and
> confidence; we would always provide childcare at meetings,
> by passing the hat around; we would form working groups as
> major issues emerged, to report back to the main meeting.[6]

The determination to keep WEL non-hierarchical made it different from organisations it has been compared with, such as the National Organization for Women in the United States. NOW began its life in 1966 with a full panoply of president, vice-presidents, chairman of the board and other office-bearers. In Australia, not only were there no presidents, there were no formal requirements for the creation of a WEL group. This was unlike New Zealand where a minimum of ten members was required and a capitation fee for each member had to be forwarded to WEL centrally. In Australia the philosophy inherited from Women's Liberation precluded such hierarchical controls and attempts to collect capitation fees were fairly unsuccessful. A group might originally be one woman and a newspaper advertisement might be used to recruit members.

'We are determined to avoid having leaders'

By January 1973 there were WEL groups in Melbourne, Sydney, Canberra, Hobart, Adelaide, Brisbane, Darwin, Alice Springs, Townsville, Wagga and many other country towns, and there would soon be a group in Perth. The urgent need to interview candidates in all federal electorates led to the multiplying of groups in rural areas and WEL became a 'huge self-propelling snowball', which at its height had some 75 groups around Australia. From Cairns to Cooma, Nhulunbuy to Nyngan, and Kalgoorlie to Kyabram, the groups were autonomous and independent, raising questions about how WEL could best operate with a national voice on national issues. There had already been one highly successful national exercise – the candidate survey. Following that exercise, pressure had to be maintained on the new federal government, quite apart from pressure on State governments and local councils. All groups were asked to prepare papers on how WEL should be organised for the first national conference in January 1973.

The NSW paper reported on a recent meeting to decide its own structure. There had been strong feeling that:

> We are determined to avoid having leaders – either convenors
> or permanent spokeswomen – or any form of power hierarchy.
> Like many other radical feminist organisations, in setting up
> a structure we want to move on from competitive masculine
> power politics, involving aggression and backstabbing, to true
> egalitarianism.[7]

Canberra members had a different view of what was needed to function as a national lobby group, believing that they would inevitably play a major role in lobbying at the federal level. Participants coming from other cities were gripped by fear that the Canberra group would suddenly gain control of WEL.[8]

Anne Summers was a keen observer of this conference and of its differences from the Women's Liberation conferences she had attended. She noted the agenda-setting papers on 'What makes a successful pressure group?' organised by Canberra WEL and given by political scientist Thelma Hunter and professional lobbyist Peter Cullen. She thought their performance 'terrifyingly convincing' on the need for a highly centralised national body with accumulated expertise and representation on departmental committees.

Nonetheless, after a day of sometimes bitter debate any move to set up a 'super-lobby' in Canberra was overturned. There had been a fierce reaction to Hunter's speech and that of Sue Butler (Ryan). Members from Sydney, Melbourne and Adelaide departed from their prepared speeches to remind conference participants of the significance of the grass-roots democratic structures of the women's movement.

Many of the country women, on the other hand, were genuinely puzzled by what they saw as anti-organisation and anti-leadership slogans and wanted a more traditional structure. Eventually a series of resolutions was passed guaranteeing local group autonomy, and accepting the need for Australia-wide agreement on national policies with only a clearing-house in Canberra.[9] National policy co-ordination across the country would be conducted by phone and telegram, with time-limits for responses and majority voting (each group to have an equal vote).

The themes raised in 1973 were to be at the heart of ongoing tensions within WEL. Metropolitan groups continued to distrust Canberra; regional groups, on the other hand, continued to lament being left out of information flows and called for more efficient dissemination from the centre. Often the metropolitan groups were blamed for leaving the regional groups out of the loop. Because the role of chair rotated, it was difficult for country members to notify the chair in advance of urgent issues they wished to raise. It was only in 1979 that WEL–NSW moved to naming in its newsletter the woman who would chair the next month's general meeting. Anti-hierarchical principles could lead sometimes to confusion – once in Adelaide a Greek-Australian member brought along another Greek woman whose English was limited. Halfway through the unstructured meeting she said: 'Don't you think we should go home? It could be midnight before they start this meeting!'[10]

Different WEL groups sometimes had different attitudes to issues of the day, or different priorities. For example, uranium mining became a priority issue for South Australian members, while WEL–NSW decided it was not a feminist issue. Sometimes long-standing differences resulted in difficulties in arriving at a uniform policy agreed on by all WEL groups – child care as a tax deduction is an outstanding example of this. Where policies were directed to State or local government this was less of an issue than where a consistent policy was required for lobbying federal government. In general, however, as community-based policy advocacy became more specialised and professionalised, the commitment to democratic collectivism became more difficult to sustain.

How WEL worked

The centrifugal pressures evident at the first national conference were to be given an additional push by one of the other conference decisions. It was agreed that Victoria would no longer publish the national *Broadsheet*, as production and postage had become a heavy burden when membership rose over 2000. Henceforth, every State was to produce its own newsletter and keep its own membership records – often jealously guarded.

Victoria ceased to have an overall role as co-ordinator of WEL activities and WEL–ACT was to be responsible for collection and dissemination of material for groups around Australia. It did not, however, have any role in maintaining membership data, and figures become somewhat rubbery from this point. By 1974 there were 52 rural and regional groups in addition to those in the capital cities. In New South Wales alone there were 35 electorate groups, 27 action groups and 1300 subscribers to the Sydney-based newsletter. Individuals formed action groups on issues close to their hearts, whether it was abortion, child care, education, Aboriginal women, environment and peace, health, media, law or employment.

In 1975 two Victorian WEL members wrote a heartfelt paper on 'Administering an unstructured organisation', emphasising the problems of relying on inefficient telephone trees and arguing for an office with a paid co-ordinator in each State to provide backup and a contact point for the media.[11] Figure 3.1 illustrates the long-standing attempt to maintain lobbying as the domain of the members and not of the 'office' or of paid staff.

An account of the structure of WEL–NSW in 1978 similarly emphasises its non-hierarchical nature and rotating chairs, the collective nature of decision making and the ability of any member to join the administrative committee or form a new action group ('no elected hierarchies or executive'). The action groups had themselves become the subject of controversy. They often developed a level of expertise in a particular area that frightened newcomers away. The position of 'contact' for the group also tended to accumulate power and a media profile, leading to initiatives to limit tenure in these positions.[12]

Some saw the energy generated by WEL's non-hierarchical structure as compensating for the lack of professional organisation. As Edna Ryan commented, 'The structural organisation of the Labor Party seems flat after the release and vitality in WEL.'[13] The level of activity

Figure 3.1 How WEL works

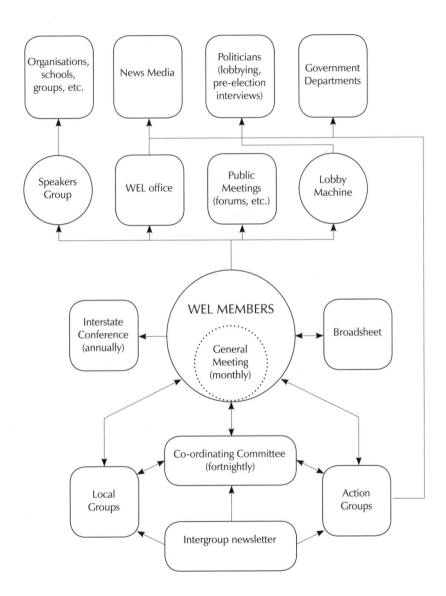

WEL–Victoria 1975.

in the 1970s was extraordinary, not only the electoral and policy work, but also the number of conferences being run annually both at national and State levels and, for a time, in regional areas. The early national conferences all attracted over 300 participants and sometimes as many as 500 (for a list of national conferences see Appendix A2). These were major feats for the volunteers who organised them. Despite the 'time poverty' of many of its members, WEL continued to organise its national conferences on a volunteer basis until 2000, to keep costs down for participants.

The momentum built up by the 1972 federal election strategy and culminating in International Women's Year (IWY) led to WEL groups proliferating all over rural Australia. Political energies were high as local groups mobilised to remove bars to women's employment, to create services and to tackle anything seen as demeaning or belittling women. This often required more courage than in the city, given rural conservatism. In Rockhampton it was male WEL members who were sent as 'front-line troops' into public bars to place 'this is offensive to women' stickers over girlie posters and advertisements.

As we have already seen, country women had different perspectives on how to organise from their city sisters, being less influenced by Women's Liberation organisational philosophy and more disadvantaged by the haphazard information flows within a decentralised organisation. The lack of formal structure within WEL caused continuing communication problems for rural branches. On the positive side, Katy Richmond reported in August 1973 that now WEL–Victoria had an office staffed every day she was circulating material to 25 regional groups.[14]

'Country conferences' began in 1973, and combined general topics with country-specific themes. For example, the conference in Wagga in December 1973 included the Prime Minister's Women's Adviser, Elizabeth Reid, Wagga's social worker, Sue Vardon, and Sylvia Baker, the Deputy Mayor of Deniliquin. A conference held in Echuca in April 1978 had speakers ranging from conservative Country Party politicians to Aboriginal women and representatives from the Rape Crisis Centre.

 Beatrice Faust and Senator Pat Giles at WEL national conference, Canberra, 1992. *Elaine Odgers Norling.*

There were also attempts to hold mainstream WEL conferences in rural areas. Efforts to hold the second national conference in Albury-Wodonga fell through and although the 1974 NSW State conference was held in Taree, there were complaints that some of the most prominent Sydney members did not turn up.[15]

The founding of an active WEL group in Cairns brought some of the frustrations over poor communications to a head. The closest group to Cairns was in Townsville – a day away by car. The convenor of the new Cairns group was told at the Women and Politics conference in Canberra that WEL groups communicated with each other by exchanging newsletters. However, when Cairns sent out their newsletter to ten WEL groups they received newsletters back from only three groups (Townsville, Melbourne and Hobart). Moreover, they had not been able to get hold of a copy of WEL's 1975 election questionnaire and were placed in the invidious position of having the Liberal candidate for Leichhardt say, 'Never mind, girls, I'll get you a copy of the questionnaire from Liberal Party headquarters'.[16]

Ceding power to Canberra?

Despite the difficulties caused by not having a national office, for a number of years there was resistance to the idea of setting one up in Canberra, close to the federal government and parliament, on the grounds that power would inevitably drift to the centre. In the United States in 1973–74 there was similar resistance to the setting up of offices in Washington by NOW and the National Women's Political Caucus. The initiation of national lobbying was seen as requiring a uniform organisational position and hence centralised decision-making; State chapters in both American organisations protested by refusing to hand over national dues, something that was to be mirrored in the history of WEL.[17]

The decision to set up a WEL national office eventually came at the 1978 national conference. This was a major breakthrough in organisational terms but there were still many reservations about ceding power to 'Canberra' or to paid staff members. The new part-time national communication officer was to be funded through membership pledges made at the conference. Officially the position was to be responsible to the annual national conference; more realistically it would be responsible to a new national management committee consisting of a representative or proxy from each State and Territory and a national treasurer. In the event, WEL–ACT always played a disproportionate role in support of the national office and in paying for its upkeep, with sporadic attempts to raise levies from State WEL groups proving largely unsuccessful.

The role of the national communication officer was hedged around to ensure she did not actually become a professional lobbyist on behalf of the organisation. Her role was strictly confined to facilitating exchange of information between WEL groups, monitoring federal government activities and supporting national campaigns. She was not to engage in lobbying herself nor liaise with groups outside WEL. She was certainly not to develop a media profile. This was similar to the situation in New South Wales, where the part-time paid co-ordinator was told *never* to make statements to the press unless instructed by an action group or simply to reiterate WEL policy.[18] Despite the part-time (ten hours) and limited nature of the new position, its significance was recognised by the nature of the selection committee chosen by national conference, which included leading femocrats and government policy experts.[19]

The national office was in Women's House in Canberra, at 3 Lobelia Street, O'Connor. The Department of Capital Territory had provided a lease for this house in 1975, as its contribution to IWY. At first the only room available was the laundry but by 1982 the office had moved into the main part of Women's House and the part-time national communication officer became the part-time national co-ordinator. At the national conference of that year Joan Bielski made a number of timely suggestions for strengthening the position.

This chapter discusses only two of the women who were to take on the role of national co-ordinator, Pamela Denoon and Jane Elix. Other national co-ordinators brought their own strengths and networks to the position (for the full list see Appendix). The new national co-ordinator in 1982, Pamela Denoon, was known for her tact, a quality needed for the sensitive task of building up the national office. She enabled it to respond to the unprecedented level of inquiries and consultations initiated by the new federal Labor government, despite the fact that she was only paid for ten hours a week. Her slight stammer made her a natural 'back-room' person and perhaps deflected the kind of anxieties engendered by the media exposure of her successor Jane Elix.

Denoon worked hard behind the scenes for the WEL team at the Economic Summit of 1983, and in putting together the coalition of women's organisations supporting the ratification of the UN Women's Convention (CEDAW), and the passage of the Commonwealth *Sex Discrimination Act*. Typical of her style was the large party she engineered on the lawns of Parliament House to celebrate the passage of the Sex Discrimination Bill through the House of Representatives on 7 March 1984.

Unlike many subsequent co-ordinators, Denoon continued to play an active role after moving to a job in the Office of Local Government. She did lobbying and media work on the Affirmative Action Bill as well as helping with the large conferences of the mid-1980s. In government she was able to work on equity issues close to her heart through the funding of a study of women in local government, *Getting the Numbers*. The setting up of the annual Pamela Denoon Lecture after her premature death from leukaemia is described in chapter 8.

Despite the development of the national office under Denoon, the new co-ordinator in 1985, Jane Elix, still had to face resistance from State groups opposed to either 'Canberra' or 'paid staff' taking too much of a public role. Thanks to the increased grant from the Office for the Status of Women, Elix could be employed for thirty hours a week. Her only preparation was experience with campus groups and the Canberra Reclaim the Night collective. There was hostility to the national co-ordinator 'speaking for WEL', even though she was the person with most day-to-day contact with media and government. Public speaking

Ruth Webber (CEP employee) and Jane Elix (WEL national co-ordinator). *Good Weekend*, 4–6 April 1986, p. 27. *Courtesy Fairfax Photos.*

was supposed to be done by convenors of national action committees in different policy areas but in practice these convenors were often in sensitive jobs, such as in the public service, and were either unable to be publicly associated with WEL or were difficult to get hold of at short notice. Elix observed that although she understood why founding WEL members believed in non-hierarchical structures and opposed specialisation of roles and functions, in practice this made it difficult to compete in the political arena of the 1980s.[20]

Inevitably the media came to the national co-ordinator, who was accessible and, in Elix's case, a highly proficient lobbyist who later worked for the Australian Conservation Foundation and the Australian Federation of Consumer Organisations. At WEL she was supported by Ruth Webber, employed by WEL under the Community Employment Program (CEP) and later a Senator from Western Australia. As has been written elsewhere:

> An advocacy organisation needs a high media profile, especially with the Canberra press gallery. It helps considerably if its chief spokesperson is articulate, readily available and skilled at providing the short dramatic quotation or the telling statistic that TV journalists and headline writers need. A high media profile helps increase legitimacy and access to main players. Ministers, their advisers and senior public servants believe an organization is important if they frequently see its spokesperson on the television news or hear them on current affairs radio.[21]

WEL was still run on a shoestring. For example, the national office did not obtain an electric typewriter until 1985 – it was a gift from Anne Summers, who wanted to see press releases look more professional. Unfortunately, the visibility and professionalism of a spokeswoman such as Elix confirmed the fears of some members in regard to paid staff. All was later forgiven when Elix, now with the Australian Conservation Foundation, addressed a WEL meeting in Sydney on 'Green girls and ecological housewives'.[22]

Moreover, times were changing. By 1997 the national co-ordinator position was renamed 'executive officer', reflecting the growing pressure on non-government organisations to become 'corporatised'. The National Management Committee was renamed the National Board, but the corporate titles were dropped again in 2001 when it was clear that they were not going to achieve the goal of secure funding.

The WEL national office moved from Women's House at the end of 1993 into space subleased from the Australian Conservation Foundation in the city. A problem here was the lack of a meeting room, and the office moved again in 1998 to Jamieson House, where other tenants included the ACT Council of Social Service, the National Women's Justice Coalition and the National Women's Media Centre. After the defunding of WEL and the other two closely associated bodies, a national co-ordinator could no longer be paid and soon the office space had to be surrendered. The WEL national office became a virtual office in 2002, a serious blow for a national advocacy organisation; national functions were then performed from members' houses and offices.

Finances

WEL began with little in the way of financial resources apart from small subs from members, with meetings taking place in members' sitting rooms and all jobs undertaken by members. It was difficult to meet even the minor expenses incurred by a lobby group. Subscriptions might be $5 a year, with a reduced rate for students or those on social security.

Suggestions to increase subscriptions were repeatedly rejected on the grounds that such a move would hurt women with no independent source of income. Many women only had housekeeping money and this factor was closely watched. In Canberra, veterinarian Gail Wilenski had to take a locum position in order to pay the WEL–ACT phone bill. Project funding, such as that provided by the Schools Commission to compile a booklet on careers for girls, was very welcome and better than running a trash and treasure stall.

Yet the success of WEL and demands both from government and from women in the community soon brought the need to acquire office space and someone to staff it. When WEL–NSW had a membership of 1200 it was still operating out of a member's house. To the volunteers doing the work, the situation was clearly untenable:

> When deadlines have to be met for Action Group submissions,
> or for Publicity's Press Releases or at election time, the
> typewriters and the duplicator run hot, the phone rings
> continuously – not just with WEL members' enquiries, but
> with women with welfare problems needing a referral to a

government department or a suitable agency, with newspapers,
radio or TV wanting opinions, stories, our view and last but not
least – cleaning up at the end of a mad day, all with children
underfoot.[23]

The need for rented office space and paid staff and the failure to raise
sufficient funds to maintain them was a *leitmotif* of WEL's organisational
history. While WEL–NSW recognised the need for an office and staff by
1974, some mistakes were made. An office was rented on Marrickville
Road, Dulwich Hill, in an attempt to move the organisation closer to
working-class women, but it proved inconvenient for most members.
It was subsequently used for the survey of migrant women discussed
in chapter 2. WEL–NSW initially voted not to apply for any of the IWY
project funds, but such high-mindedness about taking money from
government sometimes combined with thoughtlessness in exploiting
members with secretarial skills who had been trained to be too polite.[24]
A shift to part-time paid co-ordinators reduced some of this sense of
exploitation, but financing was always a problem. A Christmas raffle
might help pay the co-ordinator's salary.

The need for paid workers increased as WEL members increasingly
took up equal opportunity and women's policy positions in government in the 1980s and had little time left over for voluntary work.
The reduced time members had available for WEL meetings and other
activities also had an impact on the commitment to feminist organisational philosophy. For example, in Western Australia:

> WEL women's entry into politics and the machinery in the
> public service left them with little time or energy for specific
> WEL pursuits, so 'formalisation' of WEL's procedures was
> intended as a time-saving measure, albeit one with deeply
> ideological implications.[25]

Opportunities for commercial sponsorship of feminist advocacy activities were fairly rare. One early example was the publication – in a styl-
ish tan format – of the papers of the first WEL national conference.
Volunteers worked under the guidance of Hilary McPhee (Freeman) and

Di Gribble, later a famous publishing partnership, and cartoons were contributed by Bruce Petty. Advertising space was bought by Penguin and by the manufacturer of Delfen contraceptive foam.

The much more significant Channel 7 payment for broadcasting rights for the 'Why Should Women Vote for You' meeting in Melbourne ($3000), which is discussed in chapter 4, was exceptional. When Wendy McCarthy proposed that Sydney follow Melbourne's example by selling television rights the idea was rejected overwhelmingly. The Melbourne coverage had been deemed counter-productive because it included women booing and hissing.

One windfall for WEL in Sydney came from the Catholic Church. In 1995, rooms had been booked for the national conference at St Scholastica's College in Glebe during school holidays, but somebody told Cardinal Clancy that WEL promoted abortion and permission to use the premises was withdrawn. Babette Francis, the founder of Women Who Want to be Women, told the *Herald Sun* that she had been 'appalled to hear WEL was trying to brainwash young Catholic girls with pro-abortion and divorce theory'.[26] WEL convenor, Cate Turner, pointed out that WEL would incur substantial costs because of the cancellation. In response the Cardinal sent a cheque for $1000, apparently fearing legal action.[27]

In 1989 WEL–ACT had a somewhat similar experience when Right to Life complained to the Catholic Archbishop of Canberra and Goulburn that a workshop at Ursula College was to be addressed by leading New Zealand feminist Marilyn Waring. However, while Ursula College offered financial compensation and a bus to a new venue, ultimately all were persuaded that a workshop on feminism and the state organised in conjunction with the Royal Australian Institute of Public Administration would not be advocating abortion.

Most WEL groups decided from early on that they needed to take advantage of government funding opportunities when and where they arose. There were successful submissions by WEL groups for small IWY project grants in 1975, including Sydney, Brisbane, Alice Springs and Burnie. WEL groups also benefited from IWY grants made to women's centres which, for example, enabled the purchase of new Gestetner machines.

The next major funding opportunity arrived with the Fraser government's Wage Pause Program, which for the first time targeted the creation of women's as well as men's jobs. In order to be eligible for such funding WEL became incorporated in the ACT in 1981, with the help of the federal Minister for Business and Consumer Affairs, John Moore. *News Weekly* denounced this ministerial assistance on the grounds that any strengthening of WEL would 'increase its ability to inflict serious damage on both the Federal Government and public attitudes favouring the family'.[28]

The national office gained a paid worker for twelve months from the Wage Pause Program, while the program's Hawke government successor, the Community Employment Program (CEP), was to be even more important. Both the national office and State groups were successful in gaining temporary paid workers under this scheme. Under the Hawke government WEL also, for the first time, received operational funding to support the national office. This was never a large amount. It began with $5000 in 1983, rising gradually to about $50 000 a year until funding ceased under the Howard government in 1999. The peak year was 1993–94 when $60 000 was received.

The grants of this period were operational, rather than tied to delivery of specific projects – an important recognition by government of the role of NGO advocacy in promoting equality for women. WEL was in general a critic of the way governments were shifting in the 1990s from operational to project funding, tying NGOs to the delivery of government objectives rather than the voicing of community needs. However, the fact that the operational grants were only ever for one year meant there was never certainty about WEL's budget, and it was difficult to plan ahead or to retain staff in the national co-ordinator position. Talented young women were, not surprisingly, interested in a salary that would continue for more than a year.

WEL also received some project funds – for example, for organising the National Agenda for Women Conference for government in

1985 and a National Women's Health Conference organised with the Australian Women's Health Network in 1995. In both cases much of the money was spent in bringing large numbers of Indigenous women to Canberra. Some other assistance in staging large conferences came from the consultation funds provided to WEL representatives on the National Women's Consultative Council, such as Jo Moylan from the Northern Territory.

WEL groups also seized opportunities for project funding at the State level, such as provided by suffrage centenaries in South Australia and Western Australia. In Perth this involved the 'mile-long' banner project described in chapter 8, while the Lotteries Commission provided funding for office equipment.

The defunding of WEL–Australia in 1999 and the consequent loss of the paid national co-ordinator position was a serious blow to WEL's work as a national lobbying organisation. It was part of a more general move on the part of the Howard government to deny public fund-

 WEL–WA meeting at Katharine Susannah Pritchard House, Annie Goldflam in the chair, Perth, 1989. *Val Marsden.*

ing to advocacy organisations critical of government – a rejection of previous policy that community-based peak bodies must sometimes bite the hand that fed them in order to represent the views of their constituency.[29] WEL had never been successful in funding its national activities through capitation fees and this was again the case. In any case, State groups were also struggling. By the end of 2001 WEL–NSW was no longer able to pay for a co-ordinator and shifted back to the use of volunteers to run its Albion Street, Surry Hills office, while Victoria was in an even worse position.

The loss of a paid national co-ordinator and then the national office made national campaigns increasingly difficult. Nonetheless, when circumstances demanded it individuals stepped forward. Lisa Solomon of the 2000 IVF campaign told the *Australian*: 'We are not funded, we have no money, yet the women of Australia still answered our call. By defunding us, the Government may have thought we would be silenced. They were wrong'.[30]

Coalition building

From the beginning, with little in the way of regular income, WEL depended not only on its wits but also on the skills and networks of its members. Its middle-classness was an advantage, as members often had friends who were newspaper editors, senior public servants or even State premiers. But a problem from early on was that WEL members had a tendency to use their new political confidence and skills to establish spin-off organisations with a more specialised policy focus in areas such as child care, education, health, law reform, media monitoring and electoral politics. These more specialised organisations could become competitors with WEL for scarce resources, including the time of members, although they also provided the potential for partnerships and coalition-building.

Apart from departures for new, more specialised organisations or into new equity careers, WEL had increasing problems with recruitment. It could seem like a closed friendship group dating from a particular era of women's movement activism. Some later members reported to the history survey that they were made to feel like outsiders: 'I joined WEL with great enthusiasm, only to find there are two groups – those longstanding members and the newcomers'. Just as informal male networks had excluded women from vital information flows within organisations, friendship networks within the women's movement could perform a similar exclusionary function.[31] Older members were perceived as wanting to stay in control or to stick to issues within their comfort zone, or so caught up with trying to get policy outcomes that they neglected the mentoring of new members.

The downturn in active membership in the 1980s led to an increased reliance on coalition work with other women's organisations, including traditional ones.[32] While in most Western countries the second wave of the women's movement began with criticism of older and seemingly more conservative groups, these groups were themselves changing and their value was increasingly appreciated. In times of social movement abeyance, coalition-building is an important means of maintaining oppositional activity.[33] WEL had begun putting together coalitions in the Whitlam period but coalition-building became more important after 1975 in the face of attacks on married women's right to work and the attempt by anti-feminist groups to derail a plan of action for the UN Decade for Women.[34]

The coalitions established by WEL for lobbying purposes varied over time and place and partly depended on the personal networks of convenors and co-ordinators. WEL increasingly sought endorsement from other women's groups for its election charters and questionnaires. For the 1983 federal election, national co-ordinator Pamela Denoon brought together a coalition of nine women's organisations to push for child-care funding and women's participation in job creation schemes. Multiple endorsement of the WEL election questionnaire added weight to the telegrams sent to the Prime Minister and Opposition Leader and helped pay for the placement of advertisements in major newspapers such as the *Australian*, the *Sydney Morning Herald* and the *Canberra Times*.

While 1983 saw the election of a federal Labor government commit-ted to WEL policies of anti-discrimination and affirmative action legis-lation, this commitment was rendered shaky by the extraordinary mobilisation of conservative groups against the Sex Discrimination Bill or 'Sex Bill'. In response, Denoon stitched together another broad coali-tion of women's organisations to lobby federal parliamentarians. The inclusion of organisations traditionally regarded as part of the Liberal Party's constituency, such as the National Council of Women, was an important part of the strategy of shoring up bipartisan support for the Bill.

No sooner was this crisis over than a new threat emerged in the form of the 'broad-based consumption tax' proposed by Treasurer Paul Keating. WEL's campaign against this transfer from the 'purse to the wallet' brought together 23 organisations to co-sponsor the National Women's Tax Summit.[35] From the time of the Opposition's *Fightback* manifesto of 1991, WEL was again campaigning over the regressive effects of such taxes and their impact on low-income earners with chil-dren – predominantly women. In this new era, coalitions might include Catholic agencies, which became important partners on social justice issues.

Ad hoc coalitions, such as those WEL was initiating or joining, provide a flexible form of response to a rapidly changing political and policy environment. On the other hand, this form of response is by its nature largely reactive rather than proactive; and such relatively short-lived coalitions are unable to accumulate the resources, professional-ism or standing required for an ongoing presence in a policy commu-nity. The failure of the Australian women's movement to develop a peak organisation like those found in Canada and the United States has often been regarded as a weakness.[36]

Awareness of drawbacks such as these led to recurrent proposals for more permanent coalition structures for women's advocacy. In the late 1980s Pamela O'Neil, former Sex Discrimination Commissioner and member of WEL in Darwin, worked together with a small group from WEL and Business and Professional Women (BPW) on a proposal for a peak body. O'Neil was concerned that women were being left behind in a world where lobbying was increasingly sophisticated; they needed something comparable to other community sector bodies which were funded by government to represent their constituents in a professional way.[37] Predictably, the O'Neil proposal ran up against objections that the proposed body would be contrary to the participatory principles of the women's movement, would not adequately reflect its diversity and fluidity and would usurp the role of existing organisations.

Similar suspicions were voiced concerning a parallel initiative to create a national body for the women's movement. A group of older feminists, concerned about the increasingly fragmented nature of the women's movement, started meeting in 1988 and plans emerged for a feminist foundation to promote the ideas of the women's movement into the future. A bequest from former WEL national co-ordinator Pamela Denoon gave impetus to this development, and the National Foundation for Australian Women (NFAW) was launched in 1989.

NFAW achieved tax-deductible status with the Tax Office, meaning that through preferred donor arrangements it could assist other women's organisations. After some early euphoria, the National Foundation settled into a primary function of feminist fund-raising and initiating various forms of feminist commemoration, including the important National Women's Archive Project. After the defunding of WEL, however, and particularly from 2004, NFAW took on increased policy research and advocacy roles around the federal government's welfare to work and industrial reforms. Marie Coleman, a former head of the Whitlam government's Social Welfare Commission and later of the Office of Child Care, played the leading role in this.

A third attempt to establish a national body included a number of those involved in the first attempt. The aim of the new organisation, called CAPOW! (Coalition of Participating Organisations of Women), was to enable closer co-operation in lobbying government and preparing submissions. It was launched at the WEL national conference in 1992 when representatives of older and newer organisations sang the new 'Women's Coalition Anthem' with the help of Aboriginal singer Betty Little. The usual anxieties were expressed about another layer of hierarchy, but all agreed more effective use must be made of limited financial and human resources. The new organisation received a welcome boost when at its first conference Prime Minister Paul Keating announced amendments, long sought by WEL, to strengthen the *Sex Discrimination Act*. It attracted seed funding and then operational funding to help co-ordinate NGO preparations for the Beijing Conference of 1995.

CAPOW! initiated much closer networking of national women's organisations, with the help of the new information and communication technologies. It used a fortnightly fax-stream to disseminate information about government and parliamentary inquiries and to promote sharing of NGO submissions. It linked some sixty national women's NGOs, increasing information-sharing to an unprecedented level, particularly for those not based in Canberra. As the federal government's mode of consultation with women in the community shifted to ministerial roundtables, CAPOW! was able to take advantage of the fares paid by government to organise pre-roundtable conferences. Supplementing the fax-stream with face-to-face meetings was of great benefit in the context of the increased diversification of the women's movement.

The work of CAPOW! in the run up to the Beijing Conference resulted in Australian NGOs and their relationship with the government delegation being the envy of those from other countries. WEL national co-ordinator Ingrid MacKenzie and Jo Wainer from WEL–Victoria were accredited observers for the official conference. Wainer had been a member of the government delegation at the preceding meeting of the UN Commission on the Status of Women in New York, where she had given a presentation on Australia's experience in developing satellite national accounts that assess the value of unpaid work to the economy.

Political misfortunes, however, led to the demise of CAPOW! Senator Jocelyn Newman, already convinced that WEL was biased towards Labor, took great exception to the 1997 NGO shadow report on Australia's implementation of CEDAW. The report was critical of the new federal government's disproportionate cuts to women's and human rights agencies, and of other policy changes with disproportionate impact on women. Minister Newman described this as NGOs 'bagging their country from overseas' and claimed the report was motivated by partisan bias and provided misinformation.

The head of the Office of the Status of Women, Pru Goward, backed up the Minister's claims of misinformation in the *Australian Financial Review*. She later sent a private letter to WEL apologising for her 'mistake' in claiming that there was no legislation before parliament that would remove the complaint-handling powers of the Sex Discrimination Commissioner. Far from this being misinformation, the legislation concerned had been before Parliament for more than six months, had passed through the House of Representatives and had already been the subject of a Senate committee report.[38] Nonetheless CAPOW! was promptly defunded and WEL was also in the firing line.

In 1999 the Howard government moved to a more corporatised form of consultation with women's organisations, channelled through three and later four national 'consortia' with funded secretariats. WEL became part of the WomenSpeak consortium run out of the YWCA, and secretariat funding did provide opportunities for some meetings of NGO representatives. There was, however, a notable muting of NGO voices, with new constraints placed on the use of government funding for purposes of research or advocacy, very similar to what was happening in Canada at this time.

The arrival of the Internet

The expansion of the Internet in the 1990s was a great boon to WEL. Given the occupations of the membership, most came quickly to rely on email for communication. Email in conjunction with teleconferences enabled decision making by the WEL national management committee without the expense of face-to-face meetings by State and Territory representatives. Email is now the most significant information and communication technology used by global social movements.

But the Internet serves another important function – creating space for oppositional discourse. Given the disappearance of feminist women's pages or programs from the mainstream media in the 1990s, this was particularly significant. In January 1996, PhD student Elizabeth Shannon from WEL in Hobart outlined an exciting new initiative at the national conference. Her proposal for a feminist discussion list was somewhat overshadowed by the announcement of the next federal election but the first message was posted on Ausfem-Polnet on 1 February. It took off quickly as a forum for feminist debate on public policy and within three years had almost 700 subscribers, increasing to 900 by 2003.[39] Its aims were to link 'activists, practitioners and scholars who are actively involved with policies which aim to improve the status of women'. The femocrats on the list sometimes posted information or press releases, but rarely felt free to participate directly in debates. For the first three years Ausfem-Polnet was managed by Shannon, who completed her PhD on feminist influence on public policy during this time. It opened the eyes of WEL to the uses of the Internet for sharing policy information and for coalition-building around particular policy positions.

WEL went on to develop many email lists for its own purposes, linking its membership, as well as supporting the development of Pamelas-list, an electronic network established in 1998 linking the national women's organisations previously linked through CAPOW! Pamelas-list, which had the benefit of not requiring paid staff, was an initiative of Judy Harrison of the National Women's Justice Coalition and was supported by a grant from the Pamela Denoon Trust. In the same year WEL–ACT established a general email list called ACTWomen, for sharing information about issues and events of particular interest or relevance to women in the ACT. This linked WEL members with a broader feminist community including students in gender studies programs. While email lists were a boon, they were not fully labour-saving devices. At a minimum they required database maintenance and, to function well, a facilitator with relevant skills and knowledge.

The same could be said about electronic newsletters. *WEL–Informed* in NSW was the first to move into an electronic format, under the leadership of Jane Gardiner, and others such as *WEL–ACTivist* followed.

WEL-Australia established its website <http://www.wel.org.au> on 26 August 1995, making it the first Australian women's organisation to take this step. Overseas, feminist organisations such as Women's House in Amsterdam were moving into cyberspace in the same year. Particularly after defunding in 1999, the website became WEL's major organisational resource. It was created and maintained by the exceptional commitment of Canberra member Val Thomson. In particular the site was notable for its strict observance of access and equity protocols, making it accessible for those with disabilities or unable to afford the latest computer hardware and software. The major drawback was that only one person was able to update the site. It is notable that of the most recent cohort of members, 6 per cent found out about WEL through the website.

The WEL website became an important educational resource for students doing research on the women's movement and links to it were provided on all the major Australian politics sites. It hosted WEL submissions to parliamentary and government inquiries on issues ranging from paid maternity leave to equal pay, as well as gender analysis of federal Budgets. As a rich source for feminist perspectives on federal election campaigns it has been archived since 1996 in the National Library's Pandora Archive. Until 2004, when it was joined by EMILY's List, it was the only women's election website archived. In April 2005 the WEL website was still receiving over 1000 hits a day, despite the fact that WEL had no national staff or even an office. The WEL–Australia website has since been redesigned so more than one person is able to update it and was again archived in Pandora for the 2007 federal election.

While the WEL–Australia website was an important asset, in general the Internet could not compensate for declining interest in branch meetings and office-holding in WEL groups. In 2004 a number of core members of WEL–Victoria, including the founder, Beatrice

Faust, sought to dissolve the organisation on the grounds that more specialised organisations had taken over its role and there was insufficient policy expertise remaining in WEL for credible policy interventions. There was concern at the federal level as well that WEL no longer had the policy resources to respond adequately to an aggressively anti-feminist government. However, in 2005 WEL–Victoria started up again as an electronically-based organisation: WEL–Victoria Online <http://www.welvic.org.au>.

Talking the talk

One of the perennial issues for those seeking to influence government is the need to talk in a language that will be 'heard' by policymakers. Dominant discourses, particularly those institutionalised in government, frame reality in such a way that many messages will be screened out or literally not make any sense to those in power. This means that activists from social movements who wish to change public policy have to learn to be bilingual. Having experienced the 'click' when a feminist way of interpreting the world makes sense of otherwise puzzling experiences, they then need to latch on to the narratives understood by those in power.

We have seen how the founding members of WEL were keenly aware that the Women's Liberation message was not reaching a wider audience, or at least not in a positive way. WEL was both inclined, and careful, to present its claims within a familiar equal opportunity framework. Even at the high tide of equal opportunity discourse, however, it was rare to rely upon justice arguments alone. While WEL's childcare policy, for example, sprang from recognition of the connection between child care and equal opportunity, its case was supplemented by arguments concerning benefits to the economy, the public purse and child and family welfare. The 'derivative' nature of such arguments for women's rights, emphasising the economic benefits they would secure for society, was an example of the pragmatism of WEL's discursive strategies.

In the heyday of equal opportunity management plans in the 1980s, the intermeshing of justice goals and managerialist efficiency arguments was even more evident. While equal opportunity might be the goal, it was presented in terms of the benefits to the employer organisation, including the better utilisation of skills and talents and the better provision of services to customers. Later on, equality and trans-formational goals were to recede even further into the background, as 'managing for diversity' came to the fore.

Presenting women's claims in terms of social utility, to bolster justice claims, was not the only concern. Perth WEL member and academic Joan Eveline published an influential article in *Australian Feminist Studies* criticising WEL for framing policy claims in terms of women's disadvantage. She discussed how discomforted she was, when reading through WEL policies before the 1992 national confer-ence, to see 'how often the policies used the discourse of disadvantage and secondly by how often it was our only interlocutory voice'.[40]

Eveline argued that to talk of female disadvantage was to make men the norm and a supposedly neutral standard. Even the UN Women's Convention, with its aim of giving women equal access to the enjoyment of human rights, used men as the standard or the comparator. Instead, policies should be framed in terms of addressing male advantage. In effect, she was arguing for a return to a time when the women's movement framed the problem as patriarchy. When she raised the issue at the WEL conference many agreed that men's advan-tage was being written out of the picture in the way WEL policies were being framed. However, just as many feared the reactions from men who exercised policymaking power if the main focus became male advantage; feminist policymakers and equal opportunity practitioners were among those most concerned.

But regrets over the loss of a more radical perspective were not the only issue: by the mid-1980s seismic shifts were taking place in the English-speaking world, challenging the dominance of the equal opportunity discourse into which WEL had been able to fit quite easily. Government, or at least significant parts of government, was becoming increasingly captive to a new 'economic language', and to refuse to speak it was to put advocacy organisations out of the policy game.[41]

The time for rights talk, even if supplemented by utility arguments, was coming to an end. WEL and other feminist advocacy groups had already begun, perforce, to research and lobby in terms of the cost to the economy of phenomena such as domestic violence, rather than in terms of its impact on women's rights. Liberal Minister for the Status of Women in New South Wales, Kerry Chikarovski, had urged WEL to take up violence against women as an economic issue.[42] These broader shifts in public discourse created seemingly insuperable dilemmas for an organisation dedicated to doing something about social justice and women's rights in a world no longer receptive to such words.

The way WEL tried to preserve its social movement characteristics while performing as a lobbyist and 'talking the talk' in an increasingly professionalised policy environment was always going to pose significant challenges. The lack of financial resources further complicated the situation, as did the underlying unwillingness to become a more corporatised organisation that might be able to secure a private funding base. Whether the kind of compromises involved in becoming more corporate would in fact have secured private funding for feminist advocacy is a moot point. In any case, these organisational and financial constraints made WEL's continuing policy presence and media impact, examined in the next three chapters, even more remarkable.

4

WORKING THE MEDIA

WEL founders were determined to reach broad audiences and to influence policy makers. For both these purposes they needed to use the media, and supportive journalists recruited to the new organisation provided the media skills required. Professional packaging of the form guide for federal parliamentary candidates and the novelty value of this approach to electoral politics made WEL highly successful in gaining media attention. The novelty value wore off but WEL continued to obtain considerable if variable media coverage over the next three decades as an organisation that could be relied upon to provide a gender perspective on current issues – what used to be called 'the women's point of view'.

WEL's appearances in the media peaked in the early 1970s, declined to a low in 1986–91, then gradually rose again (Figure 4.1). All sources confirm this general trajectory although the detail is affected by the arrival of electronic newspaper archives in the mid-1980s, making media monitoring more efficient. Despite its continuing presence, WEL suffered from the short attention span the media generally afforded to social movements, even those with very long-term goals. In 1981 the *New York Times* magazine ran a cover story confidently entitled 'The women's movement is over'[1], and this theme became a media staple in Australia as well. In Sydney WEL's Eva Cox had complained even earlier: 'Because we're no longer waving placards, we're no longer news, and because people don't see us on telly they think we've gone out of existence. We haven't.'[2]

During the early honeymoon with the media most of the coverage was favourable. Of the 164 press articles about WEL which appeared in Victoria between April and November 1972, for example, only three were antagonistic. Nonetheless, the stories were often amazingly ill-informed about women's political history. One of the first big Melbourne stories proclaimed this was 'the first time in our political history that half the population (the women) have been organised into a pressure group'. Despite the journalist's lack of knowledge about women's political history this story was responsible for alerting many women to the existence of WEL and helped swell recruitment. A final paragraph claiming 'women are better off in the kitchen' probably helped.[3]

WEL's early success in attracting media attention was despite the male-dominated character of the print media of the time. As member

Figure 4.1 WEL in the media 1972–2002

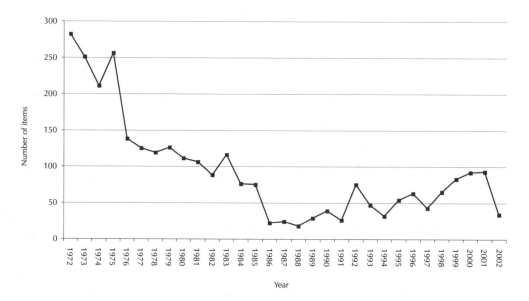

SOURCE WEL history media database

Suzanne Baker, one of Australia's top women journalists, remarked: 'There are no women in decision-making jobs in newspapers and most news gathering and feature writing is left to male supervision.'[4] Baker resigned as Women's Editor of the *Sydney Morning Herald* after finding that investigative reporting into the real world of women was not wanted. In Canberra, when member Helen Shepherd (Ester) became editor of the student newspaper *Woroni*, the story appeared under the headline 'Mother to edit ANU student paper'.[5]

Bra-burning and other media obsessions

The male authors of the honeymoon period articles, who often stressed WEL's professionalism, also felt obliged to cater to the idea that there was something inherently funny about women engaging seriously with politics and with policy. There were seemingly mandatory headlines such as: 'WEL, it's girl talk' (about the first national conference).[6] For the tabloids in particular, no matter how sympathetic the reporter, the journalistic reality was that women meant breasts. Four months after the appointment of Elizabeth Reid as Prime Minister's Women's Adviser, a position strongly supported by WEL, the *Herald* ran a story which began: 'Would the sisterhood please stand still for a moment and stop wobbling under their T-shirts? I have just been talking to the M stroke S who represents your interests in the capital ... Miz Liz – in flared jeans, tank top and no bra – was speaking in the new prime ministerial suite in Parliament House.'[7]

In 1992, journalist Lindsy Van Gelder, a contributing editor to *Ms.* magazine, revealed her role in inventing the most persistent media myth about the women's movement. In 1968, as a journalist on the *New York Post*, she was asked to cover a demonstration against the Miss America beauty contest. The press release had said the organisers would only talk to female reporters, so she was sent out to interview Robin Morgan and bring back a 'humour piece'. The organisers planned to dump bras, girdles, curlers, stiletto-heeled shoes and other instruments of torture into a freedom trashcan and Van Gelder reported that these items were to be set alight. Her story began: 'Lighting a match to a draft card or a flag has been a standard gambit of protest groups in recent years, but something new is due to go up in flames this Saturday. Would you believe a bra-burning?' The story was headed 'Bra-burners and Miss America'.

Twenty years later, Van Gelder claimed that she had been an instant convert to the planned Miss America demonstration and had been trying to give it moral weight by the analogy with Vietnam War protests. At the same time as trying to speak to the 'radicals of our generation' she was also speaking a language that 'the guys on the city desk could understand (i.e. tits)'.[8] The alliteration of bra-burning certainly helped get the story out about Women's Liberation, although in other ways Van Gelder conformed to journalistic norms of the day, describing Morgan as an 'attractive brunette'.

Ever afterwards feminists were ridiculed by the label 'bra-burners', even though no bras had been burnt. The wooden boardwalk at the Atlantic City venue was too much of a fire risk for that. The image was so pervasive, however, that even many feminists were convinced that some bra must have been burnt somewhere, sometime. Bra-burning became part of the stock-in-trade of journalism. For example, a substantial article by Maximilian Walsh, chief political correspondent of the *Sun-Herald*, was given the title 'The girls who take politics seriously' and began:

> The Treasurer, Mr Snedden, will not be making any more speeches about women burning bras – even for laughs.
> He ran into WEL – the Women's Electoral Lobby.
> No sooner had he delivered a speech at Surfers Paradise in which he said: 'burning a bra seems unlikely to be a high recommendation for selection for executive office' than a spokeswoman from WEL was on the phone complaining.[9]

The *Daily Telegraph* also ran the story, with the headline 'Don't burn your bras: Poll talks to women', and beginning: 'Women should not burn their bras if they wanted to work as executives, the Federal Treasurer (Mr Snedden) said yesterday'.[10] The statement about bra-burning came in reference to WEL having put him 'through the hoops' with their election questionnaire.

In 1975 the *Sunday Mail* in Queensland affected surprise that 'No bras burnt' at an International Women's Day Fair in Brisbane, although a popular T-shirt read on one side 'A woman needs a man' and on the other 'like a fish needs a bicycle' and the WEL stall offered pregnancy tests.[11] 'Woman needs a man like a fish needs a bicycle' was a slogan first scribbled on the back of toilet doors in Sydney in 1970 by university student Irina Dunn, something generously acknowledged by Gloria Steinem, often credited with it. Dunn was later an Independent Senator for New South Wales who, with the help of WEL members Eva Cox and Pam Simons, developed a Private Senator's Bill to increase child-care provision, in particular centre-based care.[12]

The media myth of bra-burning could make dinner parties a battleground. One early WEL member reported that although she tried to shift dinner conversations away from Women's Liberation to equality this still didn't make any difference: 'They were always asking, "When are you going to burn your bra?" But, perhaps, it really only made me more determined'.[13]

Walking the media tightrope

The media construction of Women's Liberation as man-hating lesbians had become a barrier to getting the feminist message out to a broader audience, and WEL consciously set out to present its message in a less threatening way. While Women's Liberation might be messy and adversarial, WEL would be sensible, well-briefed and clear.[14] Historian Marilyn Lake, involved in the formation of both Women's Liberation and WEL groups in Hobart in 1972, noted the difference in their media reception. The *Saturday Evening Mercury* headline about the founding of the Hobart Women's Action Group was 'This Is War, Men!' with the sub-head 'Women's Lib prepares for battle'. The headline about the founding of WEL was far less alarmist, depicting women as waking up to the fact that they had little to show for having had the vote for so long: '13 sleeping beauties ... wake up!'[15]

WEL was walking a tightrope in terms of its public presentation. On the one hand it wanted to present an image of professionalism and expertise, in order to have policy credibility. On the other hand, in order to have political credibility it needed to be seen as representing 'ordinary women' and not just a professional elite. This led to some interesting media strategies. For example, newspapers traditionally cover the birth of the New Year by covering the birth of the first babies. WEL members took advantage of this at the beginning of International Women's Year by presenting hand-painted plates bearing the IWY emblem to the first-born girls. One of those involved in Canberra was Chris Ronalds, later a prominent barrister and architect of the Commonwealth *Sex Discrimination Act*, but here complicit in exploiting a very traditional media ritual.[16] It was an effective way to promote IWY and its emblem – a peace dove incorporating female and equality symbols. Letters to the Editor were another way of providing linkages between the stories of 'ordinary' women found in the media and the policy issues being pursued by WEL: for example, a story about cruel treatment of a widow by officials could be used as a hook for a letter promoting the reform of death duties and pointing to similar legislative reform taking place elsewhere.[17]

In its first three years it was WEL's electoral interventions that gained the most media coverage and, in particular, the 1972 questionnaire and rating of federal election candidates. The presentation of findings in the form of a racing form guide helped the ratings fit into existing 'horse-race' frames for media coverage of elections. One of the first articles on WEL was subtitled: 'Full form on all the runners'.[18] The ratings for Victorian candidates indeed looked like a racing guide when they were published as a lift-out Green Guide in *The Age*. Elsewhere the form guides were written up in the *Sun-Herald* and *Sunday Telegraph* for New South Wales, the *Advertiser* for South Australia, the *Courier-Mail* for Queensland, the *Mercury* for Tasmania, and the *Canberra Times* for the ACT, while the *West Australian* reported on the Sydney form guide and the *National Times* reported nationally. Local newspapers ran material relevant to local candidates.

Similarly, in New Zealand it was WEL's first election survey, in 1975, which attracted most media attention. As in Australia, interviews were conducted by WEL members in pairs and survey responses were scored to provide a form guide. Headlines included: 'Lowest scorers condemn WEL MP poll' and 'Scoring with the ladies'. Choice extracts from candidate interviews were put up on the walls at the press conference launching the survey results, such as 'Rape is so traumatic that I question whether the law should cope with it'. Cartoons included 'The Judgement of Clarice' showing the party leaders posing before WEL, who is pondering which of them should be awarded the lemon.[19]

In Australia, WEL's federal election activity in 1974 and 1975 continued to attract coverage, as did its interventions in State and local elections. Many of the responses by sitting conservative politicians were sufficiently archaic to be newsworthy and WEL made the most of these. In response to questions about employment in 1974, Senator Laucke (South Australia) stated that 'women are ennobling in their own particular provinces'; Senator Wright (Tasmania) believed 'The female is especially adapted to teaching and nursing'; while Senator Greenwood (Victoria) suggested 'Most women do just want to be wives and mothers'.[20]

While WEL was more interested in raising awareness of feminist issues than directly influencing votes, the question of whether the organisation could affect the outcome of elections was of more interest to the media than the policies. Perhaps inevitably, because WEL needed the media, and hence became complicit in the horse-race frame, this did divert attention from the issues. The high ratings given to minor party or single-issue candidates on the basis of their understanding of women's issues were often later used against WEL. Critics suggested that the fact that candidates with top ratings polled poorly showed that WEL was unable to swing votes.

The prime example was the Parramatta by-election in 1973. WEL received national television and radio coverage (including a *Four Corners* program) and attracted 350 people to its Meet the Candidates meeting. The outcome of the election was that Philip Ruddock was elected to federal parliament for the first time and the Defence of Government Schools candidate, to whom WEL gave the top rating, did very poorly. The experience convinced a number of members that it was futile to interview or rate single-issue candidates when the main aim was to get the major parties to implement WEL policy.

The one exception to the general lack of media interest in WEL issues in the election context was abortion, which easily became ammunition in partisan controversy. In 1972 the flagging political fortunes of Prime Minister William McMahon persuaded him to try to use abortion as a wedge issue against the ALP in a late stage of the campaign. In order to avoid a repeat of this kind of partisan hijacking, WEL left questions about fertility control out of its 1974 federal election survey, focusing simply on child care, employment and education issues.

Women grilling politicians

As mentioned in chapter 1, candidate surveys were not the only item in WEL's electoral repertoire. Meet the Candidate meetings were often newsworthy for their reversal of gender roles, with women subjecting male candidates to expert examination. These meetings were held in country towns as well as in the cities and the ABC thought this such a novel idea that a television crew was sent to Wagga Wagga in New South Wales to film the local group's candidate meeting for a 1972 *Four Corners* program on WEL, 'The Hand that Rocks the Ballot Box'. Three other television current affairs programs also ran segments on WEL in this election.

In 1972–73 media stories frequently used terms such as women 'grilling' or 'quizzing' the candidates, or even 'candidates under fire from women'.[21] WEL exploited this angle in its media strategy. The formula 'Women quiz candidates' was used in a template press release provided to groups rating candidates in the 1973 Victorian local government elections. It was widely reproduced by suburban and regional papers reporting on the WEL ratings. Thirteen local papers used the exact formula while the quizzing activity was reported by many others.[22] In the 1975 federal election the media story was still 'Candidates face trial by women' when 150 women assembled in Launceston to gauge the quality of eight federal candidates, while in the 1989 State election in Western Australia the premier and opposition leader were photographed at a WEL breakfast meeting, with the caption 'Leaders escape at early grilling'.[23]

Sometimes the reactions of those on trial helped promote the story. For example, during the 1974 Queensland State election, WEL–Townsville held a Meet the Candidates forum chaired by Dale Spender wearing diaphanous green (before she took to purple). The ten male candidates were somewhat uneasy at being confronted by 150 women, despite cocktails beforehand. Most displayed an 'abysmal ignorance'. They were totally confused by a WEL member heavily pregnant with twins asking for their views on the decriminalisation of abortion. Subsequently the Member for Townsville South, Tom Aikens, denounced this experience in a parliamentary speech, saying: 'We should consider the ordinary women – the workers, the toilers, women in offices and in homes who do the jobs women are supposed to do and are good wives and mothers. They are the women I am concerned about. They do not run along to public meetings.' His grossly offensive statement, 'Probably some WEL members would feel elated if they themselves were raped', ensured that Margaret Reynolds, publicity officer for WEL–Townsville, was able to respond to him in a televised debate. Her performance gave her a boost in confidence and encouraged her to think about a political career.[24]

A particularly successful example of the 'women grilling politicians' genre was the public forum 'Why Should Women Vote for You?', held on 7 May 1973 during the Victorian State election campaign. For the first time all the party leaders appeared on the same platform, at the Dallas Brooks Hall in Melbourne. They included the State Premier, the Leader of the Opposition, the Leader of the Country Party, the State Secretary of the DLP and the Convenor of the Australia Party.

WEL–Victoria State election forum, May 1973. L to R, Rupert Hamer, Liberal Premier; Clyde Holding, Labor leader; Peter Ross-Edwards, Country Party leader; Frank Dowling, State Secretary, Democratic Labor Party. *Sun*, 8 May 1973, p. 2. *Courtesy Herald & Weekly Times.*

Two thousand tickets were sold in advance and hundreds of other people had to be turned away, according to Eve Mahlab, who chaired the meeting. While conventional in some respects, social movement legacies were apparent in the booing, hissing and cheering from the audience, captured in the television coverage. WEL–Victoria had sold the rights to broadcast the event to Channel 7 for $3000. The forum was rebroadcast within three days due to popular demand. A similar State election forum held in Perth in 1974 attracted over 500 people to hear WA party leaders explain 'Why Women Should Vote for My Party'. Again the forum was televised and the broadcast the following evening took up the full half hour of the ABC program *This Day Tonight*.[25] In New Zealand, WEL was inspired to run four successful lunches with party leaders in the 1975 election, including with Opposition leader Robert Muldoon, who was antagonistic, and with the more sympathetic Prime Minister, Bill Rowling.

Despite these media successes, in an address to the Melbourne Press Club later in 1973 Eve Mahlab was highly critical of the print media's trivialising treatment of the changes taking place in women's lives. She described how print journalists simply reported the Victorian election forum in terms of 'screaming hysterical women in wobbling T-shirts'. They ignored the real news from the forum, including the Premier's commitment to enact anti-discrimination legislation, to extend the minimum wage to women and to remove the ban on the advertising of contraceptives. Mahlab also wrote a weighty letter to the *Australian Financial Review*, complaining that it too had left out such commitments in its coverage of election promises.[26]

Staging media events

The Women's Liberation slogan of 'Free, 24-hour childcare' has been described as one of the most disastrous political slogans of all time, making it easy for opponents to dismiss feminists as 'unnatural mothers'. The slogan originated in the United Kingdom and was an attempt to try to break out of middle-class perspectives and cater for the needs of shift workers. Despite the initial handicap presented by poor policy labelling, the demand for at least accessible child care was one whose time had come. It was a policy demand that lent itself to visual strategies, and WEL was not slow in devising these. As we have seen, major child-care commitments were made by the ALP in the run up to the 1974 federal election but after the election the Treasurer made drastic savings to the funds. WEL had to run an extensive media campaign to wrest them back.

Media events with children and good photo opportunities were organised around Australia, including events in Melbourne, Canberra and Sydney, and a full-page advertisement in the *Australian Financial Review* to explain their purpose.

**MR WHITLAM
AND MEMBERS OF GOVERNMENT**

**KEEP YOUR MAY PROMISES
LET'S START ON CHILD CARE NOW**

**CAN THE THOUSANDS OF CHILDREN IN NEED NOW
WAIT A YEAR AT THE TREASURY'S PLEASURE?**

**IT'S TWENTY MONTHS AND VERY LITTLE HAS
HAPPENED FOR THOSE MOST IN NEED**

WE NEED:

1. A child care body to be established with an appropriate Act so that it can start to implement a co-ordinated program with full-time commissioners, and staff to make this effective.
2. Priority to be given to those programs that cater for single parents and families where both parents work.
3. After-school care to be included as an urgent priority as it is EXCLUDED under the present Child Care Act.

WEL **WEL Australia**

Child care ad.
*Australian Financial
Review,* 1 August 1974.

In Melbourne a WEL child-care demonstration leading from Collins Street to State Parliament was well covered in the news on Channels 0 and 9, but the main child-care demonstration, the following week, was held in front of Parliament House in Canberra. It took the form of a children's party and invitations adorned with elephants and flowers had been sent to politicians. A fire engine was organised to give children rides around Parliament House, and a carousel and a marquee were hired. Balloons and toffee apples were handed out under placards reading 'Promises, Promises' and a 1974 election poster reading: 'Only Whitlam has a programme for child care' overstamped with the word 'cancelled'. A number of government and opposition parliamentarians joined the 300 at the party. Former Minister for Social Services, W.C. Wentworth, wore a pink party hat and said he thought married women with children were getting a raw deal. Liberal Shadow Minister for Education, Jim Killen, told ABC Radio he was impressed with the novelty of the protest and thought that 'those of us who sit in parliament should take heed of it'.[27] The party provided excellent 'visuals' for television and press photographers in addition to impressive WEL spokeswomen.

In Martin Place in Sydney the demonstration included black and white balloons. For every white balloon there were ten black balloons, symbolising that for every child who had a child-care place ten had nowhere to go. The demonstrators again used the 'cancelled' child-care poster. NSW Labor leader Neville Wran joined the demonstration and said he believed that the federal government had got its priorities confused: 'I would rather have more potholes in the roads than have a deferment in our program for childcare and preschool centres'. The NSW shadow minister would go to Canberra to discuss the issue with his federal counterparts.[28] Even the rude refusal of a prominent Labor

Foreground: Elizabeth Bilney and Meredith Edwards at WEL child-care demonstration, Canberra, August 1974. *Chris Ronalds*.

politician to attend the Canberra party became the subject of major stories in the *Australian Financial Review* and the *Australian* (Australia's two national newspapers) and in tabloids like the *Daily Mirror.*

As a result of this campaign, the Whitlam government was persuaded to return some of the funds to the community-based children's services program. As early femocrat Sara Dowse observed: 'There would have been less had WEL not protested'.[29] In September the program was allocated $75 million and an Interim Committee for a Children's Services Commission was set up to deliver it. Despite this noisy and successful effort to win back child-care funding, WEL was later accused of having said nothing about Labor child-care cuts, in contrast to its outcry over Fraser government cuts to child care and legal aid.[30]

Some of WEL's policy work was in relatively technical areas such as machinery of government, where it tended to attract media for losses rather than gains. For example, there was extensive coverage for its stand over the resignation of Elizabeth Reid as Prime Minister's Women's Adviser in 1975. The *Australian* led on its front page with 'Keep top women's position WEL tells PM'.[31] Coverage was helped along by media events. There was a 24-hour vigil by fifty members of WEL–Brisbane in King George Square, with visuals including the IWY symbol being ejected from Parliament House in Canberra. The vigil promoted WEL demands for an adequately staffed women's affairs branch in the Prime Minister's Department, headed by someone with direct access to the Prime Minister.[32] A protest in City Square in Melbourne, in conjunction with Women's Liberation and the Union of Australian Women, also gained media coverage. Placards included 'Permanent Women's Adviser Now' and some 250 women sang 'I Am Woman, Hear Me Roar'.[33]

In 1997, when the federal Status of Women portfolio was given to a junior minister outside Cabinet, Prime Minister John Howard claimed she would be called in whenever there were decisions affecting women. WEL cast doubt on whether she would be in Cabinet for all the vital economic decision-making affecting women, 'otherwise

WEL members Alison Hollingsworth, Delma Brunello and Heather Williams at vigil in Brisbane's King George Square. *The Australian*, 8 October 1975. *Newspix/Jim Fenwick.*

she would be a Cabinet Minister'. The *Courier-Mail*'s story about this demotion of women's affairs featured WEL members involved in the Brisbane vigil over the same issue more than twenty years before.[34] On a more positive note, when WEL members picketed the major party campaign launches at the 1983 WA State election, there was television coverage of a WEL member wearing a sandwich board saying: 'Vote 1 – Women's Advisor'.[35]

Thanks to the media savvy of key advocates such as Edna Ryan and Lyndsay Connors, WEL's detailed policy work on the minimum wage and labour market training also received good coverage in both broadsheets and tabloids. For example, a Canberra WEL submission on how existing employment training options failed women trying to re-enter the labour market was covered by the *Australian Financial Review*, the *Australian*, *Canberra Times*, the *Examiner*, the *West Australian*, *The*

Age, the *Herald*, *Daily Telegraph* and *Canberra News*. The most extensive coverage was in the *Australian Financial Review*, which reproduced all the key points of the submission (64 paragraphs).[36] This combination of policy expertise and media skills also resulted in extensive media coverage of WEL's position on tax, where Meredith Edwards was the key spokeswoman.[37]

WEL's media strategies did not rely purely on media contacts and good policy submissions, however, and 'dissent events' continued to be staged. For example, while WEL's evidence to the full bench of the Arbitration Commission on the minimum wage was receiving extensive media attention in 1974, direct action in Adelaide also made the news. A tyre dealer advertised for three women tyrefitters and a woman mechanic, on the grounds he would not have to pay them the kind of over-award wages he would have to pay to men. WEL members picketed his business, carrying placards with slogans such as 'Same work, same bosses, same machines, same hours, same sweat, different pay'.[38] Later in the same year in Adelaide, WEL members protested outside the Gepps Cross Abattoirs in support of four women who had been employed as cleaners. The arrival of the women had resulted in 1220 men walking off the job, claiming that married women should not be employed while there were men without work.[39]

Similarly, in 1975 WEL members conducted a vigil outside Government House in Sydney and demonstrated outside Parliament House in Canberra to protest over a House of Lords rape ruling.[40] Such action prepared the way for WEL to have lasting influence on rape law reform, thanks to the careful drafting and legal argument of barrister Jocelynne Scutt. Sometimes WEL received extensive media coverage for issues not very high on its policy agenda, simply because they provided good pictures. For example, in 1974 Canberra members, accompanied by Senator Ruth Coleman, received extensive national television and press coverage for their invasion of a male-only bar at the Canberra Rex Hotel and a triumphant return a week later.

New media opportunities

WEL made good use of regional and suburban newspapers, which were often hungry for ready-made stories or even weekly columns. In 1972 there were 171 newspaper stories about WEL logged in Victoria, of which 93 were in local papers.[41] A Master's thesis on WEL–Victoria, covering a slightly different period, logged 120 stories in 1972–73, of which 41 were from suburban or regional papers.[42] As we have seen, many of these were on the topic of WEL 'quizzing' candidates in the 1973 local government elections. International Women's Year also provided a useful peg for requests for media space, and WEL acquired weekly columns in newspapers such as the *Townsville Daily Bulletin* and the *Weekend News* in Perth.

Local radio stations were also often accessible. For example, in 1975 WEL groups were doing weekly broadcasts on 4TO in Townsville and 7BU in Tasmania and in a number of other places. Local television also provided opportunities. One early WEL member in north-west Tasmania contrasted the ease of getting onto television with the intransigence of the local newspaper:

> press releases issued by WEL were included in the social
> pages (if at all). A meeting with the Editor demonstrated just
> how difficult this would be to change. He insisted that we be
> identified by our husband's name – Mrs. JOHN Smith etc, and
> wanted to send the social reporter to any WEL functions, to
> describe our fashions!
>
> We concentrated on developing our skills in this area –
> writing, being interviewed for radio and speaking at meetings.
> Later, as community video facilities became available, we
> not only learned how to use it but used it effectively to train
> ourselves how to perform capably before the camera. The
> result was that most issues were commented on by WEL
> members, as local TV producers realised that an interview with
> a spokesperson who didn't 'um and er' or freeze with nerves
> was a relatively easy option.[43]

In Adelaide WEL obtained a regular segment in a new daytime television current affairs program and was able to introduce issues such as the need for workers' compensation coverage for unpaid work in the home. The going was not necessarily smooth in the electronic media, however. Katy Richmond reported that Border WEL ran a candidates' meeting before the 1972 federal election that was four times the size of any political meeting in Wodonga for the previous decade. Yet when she asked a local radio reporter what she would say about the meeting the reply was: 'Who do you WEL women think you are? We mentioned WEL in a programme eight weeks ago, and you must remember we have 300 churches in this area to report also.'[44]

The advent of community radio at the end of the Whitlam era presented an important media opportunity. A range of interests were involved, including ethnic community leaders wanting community language programs, classical music buffs wanting more music, and social movements that had become impatient with mainstream media bias or inattention – for example the coverage of the 1971 protests against the Springbok tour in Brisbane. The women's movement had been particularly incensed by media bias during International Women's Year. It seemed increasingly important to be able to get the message out in unmediated form and WEL members became leaders in the push for community radio licences.

The Whitlam government supported the development of community broadcasting in the face of fierce opposition from entrenched broadcasting interests. The new Minister for the Media, Moss Cass, managed to get Cabinet approval for the granting of twelve community radio licences, each associated with a tertiary education institution, against the advice of the Attorney-General's and Postmaster-General's departments. Unfortunately this happened late in 1975, and the licences had yet to be issued when the Whitlam government was dismissed. Energetic action by proponents at the Lismore and Bathurst Colleges of Advanced Education, both in marginal Country Party seats, saved the day and persuaded the new Country Party media minister to go ahead. Having survived the dramatic change of government, community radio survived and expanded under the Fraser government.[45]

Community radio was an ideal medium for increasingly articulate

WEL women, and WEL groups all over Australia took up the oppor-
tunity to provide regular radio programs. These included *Alive and
WEL*, a 30-minute program at lunchtime every Wednesday on 3CR in
Melbourne, which ran from 1976 to 1984, largely presented by Alma
Morton. The tapes were made available to other WEL groups running
their own radio programs, such as WEL–Geelong.

On 6NR in Perth the Women's Broadcasting Co-operative also
produced a 30-minute program, *Out of the Gilded Cage*, every week
between 1976 and 1981. The Co-operative was made up of a number of
women's groups, but those most frequently on air were WEL, Women's
Liberation, Women's Study Group and Amazon Access. Apart from the
programs put on by WEL groups themselves, community radio stations
were sometimes targeted as part of campaigns such as that on child
care as a tax deduction, discussed in chapter 6.

Shortly before the fall of the Whitlam government, Brisbane
WEL member Pam Gorring chaired an interim committee to set up a
women's radio station. Hundreds of women attended highly contested
meetings after an inflammatory flyer was circulated to church women
suggesting that the station would promote abortion on demand. This
was despite the broad spectrum of women represented on the interim
committee, ranging from WEL through the Country Women's Association, Liberal Party representatives and two Catholic nuns.[46]

In Sydney in the 1980s WEL had a regular slot on 2GB, while in
the early 1990s Pat Richardson gave weekly broadcasts on 2SER-FM
about the personal and political journey of 'Belle', a WEL member who
had spent much of her life in the country. The stories, most of which
(somewhat confusingly) had a gay male narrator, were published in two
volumes, *Belle the Bushie* and *Belle on a Broomstick*. 'Belle' describes what
a revelation WEL was for her, having been brought up never to discuss
politics or religion. She 'woke up' after reading the 1972 WEL survey
and discovering that her local member of parliament knew nothing
about women's issues or lives. When she travelled to WEL conferences
in the early seventies she found hundreds of women 'trotting from
room to room, from one workshop to another, holding discussions on

every subject under the sun, no holds barred'. Her broadcasts included experiences such as marching for abortion rights or for International Women's Day ('a lovely march … geared to the pace of the young women pushing their babies in prams'), working part time in the WEL office, campaigning in a State election, and even issues such the 'new federalism' of 1991.[47]

The Fraser years

With the dismissal of the Whitlam government and the election of the conservative Fraser government, WEL's membership declined. The euphoria of changing the world was over. In many parts of Australia members could no longer see any immediate return for the effort they put into policy work or lobbying. In terms of media coverage, WEL was no longer a new and unpredictable element in the electoral scene and coverage of its federal electoral interventions dwindled. The novelty of women 'quizzing' politicians by its nature could not last. Although the rating of politicians and policies remained part of WEL's repertoire it slid out of the headlines, as had happened with WEL's predecessors. The year 1982 represented a low point in the organisation's media impact. When an *Age* journalist suggested contacting WEL for feminist comment on a story the response was: 'WEL? No one takes notice of them anymore. They're faded, burnt out.' That year a media release from the WEL national conference suggested that the Australian ethos remained: 'If it moves, shoot it, if it stands still, cut it down and, regrettably, if it's female, ignore it'.[48]

One notable success during the Fraser period was the achievement of wide media coverage of gender issues in tax policy.[49] After the 1980 federal election, conservative politicians were engaged in a push for income-splitting or family-unit taxation. While the issue was of crucial importance for secondary earners, usually women, it did not lend itself to visual strategies and was not in itself a media magnet. It was the policy expertise and media savvy of economist Meredith Edwards that enabled WEL to get the message out to the public about the impact

WEL–NSW with banners against the Lusher motion.
International Women's Day, Sydney, 1979. *Search Foundation-Tribune, Mitchell Library, State Library of NSW.*

that a shift from the existing basis of the tax system would have on women. In 1981 alone, Edwards gave over twenty public presentations on tax and child care, always lining up key journalists to ensure media coverage.

Successful media coverage required both tax expertise and the ability to present complex issues in simple language. As many journalists were unschooled in gender analysis, WEL had to provide a quick introduction to the distributional effects of shifting from the individual to the family as the unit of account in the tax system. A family-unit tax would benefit the high-income earner in the family (almost invariably the husband) by reducing his tax. It would increase disincentives for second earners, who would be taxed at the higher marginal rates and lose access to the tax-free threshold that acknowledges the cost of earning an income. Instead, WEL and other women's groups wanted an increase in family allowances as a means of getting income to mothers and improving family welfare without providing disincentives for women's workforce participation.

Another policy area where WEL was on the defensive but still gaining considerable media coverage was that of access to abortion. In 1979 WEL came out strongly against the 'Lusher motion' introduced into the House of Representatives in an attempt to deny Medicare funding for abortions. The House of Representatives was once again an all-male body and new members of parliament such as John Howard and Philip Ruddock were supporting Lusher. The Lusher initiative galvanised WEL responses from around Australia.[50] The following year WEL mobilised again over a draconian anti-abortion bill introduced into the Queensland parliament. It obtained bulk copies of the *Women's Weekly* to deliver to all State and federal politicians, stapled open at a survey of 30 000 women showing 62 per cent were in favour of abortion being freely available and a further 32 per cent in certain circumstances.[51] A less successful strategy was a 'pray-in' in Sydney. The minister made reference before and during the sermon to the discriminatory nature of the Lusher motion and urged the signing of petitions that WEL members had brought along, but the media stayed away.[52] It was a rainy day.

The Hawke/Keating years

The election of the Hawke government saw renewed progress on a number of WEL's policy priorities, including the introduction of federal sex discrimination legislation. WEL attracted media coverage for its support for the ratification of CEDAW and the passage of the *Sex Discrimination Act 1984* but the party it organised to celebrate the passage of the Act was reported without acknowledgment of WEL (see the next chapter).[53]

WEL's criticism of the Green Paper on Affirmative Action and the absence of sanctions from the *Affirmative Action Act* also received considerable coverage.[54] Under the Keating government, the *Sex Discrimination* and *Affirmative Action* Acts were strengthened following the Lavarch inquiry that reported in 1992. WEL was closely involved in this inquiry and Michael Lavarch was also a skilled media player, resulting in headlines such as 'Men still chain women to the kitchen sink'.[55]

The Hawke years were a time when WEL was trying to focus attention on the gender dimension of economic issues. This started with WEL's contribution to the National Economic Summit in the first year of the Hawke government and was followed by the organising of two major conferences on women and taxation. The strategic intervention by WEL before the government's 1985 tax summit – the National Women's Tax Summit – received extensive media coverage in both the electronic and print media.[56] The conference communiqué stated that organisations 'representing five million Australian women' were opposed to Treasurer Paul Keating's proposed broad-based consumption tax. Such a tax would mean a transfer from purse to wallet – the costs being paid by women who did most of the household shopping and the benefits in terms of income-tax cuts going to those who earned above average wages, mostly men. The success of the National Women's Tax Summit was important in convincing the ACTU to adopt the 'equity' option (rather than tax cuts for its better-paid blue-collar workers), and hence in defeating the proposal favoured by the Treasurer.

WEL organised a follow-up Women's Tax Convention in partnership with the Hawke government's National Women's Consultative Council, with forty participating organisations said to represent two million women. The Convention was held in March 1989 in the new Parliament House, Canberra, but in the absence of the Treasurer.[57] The Convention resolved that the tax cuts promised by government should be targeted to low-income earners and those with children. As is so often the case, tax cuts had been mooted only for those earning above the female average wage.

WEL re-engaged in the campaign against a broad-based consumption tax in 1992, this time opposing the Coalition's proposal for a Goods and Services Tax (GST). WEL–Brisbane got nationwide media coverage for its survey *The GST: Its impact on the household budget*. This was the first analysis of the impact of the GST based on the expectations of retailers, covering 36 local and national businesses. It was a substantial piece of work, endorsed by university economists. WEL found that of 499 household items, 454 would cost more under a GST. Many retailers were reluctant to commit themselves to any price cuts, despite the cuts in business taxes that were supposed to offset the impact of the GST on shelf prices. The survey was a major setback for Liberal leader John Hewson, with front-page headlines such as 'Libs admit flop on *Fightback*: Women find 90 per cent of prices up'.[58] One interesting aspect of the newspaper coverage was that because it was an 'economic' issue, all the articles were written by male journalists.

The reaction of Liberal politicians to the survey was very hostile, and local Liberals called the police when WEL launched the report outside a Brisbane supermarket. Queensland Liberal leader Joan Sheldon launched a vitriolic attack in State parliament, describing the WEL researchers as 'airheads' who had compiled a 'rather silly shopping survey'. She alleged a link between the revival of WEL in Brisbane and the appointment of Anne Summers as adviser to Prime Minister Paul Keating: 'Dr Summers was, of course, a foundation member of WEL when it was set up to manipulate the women's movement and help the Whitlam Labor Government. It looks like Dr Summers put the word out again'.[59] This ignored the fact that Anne Summers was a critic rather than a member of WEL in the 1970s. An attempt by a commercial television presenter to get the WEL group to respond in kind, to feed into the popular media image of 'women at war', was easily fended off. When the television crew arrived to film the WEL meeting, they found not 'jean-clad feral lefties' but WEL members dressed in their Sunday best ('we could have been attending a Buckingham Palace garden party') and acting as sweetness and light personified.[60]

Federal politicians were also getting into the action. On 5 May 1992, the day WEL's survey hit the headlines, Wendy Fatin, Minister Assisting the Prime Minister for the Status of Women, issued a press release headed 'GST Study Essential Reading for Women'. Peter Reith, Shadow Treasurer, countered with a press release headed simply 'WEL

WEL–Brisbane members Sherrill Molloy and Margaret Carroll working on the GST survey. Greg Abbott, *Sun-Herald* (Brisbane edition), 7 June 1992, p. 7.

Survey Wrong.' Further publicity and parliamentary debate resulted from allegations of abusive and threatening phone calls to WEL, one of which came from an endorsed Liberal candidate for a Queensland State seat.

Not receiving as much press, but still of considerable importance, was WEL's 'statement of concerns' prepared for government and employers on the likely impact of enterprise bargaining on women's wages and conditions. The Australian Industrial Relations Commission had adopted the enterprise bargaining principle in 1991, after an initial delay caused by concern over gender impact. The media reported both on WEL's statement and on how the Minister for Industrial Relations was attempting to accommodate its concerns by safeguards inserted in the *Industrial Relations Reform Act* to ensure women's workplace gains such as work/family provisions could not be bargained away at enterprise level.[61]

The Howard years

Some of WEL's concerns under the Howard government consisted of unfinished business, such as the long campaign for paid maternity leave and for decriminalisation of abortion at the State level, while others were primarily defensive in character, opposing shifts in the tax system, defending the *Sex Discrimination Act* and resisting the deregulation of the industrial relations system.

One of the more colourful actions, and one that generated the impression WEL was being regenerated by youthful and vigorous leaders, was the campaign for the exemption of sanitary products and lactation aids from the GST. As an earlier election slogan had it, in 2000 the GST was about to make it more expensive to be a woman in Australia. The campaign, which stretched over January and February 2000, generated wide support among women and a huge amount of media coverage. The Minister for Health, Dr Michael Wooldridge, spurred it along with his ill-advised comment that 'If I was a bloke I'd like shaving cream exempt, but I'm not expecting it to be'. After a certain amount of furore, he apologised for equating tampons with shaving cream but went on to accuse WEL of taking money from the tampon industry and to suggest the whole issue had been contrived by the Labor Party.[62]

Meanwhile an electronic petition was whizzing around women's workplaces, collecting over 10 000 signatures (at that time the largest electronic petition to be tabled in Parliament). Downloadable labels such as 'No taxation on menstruation' were also available from the WEL website. Many women became angry at what was seen as a discriminatory tax, with tampons already an expensive item. The Australian Education Union pointed out that Treasurer Costello had been asked at a national women's round table whether the new tax package had been subject to a gender impact assessment. In fact, such assessments were no longer being conducted.[63] When Parliament resumed some MPs were put out to find women wearing T-shirts declaring 'I bleed and I vote', and the young WEL national co-ordinator presenting a declaration attached to sanitary pads to the Health Minister. In the NSW coastal town of Nowra 'menstrual avengers' clad in red capes pelted government ministers with tampons, while further north the Prime Minister was confronted by protesters including 'Tanya Tampon' dressed as a tampon. News of what was making Australian women 'see red' went round the world on the US-based 'Feminist Wire'.[64] Unfortunately this lively campaign did not succeed in removing the tax on being a woman.

The standout issue for WEL in the media in the Howard years was, however, the defence of the Commonwealth *Sex Discrimination Act* and particularly its prohibition of marital status discrimination. Led by Lisa Solomon, WEL–Victoria briefed legal counsel to intervene in a High Court case (*McBain v State of Victoria*) in support of the right of single women to obtain IVF treatment. The Federal Court had already ruled that a Victorian law restricting such access was inconsistent with the Commonwealth Act and hence invalid. Dr John McBain, a

Erica Lewis, WEL acting national co-ordinator, on the national day of action against the GST on sanitary products. Canberra, 25 February 2000. *Erica Lewis.*

WEL members demonstrate outside the High Court with Leesa Meldrum. Kate Callas, *Sydney Morning Herald*, 5 September 2001, p. 6.

Melbourne IVF specialist, had challenged the Victorian legislation on behalf of his patient, Leesa Meldrum, a single woman in her thirties. Meanwhile the Commonwealth Attorney-General had issued a fiat allowing the Australian Conference of Catholic Bishops to appeal to the High Court to overturn the Federal Court decision.[65] The challenge not only threatened single women's access to IVF, but also the marital status provisions of the *Sex Discrimination Act 1984* more generally. Both WEL–Victoria and the Human Rights and Equal Opportunity Commission (HREOC) intervened in the proceedings to support the Federal Court decision.

This case was the first time a women's group had been granted status in the High Court. Australia has been unlike North America insofar as women's organisations have rarely pursued litigation strategies, both because it has been harder for public interest groups to obtain 'standing' in Australia and because other elements of the opportunity structure have been more accessible than in North America. The

Australian bureaucracy, for example, was more open to the recruitment of feminists into women's policy agencies, and feminists outside government were more inclined to see these agencies as internal advocates for their demands. This Australian tradition of 'looking to the state' differed from a more rights-based approach relying on the courts to advance gender claims.[66]

WEL had first applied for *amicus curiae* ('friend of the court') status before the High Court in 1996 in *CES v Superclinics*, but ultimately that case was settled out of court and WEL did not have to proceed. In 2001 there was a highly charged atmosphere as WEL women with placards demonstrated outside the Court while inside WEL counsel prepared to oppose the bishops. According to the *Australian*:

> WEL has seen the battle flag and marshalled its forces
> accordingly. The call has gone out via email and telephone
> call: 'WEL and all other supporting organisations are calling
> on women to attend the High Court, to fill the public gallery,
> to mass on the steps – to show the Catholic church and the
> Australian Government, as well as the rest of the world, that
> Australian women will not stand for this kind of attack and
> that we take our human rights seriously.'[67]

While Australian women did not exactly mass outside the High Court, WEL stalwarts were there.

WEL's case was three-pronged: first, to oppose the standing of the bishops; second, if the bishops were granted standing, to be the other major party; and third, if that failed to be granted *amicus curiae* status to put arguments on behalf of women. 'How bishops' IVF bid galvanised feminism' and 'Women's lobby challenges church' were some of the headlines.[68] In the end the High Court ruled that those such as the Catholic Bishops Conference who had not been parties to a case did not have standing to appeal the decision. Hence the Federal Court decision stood. It was not the end of the story, as the government persisted with its attempts to amend the *Sex Discrimination Act* to allow marital status discrimination in access to infertility treatment and WEL continued to take a lead in community resistance to this.[69]

Many media commentators, such as those on ABC-TV's *7.30 Report*, saw WEL, rather than HREOC, as the main player defending women's right to make choices regarding children, regardless of marital status.[70] The Internet search engine Google records 473 media items about WEL's intervention in the High Court case, reflecting the new media environment in which WEL was operating.[71] Whereas in the 1970s WEL took advantage of the new medium of community radio, now it had its own significant on-line presence. Its challenge to the bishops was also recorded in on-line versions of metropolitan newspapers and the ABC, transcripts of television current affairs programs and in the on-line publications of many organisations.[72]

While the defence of the *Sex Discrimination Act* did not have the immediate visual appeal of some of WEL's other campaigns, the 'WEL Stands for Women' placards outside the High Court were photogenic; other tactics included Young WEL–ACT's participation in the delivery of a turkey baster to the Prime Minister. An enclosed letter pointed out that this would be the safest way that infertile single and lesbian women would be able to become pregnant under proposed changes to the Act.[73]

Analysis of WEL's media coverage confirms that media priorities on WEL issues did not always correspond to either the priorities of members or the focus of policy submissions. Whereas policy submissions and policy advocacy sometimes had fairly direct impacts, as in the case of the amendments to the *Sex Discrimination Act* following the Lavarch inquiry or the ILO inclusions in the *Industrial Relations Reform Act*, this impact was not necessarily covered by the media. Nonetheless, the initial build-up of favourable media coverage over WEL's electoral interventions in the 1970s was undoubtedly important in preparing the way for acceptance of its proposals on matters such as anti-discrimination legislation and women's policy machinery within government. The latter, in particular, was typical of an issue where WEL had a high degree of influence but there was little media interest – except in the case of flashpoints involving resignations or relocations.

There was also a changing media environment over the thirty

years, including an increase in the number of women political reporters but a decrease in dedicated women's pages or programs. Such pages
and programs had been 'turned around' under the influence of second-
wave feminism and became useful vehicles for news on gender-related
policy issues. For example, the women's section in the *Sydney Morning
Herald* changed significantly between June 1970 and June 1975. In 1970
it was almost entirely devoted to home decoration, children and social
reporting, with articles such as 'Protocol for the Family Christening'
and 'How to Curtsey with Aplomb'. By 1975 it covered issues such as
a conference on abortion law reform, the rape crisis centre, the *Family
Law Act* and the campaign by WEL to obtain benefits and training for
unemployed women.[74]

Women's sections in the media which were particularly helpful
in promoting WEL issues included the long-lived 'Accent Page' in *The
Age* (1966–97), particularly under editor Rosemary West, and 'Corporate Woman' in the *Australian Financial Review* (1988–98).[75] For a decade
from 1991 the less mainstream *Green Left* also provided a weekly feminist commentary on policy issues ('Ain't I a woman?'). On radio, the
most significant program for WEL was the ABC's *Coming Out Show*. It
was established by the Women's Broadcasting Collective as an International Women's Year project in 1975 and lasted until the end of 1994,
before being renamed the *Women Out Loud* program and then abolished
at the end of 1998. Despite the disappearance of much dedicated feminist media space in the late 1990s, some feminist programs survived on
community radio, such as 3CR's *Women on the Line*, which celebrated
twenty years of chronicling 'defining moments and debates in the
women's movement' with the release of a CD in 2006. Given all these
vicissitudes, WEL was remarkably resilient in the Howard era.

WEL in the federal parliament

An example of the seriousness with which WEL was treated in Parliament in the Whitlam period was the answer given to a Liberal Shadow
Minister's question on a WEL submission entitled 'Aspects of Women

in the Workforce'. The Minister for Labour, Clyde Cameron, responded comprehensively, traversing what had been done to implement concerns outlined in the submission relating to equal pay, equal opportunity, maternity leave, training, vocational guidance and employment services available to women.[76]

Other examples included references to WEL's campaign on probate and the inequitable tax treatment of widows. Liberal Senator Peter Baume drew on the authority of WEL to advocate schemes for flexible part-time employment to improve retention of women health professionals, while Labor Senator Ruth Coleman used WEL data on turn-away rates at women's refuges and the shortfall in provision in Western Australia.[77] In contrast was a campaign waged by Independent Senator Brian Harradine, who was convinced WEL was using government money to promote abortion. He read into Hansard a parable, 'The witch who came in from the cold', presented by Sara Dowse at the 1978 WEL National Conference. The parable dealt with the short-lived kingdom of Craminalot, where the lady-in-waiting wove magic to ensure girl babies were no longer sacrificed, and the tree of magic that grew outside the palace walls had purple flowers and was tended by wise women. Harradine was convinced that the tree of magic that was the source of power of the handmaidens in the palace was WEL. He understood the parable as saying that Dowse's first loyalty as head of the Women's Affairs Branch had been to WEL rather than to the government.[78] Furthermore, he believed advice coming from sources such as WEL was destructive to the principles of family life. His 'evidence' included an Education Department journal describing a women's affairs adviser as having 'a husband and two cats'.

Defunding created a peak in WEL's coverage in parliamentary debate (see Appendix A5). The previous peak, in 1997, came at a time when WEL was being publicly attacked by government spokeswomen for providing 'misleading' information to the United Nations. WEL continued to receive favourable mentions from some government ministers, for example for its role in the insertion of a definition of merit in the Public Service Bill, while the Opposition and the Australian Democrats referred favourably to WEL submissions on affirmative action and human rights legislation. WEL's critique of the failure of the government to include a woman in the large delegation to the ILO conference on maternity leave was also picked up. But most often in the Howard era, WEL was referred to in Parliament as the outstanding example of the way government was defunding NGOs that were critical of government policy. In other words, it had become a stick to beat the government with.

Although supposedly in decline since the 1970s, WEL remained the women's organisation most frequently referred to in debate in the federal parliament in 1981–2005. It was significantly ahead of the next most frequently cited organisations, the National Council of Women and the YWCA.

'Women at war'

While WEL was successful in gaining media attention, media priorities were often at odds with serious coverage. Apart from the horse-race frame imposed on its electoral interventions, another popular media frame was that of conflict between women, with the subtext that women could not be significant collective actors because they were 'their own worst enemies'. A staple topic in the early media coverage of WEL was the differences between WEL and Women's Liberation. When the Women's Action Alliance (WAA) was founded to contest the influence of WEL over government, joined later by Women Who Want to be Women, this provided new potential for stories about conflict among women (for the founding of these and other new women's groups see Appendix A4).

In 1976 a number of stories appeared in *The Age* highlighting the differences between women's groups, or 'how the female ranks divide'.[79] Leonard Radic, for example, wrote a three-part series contrasting the radical feminists of Women's Liberation and WEL with the women of WAA. He quoted the WAA founder, Joan Adamson, as saying that 1000 women had packed the Royale Ballroom to hear speakers attack 'feminists and Women's Libbers' when the WAA was founded during

International Women's Year. In another big 'women at war' article for
The Age three years later, David Elias quoted Adamson as saying that
feminists had gone quiet because they were now inside government
and didn't need to make a noise anymore.[80]

In the 1980s the 'women at war' stories were partially displaced
by the 'women's movement is over' stories also prominent in the US
media in this period. 'How the shout of the '70s became just a whimper'
is an early example.[81] Ironically, just as the media were proclaiming the
women's movement was over, the numbers of women in Australian
parliaments began to build up, bringing women's movement discourse
into a new arena.

A decade later, the early conflict stories were succeeded by generation war stories. In the mid-1990s there was saturation coverage of two
controversies. The first arose from Anne Summers' 'Letter to the next
generation' criticising the lack of activism by young feminists. The
second was sparked by Helen Garner's book *The First Stone*, which was
censorious of young 'victim feminists' for bringing a sexual harassment
case against the master of a university college. All of these became part
of a narrative of conflict between the baby-boomer WEL generation
and the succeeding X and Y generations. Leading conservative journalist Piers Akerman epitomised the conservative discourse on the war
between women:

> For 30 years the Australian feminist movement has been
> dominated by the women who want to be men brigade. But
> the tide has now turned.
>
> The ageing radicals who led the movement in the 60s and
> 70s are being challenged by younger women, who believe
> in feminism but don't believe that it is necessary to reject
> motherhood – the most important female occupation – or other
> family-oriented goals to demonstrate their credentials.
>
> The burn-the-bra brigade, which found a haven in the
> Whitlam Government and established guidelines for successive
> Labor governments, has passed its use-by date but has left a
> destructive legacy.[82]

This piece relies on many conservative media staples – including the 'burn-the-bra' myth and the construction of an 'anti-motherhood' image for a generation of activists, many of whom had emerged from Parents and Citizens associations. But above all, the piece is characterised by the attempt to erase its own conservative footprint – it is 'today's young women', not conservative journalists, who are saying that old-guard feminists devalued motherhood and ignored women's psychological and physiological needs.

The increased dominance of conservative discourse in the latter part of the 1990s created an unsympathetic media environment for WEL's policy messages. Neo-conservative and neo-liberal columnists combined to depict WEL as some kind of feminist dinosaur committed to the use of the public sector to promote gender equity and standing in the way of other women's desire either to become individual entrepreneurs or to achieve their true destiny as wives and mothers. Lack of influence on government in this new environment also meant that WEL was no longer seen as a significant commentator on government policy. Although the Internet created new opportunities for WEL commentary on public affairs, e-lists and websites were most often 'preaching to the converted'. WEL remained the organisation most often sought after by those seeking feminist perspectives on public policy, but this was a diminishing group. By this stage WEL was more often regarded as of historical interest by students and others, rather than a significant political actor in the new 'post-feminist' environment.

5

MAKING GOVERNMENT
WOMEN-FRIENDLY

Outside Australia, WEL is best known for its role in initiating what has been called Australia's 'femocratic experiment'. Femocrat was initially a term of abuse for feminists entering government but became a label worn with pride, in the same way that 'black' turned from a term of abuse into an expression of identity. WEL wanted to make government responsive to women and to ensure that those developing policy had to take note of its impact on women. WEL members who had been undertaking gender analysis on an unpaid basis within the community sector were now able to take their expertise into new positions being created in government.

The interest in policy structures was distinctive in international terms and also in relation to other parts of the Australian women's movement. It reflected both the opportunities of the time and a relatively positive attitude towards what could be achieved through government, given political will and good institutional design. WEL was both responding to opportunities and creating them. Where social movement organisations often exercise influence through making problems newly visible, rather than developing detailed policy solutions, WEL undertook both – helping introduce women's movement discourses into public policy arenas and promoting a particular model of women's policy machinery.

In Canberra, in particular, WEL had a close-up view of strategic opportunities. It used the historic Royal Commission on Australian Government Administration (RCAGA, or Coombs Commission) to try to work out how best to make government policy women-friendly. Its 1974 submission recommended taskforces in the central areas of all departments and authorities to monitor policy development and program administration, initiate research, maintain liaison with target groups of women and brief inter-departmental committees and advisory councils. The submission was a milestone in setting out the 'wheel model' of women's policy machinery. This model, with a hub at the centre of government, spokes in line departments and a focus on policy advice and policy monitoring rather than program delivery, was the 'good practice' model for which Australia became noted. It was disseminated internationally as well as at all levels of government at home. It was a forerunner of the 'gender mainstreaming' approach adopted by 189 governments at the Beijing Conference in 1995.[1]

WEL's thinking was taken up in the RCAGA discussion paper, *Sexism in Public Service*, which canvassed options for women's policy machinery, focusing on the co-ordination role. These included expanding the existing women's affairs section within the Prime Minister's Department to division status while recognising the 'difficulty of channelling advice through hierarchies that epitomise male dominion in public policy-making'. Another option, a self-standing bureau or commission, would provide greater independence, but a 'critical weakness' would be remoteness from the day-to-day working of the bureaucracy.[2]

In response to *Sexism in Public Service* WEL further elaborated its position, stressing the need for departmental units and for reporting mechanisms to ensure women's needs were integrated into programs and policies at an early stage of development. Meanwhile responsibility for policy co-ordination in areas crossing portfolio boundaries, such as women's refuges, would be retained at the centre. WEL's 1975 federal election policy statement included two pages on women's policy machinery reiterating the need for units with adequate seniority for the policy monitoring role and for central co-ordination by an office that would initiate and support cross-portfolio projects.[3]

In the final analysis, RCAGA recommended that the model put forward by WEL be trialled. The Women's Affairs Branch in the Prime Minister's Department would be the hub, while the spokes would be in functional departments. It was different in conception from other new policy departures, where location in the Prime Minister's Department was seen as a prelude to the setting up of a department with program responsibilities. With the WEL model, the primary goal was to monitor and audit policy, not to deliver programs. In 1976 a network of twelve women's policy units came into being (but not a unit in Treasury, as WEL had recommended). An Interdepartmental Working Group, which set up taskforces with experts from outside as well as inside government, was established to advise on issues like the funding of women's refuges, anti-discrimination policy and migrant women.

In 1976 WEL was also making detailed recommendations to Prime Minister Malcolm Fraser on the structure of his proposed Women's Advisory Council, wanting it to have the capacity to commission and publish research like the Canadian equivalent. In a series of meetings with women's organisations, the Prime Minister, the Treasurer and four other senior ministers heard detailed points presented by WEL on administrative and reporting arrangements for a Council.[4]

A working party elected from these meetings was chaired by Dame Beryl Beaurepaire of the Federal Women's Committee of the Liberal Party. Fifteen WEL groups, including regional groups in Rockhampton, Cairns, Townsville, Burnie and Cooma, made submissions on how the advisory body should operate. The Council set up by the Fraser government did indeed have considerable independence and was able to commission important policy research, not only on financial arrangements within families but also on legislative means to address domestic violence, such as apprehended violence orders.[5] WEL went on to be closely involved in the design of advisory bodies at other levels of government, seeking broad-based councils that would garner bipartisan support for women's policy machinery while also having an independent voice.

WEL's close relationship with the emerging 'women's state' gave rise to a partnership not found in other Western democracies during the 1970s. The porous relationship between the women's movement and the women's state in Australia was epitomised by the government delegation to the IWY conference in Mexico City – Australia was the only country to have its official delegation headed by an avowed feminist (Elizabeth Reid). Elsewhere feminists either felt greater distrust of the state or had fewer opportunities for policy innovation from within it. Even in Canada, also developing its women's policy machinery at this time, the women's movement paid relatively little attention to it, raising no outcry when it was moved out of the Privy Council Office, the central policy co-ordination body in government.[6]

By contrast, WEL responded immediately when the Whitlam government decided to move the Women's Adviser, Elizabeth Reid, from the Prime Minister's office into the Prime Minister's Department. Reid resigned over what she viewed as an attempt to silence her, and WEL spokeswomen around Australia gave media interviews expressing their anger.[7] In Brisbane WEL set up a vigil in King George Square, while the group in the NSW electorate of Wentworth initiated a national 'Send a pig campaign'. The postcard showed a male chauvinist pig about to gobble up the International Women's Year symbol and was captioned 'MCPs lose women's votes'. The Prime Minister claimed that fortunately it didn't look like him.[8] In light of unrelated political developments that were to lead to his dismissal, the campaign was short-lived and telegrams were sent to all WEL groups calling it off.

Despite the political turbulence, WEL continued to press the Prime Minister on the detail of women's policy machinery:

> There has never been any doubt in our minds that the women's affairs section in your department needs to be expanded and upgraded ... There is also an urgent need for women's policy units within other important co-ordinating departments, such

as Treasury, and social policy departments such as Urban and
Regional Development, Social Security, Health and Education.[9]

After the dismissal of the Whitlam government and the election of the
new Fraser government, the preservation of programs became a key
concern. While the new government had made an electoral commitment to maintain the Women's Affairs Branch in Prime Minister and
Cabinet, a number of programs were less secure. In January 1976
WEL received coverage in media all around Australia as it pinpointed
programs at risk, including the Children's Commission, Legal Aid, the
Supporting Mother's Benefit, the National Employment and Training
Scheme (NEAT), the Royal Commission on Human Relationships and
the final grants for International Women's Year.[10] Women were said to
make up two thirds of those using legal aid services while NEAT was a
bridge for women re-entering the labour market.

In the event only the Children's Commission and NEAT were lost,
but there were cuts to children's services, legal aid and refuges, the
loss of paternity leave in the Australian Public Service and continuing threats of devolution of responsibility for women's services to the
States. The protection of legal aid services was to be a major issue over
the next two decades, as funding cuts meant those facing imprison-
ment were prioritised over those needing legal aid for family law cases,
who were predominantly women.[11]

In 1977–78 WEL was again in full cry around Australia over the
government's decision to transfer the Office of Women's Affairs from
the most powerful government department to the Department of
Home Affairs, ranked 26 out of 27. 'Dumped among museums, archives
and the Australian War Memorial,' as one WEL spokeswoman said.
Women's Adviser Sara Dowse resigned over the decision – helping
put the location of the Office on the Opposition's agenda. With the
election of the Hawke government in 1983 there was a triumphant
return of what was now the Office of the Status of Women (OSW).
Not only was the Office back in Prime Minister and Cabinet but it soon
took responsibility for an important 'whole-of-government' initiative,
the Women's Budget Program. All portfolios were required to provide

Male chauvinist pig postcard,
October 1975.

breakdowns of the impact on women of Budget outlays for an official
Budget document. Women's budgets were gradually adopted by all
Australian governments at the urging of WEL and feminists within
government. International bodies adopted the idea as an example
of good practice and many countries introduced 'gender-sensitive
budgeting'.[12]

Separate from women's policy machinery was the development
of equal opportunity units responsible for removing discrimination in
public sector employment. Just before the fall of the Whitlam government Gail Radford was appointed to the Public Service Board to
develop equal opportunity policy. WEL had long been calling for a more
proactive approach to equal opportunity in the Public Service, including measures to overcome the effects of past discrimination.[13] There
were also inherited problems such as the lack of a career structure in
the female ghetto of keyboard work. The *Public Service Act* was finally
amended in 1984 to require the development of equal employment

opportunity (EEO) plans by departments and agencies staffed under the Act. In 1987, however, in a sudden move announced on Bastille Day, the Public Service Board was abolished and responsibilities for personnel and EEO devolved to departments and agencies, even before some of the latter had submitted their first EEO programs. WEL and EEO practitioner groups lobbied vigorously against the changes on the grounds that change required strong central direction and that central monitoring and expertise, including statistical expertise, was essential for the success of EEO.

Thanks to this campaign, backed by politicians such as Senator Pat Giles, Senator Susan Ryan and Wendy Fatin[14], the statutory reporting requirement was retained along with a small monitoring unit in the new Public Service Commission. This was insufficient safeguard, however, given the new philosophy of 'letting the managers manage'. Gail Radford's position was axed in 1990, and in 1991 WEL members reported to a parliamentary inquiry that EEO in the Australian Public Service had become a 'sad farce'.[15] EEO plans were filed but not assessed. At State and Territory levels too, WEL members had helped dismantle discriminatory barriers in public sector employment only to see equity concerns later eroded under the influence of private sector models of corporate governance. During the 1990s the equality concerns that underlay equal opportunity programs were being displaced by a new focus on managing or harnessing the productivity gains to be made from diversity.

Making State governments women-friendly

In Hobart, as in Canberra, WEL members had kept a close eye on machinery of government and public sector employment issues. In the 1970s Tasmanian ministers and heads of department were busy answering a stream of WEL letters concerning discriminatory advertising of vacancies, like the large advertisement headed 'Career Opportunities for Young Men' offering appointments as clerks, cadets or trainees and juxtaposed against an advertisement offering positions as junior typists or office assistants to girls under 21 (closing date 3 January 1973). WEL was also pursuing the cause of flexible working hours and paternity leave in the State public service and lobbying energetically for the appointment of a women's adviser. In Adelaide WEL was seeking the employment of a women's adviser as well as providing detailed evidence on pay inequities and employment discrimination in the Public Service.

In Tasmania there was a false start in May 1975 when the premier announced the appointment, without advertisement, of a Mrs Barbara Knight to a position described as Adviser on Women's Affairs, the duties of which included arranging dinner parties for the Premier. WEL–Tasmania was acerbic about this blunder[16], and in January 1976 WEL member Kim Boyer became the Tasmanian Women's Adviser, this time a full-time position with an appropriate range of duties. Boyer was a journalist and postgraduate student who in 1973 had become the first woman lay coroner in Australia.

 First State-wide meeting of WEL in Tasmania, 1974. *Kim Boyer.*

Both Boyer and Deborah McCulloch, who became South Australian Women's Adviser a few months later, had young children and were particularly keen to improve employment conditions for women in the same circumstances. Barriers included rigid hours and requirements for continuity of service. In 1979 the benchmark federal *Maternity Leave Test Case* resulted in twelve months unpaid maternity leave for workers under federal awards. Similar provisions were introduced for Tasmanian public servants in the same year, as well as a raft of equal opportunity initiatives in employment and education, rape and domestic violence law reform, child care and women's refuges.

In Tasmania, as later in the other States, new structures were developed to give women, including particular groups such as migrant women, greater access to government. Advisory committees and task forces came into being, in addition to women's information services. As a pioneering women's adviser, Boyer was able to give WEL members from other States ideas on what kind of policy machinery was likely to be effective. Eva Cox, for example, took ideas from Hobart back to Sydney to use in lobbying the newly-elected Wran government. Cox was joined by others, including Joan Bielski, Juliet Richter, Elizabeth Windschuttle and Anne Conlon, in developing the NSW machinery submission.

A change of government in Tasmania 1982 saw the abolition of the women's adviser position by the incoming Liberal Premier, who stated that as he had a wife he didn't need a women's adviser. His all-male Cabinet was sufficient to provide good government. WEL and the Support Women's Adviser Team (SWAT) campaigned hard over the loss of the position, both as an access point for women to government and as a means to ensure systematic monitoring and gender analysis of Cabinet submissions.[17] Thanks to this political mobilisation it was restored with the return of a Labor government in 1989.

There was also a less than happy experience in Victoria, where women's policy machinery was first established in 1976 under the Hamer Liberal government but the inaugural women's adviser resigned after adverse publicity. She was replaced by Yolanda Klempfner, who was appointed as co-ordinator of women's affairs in the Premier's Department in 1977.

In 1977 New South Wales became the fourth State to set up a women's adviser. Founding WEL member and TAFE teacher Carmel Niland was appointed, heading the Women's Co-ordination Unit in the Premier's Department. Thanks to WEL, the position, unusually, had direct access to the Premier without having to go through the departmental hierarchy. At her first meeting with Premier Wran she asked about his priorities. He responded: 'The anti-Discrimination Bill. I introduced it as a Private Member's Bill, but WEL says there are problems with it. Sort that out. Then the women's refuges ... And childcare centres.' WEL was seen as not only setting the agenda, but as having trained and shaped the bureaucrats who went into many of the significant jobs of the era.[18]

Once a network of women's advisers had come into being around Australia (for the full sequence see Appendix A6), regular Commonwealth/State Women's Advisors meetings were initiated, providing a safe space to float ideas and share best practice information. In October 1978 WEL–Tasmania hosted a dinner for the Commonwealth/State Women's Advisers meeting in Hobart, on a 'bring your food and friends' basis.

In 1979 WEL–NT started the ball rolling for women's policy machinery by convening a forum called 'A Women's Adviser: Does the Territory need one?' The keynote speaker was Sara Dowse, former Commonwealth Women's Adviser. The forum called on the Northern Territory Government to appoint a women's adviser without further delay and to stop avoiding its responsibility towards women in the community.[19] WEL subsequently produced a 50-page submission outlining the case for a women's adviser and office of women's affairs located in the Chief Minister's Department with access to Cabinet submissions from across government.[20] When this made no impact on a Country Liberal Party Chief Minister convinced it was about the needs of a 'special interest group', WEL took to shopping centres to gather signatures for petitions.[21]

In 1982 the Chief Minister finally responded by appointing a women's adviser, although without advertisement and not from the women's movement. Nonetheless WEL welcomed the appointment and a delegation promptly called by to provide information on how women's advisers operated in other States. Unfortunately the appointment was not a success and the adviser lost further credibility by attacking the UN Women's Convention on International Women's Day. Julie Ellis responded for WEL on ABC Television. After the adviser's resignation there was a change of heart and someone with policy credibility and commitment was appointed – WEL activist Chris Sylvester. Meanwhile WEL–NT had been pressing for the appointment of a full-time adviser on sexism in education and for action on domestic violence. There was a need to overcome persistent assumptions this was a problem peculiar to Aboriginal communities and that victims, whether Aboriginal or not, had easy recourse to the law despite being economically dependent on their aggressors.[22]

WEL's focus on the need for machinery to make government responsive to the needs of women has been nicely summarised by Val Marsden in her account of WEL–WA and its long campaign for women's policy machinery, advisory structures and information services in that State. Marsden had moved across Australia to Perth in 1977, after joining WEL on the Gold Coast and helping found the first family planning clinic there:

> I became active in WEL almost immediately after my arrival in Perth. My experiences, and those of others, made us very aware of the importance of getting policies in place that gave formal recognition to the needs of women. The first step in doing that was to get a woman's adviser to the premier; someone who could provide a woman's perspective to decision-making at the highest level. As well, we wanted consultation with women in the community so that the advice given could reflect the variety of women's experience. And, finally, we wanted somewhere for women to go to receive the kind of information needed to enable women to take control of their lives.[23]

The campaign described by Marsden finally bore fruit when the Burke

Labor government was elected in Western Australia in 1983. The previous year the Labor Women's Organisation had successfully moved to have equal opportunity legislation and women's policy machinery included in the party platform. As we saw in chapter 4, WEL picketed the campaign openings of both Liberal and Labor parties during the election, promoting issues such as refuge funding and the need for a women's adviser. Soon after the election, Deborah McCulloch was called in from South Australia as a consultant on the setting up of the women's interests division within the Premier's Department, a Women's Advisory Council, a women's information and referral service and equal opportunity legislation.

WEL member Liza Newby was appointed as Women's Adviser and the Community Employment Program was again helpful in funding the initial positions in the women's interests division as well as the thirteen positions in the information service. The WA Women's Advisory Council became the best resourced and most independent of its kind around Australia. A WEL founder, Dot Goodrick, became its first president, followed by Janet Pine, another WEL member.

In 1985 WEL–ACT member Ann Wentworth was appointed as the first women's adviser in the ACT. She had a difficult time at first and much of the energy of the ACT Women's Consultative Committee went into pushing for adequate resources to support her position. Nonetheless, Wentworth played a key role in the development of women's services, such as the 24-hour domestic violence crisis intervention service, which attended incidents along with police, and the women's health service. Moreover, the situation improved with the anticipation that the new ACT government would be headed by a woman. In May 1989 Rosemary Follett became Chief Minister at the head of a minority Labor government. Wentworth was always a very active member of WEL and after moving out of the bureaucracy became WEL national co-ordinator in 1991.

In 1998 WEL–ACT's election questionnaire was almost wholly devoted to strengthening machinery of government, which had been eroding under a Liberal government. The questionnaire (endorsed by other women's organisations) asked detailed questions about support for return of a women's policy unit to the Chief Minister's Department, planning mechanisms and gender budget reporting, the funding and location of the Women's Information and Referral Centre, women's advisory or consultative mechanisms, and support for a co-ordinating network of women's community organisations. When Labor was returned to government in the ACT in 2002 most of these machinery proposals were implemented, at least for a time.

The 1983 WA election campaign sandwich board asking people to vote for a women's adviser was symptomatic of WEL's use of the opportunities presented by election campaigns, although their efforts did not always bear fruit. In Queensland, WEL took credit for the setting up of a Status of Women Inquiry in 1973 but its long campaign for a women's adviser made little impact on the Bjelke-Petersen governments of the 1980s.[24] They had to wait until the 1989 election of the Goss Labor government, which established a Women's Policy Unit in the Premier's Department in 1990. This was a case of combined and uneven development, with the late-arriving women's policy unit being able to take advantage of the experience of other States and quickly introduce whole-of-government initiatives such as women's Budget statements.

Supporting women in government

WEL also served as a political base and support network for EEO and women's policy officers outside election periods. A large workshop held at the end of the 1980s by WEL–ACT in conjunction with the Institute of Public Administration illustrated this role. It was addressed by Marilyn Waring and Sara Dowse, among others, and focused on strategies to support women trying to preserve feminist values in government. The many public servants at the workshop brought forward issues such as the need to use economic rationalist language to get on the agenda, despite the hostility of economic rationalism to the forms of social investment needed by women. Feminists in government had to be bilingual, speaking the official language while trying to retain feminist idealism and direction. There were also the effects of managerialism: the pressure to compete against other women and produce showy 'runs on the board'; the discounting of participatory processes; and 'hierarchical seduction', whereby women were enticed away from group solidarity and collective effort.

Strategies included the need to rebuild pressure from outside, whereby feminist policy makers were supported and fed by a women's movement moving ahead of public opinion. More letters needed to arrive at ministers' offices to counter the perception that cuts at the expense of women were not particularly 'sensitive'. It was important to use community education programs to strengthen community networks, as with the domestic violence education program, rather than giving them to advertising agencies. Participants found the workshop a positive example of feminist networking, enabling women to name their experiences in the bureaucracy and to deconstruct them.[25]

'The Song of the Femocrat', written by Jenny Pausacker, summed up some of the experience of those 'inside':

> One day I came home to my flat
> I took off my femocrat hat
> I was starting to bleed, I was too tired to read
> So I stared at the TEEV and felt flat.
> I woke as I started to snore
> And thought I have been here before
> A fourteen-hour day is too much for the pay
> It's turning me into a bore.
>
> ... So try to change the system sisters
> Don't let it change you
> Even if the change comes slowly
> Keep the end in view
> We're still mainly on the margin
> But the margin is enlargin'
> And you can try to change the system sisters.

Almost ten years later, in February 1998, another strategic workshop was held in Canberra, organised at the ANU as part of a 'Reshaping Australian Institutions' project and this time piggy-backing off a Commonwealth/State meeting of women's advisers. Some of the issues remained the same, such as the lack of external pressure coming from the women's movement and the difficulty of implementing long-term projects such as improving the status of women within a managerialist environment. There was also the erosion of gains within government: women's co-ordinating units were being moved out of premier's departments, other women's units and policies were being abolished in the name of 'mainstreaming', and issue-specific inter-governmental bodies were being lost. Moreover, by 1998 only two of the women's advisers were still from the women's movement, the others being party or bureaucratic appointments. One of the WEL participants in this workshop, Elizabeth Shannon, not only sang to restore flagging spirits but also organised a follow-up workshop in Tasmania to promote the networking of policy practitioners, policy experts and policy activists.

Apart from sporadic initiatives such as the Canberra workshops, WEL women such as Pat Giles played an important role. Once Giles arrived in Canberra as Senator for Western Australia in 1981 she set up the Caucus Status of Women Committee, which she chaired until her retirement in 1993. It met weekly during sitting weeks and was a source of support for feminists within government. It promoted and salvaged initiatives such as gender budgeting, and initiated structures such as women's advisory groups for inter-governmental ministerial councils. International comparative research has found that such party committees, through mandating a focus on gender and gender impact, are a significant factor in reinforcing women's policy machinery and in enabling women in parliament to make a difference.[26] Giles used her position as senator to provide timely letters praising the work of a women's unit within government or helping to clear away bureaucratic blockages.

While women such as Giles were 'critical actors' within Parliament, WEL outside Parliament had the advantages of voice unconstrained by party or factional discipline. When women's units or women's programs were threatened or downgraded, WEL could be relied upon for a press statement and other action. As we have seen, Tasmanian WEL members led resistance to the early decision to abolish State women's adviser and EEO positions.[27] In Sydney WEL members rallied around the Women's Co-ordination Unit when it was moved out of the Premier's Department by a Liberal premier in 1988. On the other side of the country WEL protested against a Labor government for downgrading the women's interests division of the WA Premier's Department, in 1990 convening a public meeting attended by over 400 women under the banner 'Has Labor Dumped Women?' One member commented: 'Without the presence of WEL in Western Australia … it is likely that many more women-oriented services in the public sector would be "mainstreamed" quietly, watered down, shut down or disappeared into generalised services'.[28]

Unfortunately, under the federal Howard government such mainstreaming continued apace, with most women's units, including the venerable Women's Bureau, being closed down soon after it came to office. WEL wrote to the Prime Minister saying:

> you would acknowledge that people in small business have special needs, for example, or farmers, or self-funded retirees. Women have always banded together to form a whole variety of groups, recognising their distinctive characteristics and special needs. These distinctive characteristics and special needs should not be ignored and dismissed by mainstreaming government units devoted to women's issues.[29]

Unfortunately such protests now fell on deaf ears. In 2004, when WEL contested the NSW Labor government's decision to abolish the Department for Women, an Opposition spokeswoman suggested that its demise was somehow WEL's fault, for being insufficiently vigilant when the Department developed an 'obscure commitment' to gender analysis.[30] At the Commonwealth level, WEL spoke out in the same year against the decision to move the renamed Office for Women from the Department of Prime Minister and Cabinet to the Department of Family and Community Services, a move which confirmed the abandonment of any serious policy co-ordination role across government.

During a national consultation among WEL members over priorities for 2008, Jan Roberts commented that for WEL in Wagga, machinery of government was the one big issue:

> We have watched as successive governments, both at state and federal levels have dismantled the structures whereby women's voices were given importance and priority. We now have lip service to a 'whole of government' approach to women's issues, which if there was any real intention to do it would have been a positive move. However, women and their issues have slipped back into family affairs.[31]

Getting information out to women

From the time that WEL achieved a media profile in its first year of existence, it found itself dealing with a rush of demands from women for information, whether about social security, health issues or services. Many women in the community suffered from the loss of self-esteem associated with the status of 'housewife' and lacked the confidence to approach government directly for information. The women's centres or houses set up in the 1970s, with many of which WEL had been involved, found themselves providing a vast amount of information and advice, as well facilities such as a library and the ubiquitous Gestetner. In 1974 in Canberra, for example, an information service set up by WEL and Women's Liberation members, and co-ordinated by Chris Ronalds of WEL, ran for four hours a day and dealt with several hundred enquiries in its first four months.[32] As similar patterns were found elsewhere, it quickly became evident that the demand for non-patronising information and referral services could not be met on a volunteer basis alone. Voluntary, unpaid work simply shored up the inadequacy of public provision and added to the exploitation of women. WEL pressed for governments to take responsibility for meeting this need for information, and members with experience in providing services as volunteers played a central role in establishing the first government information services, including those in Adelaide, Canberra and Perth.

Founding WEL member and SA Women's Adviser Deborah McCulloch established the pioneering Women's Information Switchboard (WIS) in Adelaide in 1978. She obtained funding for five positions under the State unemployment relief scheme and seconded the officer who had written the funding submission to act as co-ordinator for the new service. WIS was dedicated to taking every request for information seriously, a commitment put to the test when the first caller wanted to know where she could hire a bridesmaid's dress.[33] The pilot project soon became a permanent government service, run on democratic lines and successfully reaching out to immigrant and Aboriginal women. Somewhat controversially, it used a lot of volunteers but this was justified by ensuring they received sufficient skills development, including a 12-week training program, to enhance their future options in the paid workforce.

WIS became a model for other government-funded women's information services around Australia and overseas. WEL helped fireproof it against a change of government through setting up a broad-based WIS Support Group. This encompassed about 100 organisations, including church groups, and was chaired by a WEL member. WEL was also instrumental in setting up the Working Women's Centre in Adelaide to provide information, support and advocacy to working women. In Canberra the inaugural WEL–Townsville convenor, Patti Kendall, became the co-ordinator of the Women's Shopfront, a Commonwealth Government initiative that followed hard on the heels of WIS in South Australia. When the ACT achieved self-government the shopfront became the Women's Information and Resource Centre of the ACT Government.

In Perth, WEL members had provided a WEL–TEL service for a number of years before the election of the Burke Labor government enabled a government service to be set up in 1984. Deborah McCulloch, in Perth to advise on equal opportunity legislation, also advised on the new service, the Women's Information and Referral Exchange (WIRE). In addition to a democratic structure, WIRE acquired an outstanding

L to R, Pat Fuller, secretary of SA Women's Unit, Deborah McCulloch, SA Women's Adviser, and Rosemary Wighton, incoming Women's Adviser, June 1979. *Deborah McCulloch.*

shopfront premises in St Georges Terrace, in the heart of the main business district of Perth; Val Marsden became the first co-ordinator.

WEL's role in these developments has been acknowledged in the history of WIRE (published in 2003), which describes the volunteer work of WEL and the 'dedication and commitment' that preceded the introduction of government machinery for women in 1983–84.[34] As we saw in chapter 3, WEL was also a jealous guardian of the non-hierarchical and collectivist structure which characterised WIRE's early years. In 1991, when the service came under sustained attack from the *West Australian* newspaper for having allowed the fraudulent Western Women's Finance Group to use its premises, WEL reactivated the 'Friends of WIRE' to defend it. The service was salvaged under the name Women's Information Service, but is now only a telephone-based service staffed by volunteers, assisted by a volunteer support officer in the Office of Women's Policy.

Also in 1984, a Women's Information and Referral Exchange was established in Melbourne. WEL and the Young Women's Christian Association (YWCA) had made the original proposal for the service in 1981. WIRE's commitment to collectivism caused a certain amount of friction with government funders but, after some compromises, WIRE in Melbourne is still flourishing with seven core staff and around 100 volunteers.

In New South Wales, lobbying for a government-funded women's information service took far longer than in other States and Territories, despite the creation of some specific services such as the Immigrant Women's Resource Centre. Queensland and Tasmania were also late starters, with the Commonwealth Office of the Status of Women running women's information services in those States until the 1989 election of Labor governments which took over responsibility.

In general, the story of women's information and referral services confirmed WEL's view that where a need had been demonstrated, in this case for women-friendly information and service delivery, government should take over the funding. As we have seen, volunteers were sometimes used, but care was taken to ensure that adequate training and support were provided so that rather than exploiting women these services were a stepping stone to new employment opportunities. The preservation of non-hierarchical and collectivist structures proved more difficult.

Tackling discrimination in employment

From its founding in 1972 WEL was always at the forefront of lobbying for the introduction of anti-discrimination legislation. One of the great disappointments was the sacking of the Whitlam government before sex discrimination legislation was achieved. In the event, the ratification of the ILO Convention on employment discrimination and the setting up of employment discrimination committees (EDCs) at State and federal levels in 1973 enabled WEL to use this new complaints mechanism.

In Port Pirie, South Australia in 1973, the local WEL group successfully filed a complaint against four major employers, including the local Council and BHP, who were forcing women to resign on marriage – the marriage bar was supported by employers and unions both. The secretary of the Port Pirie Trades and Labour Council stated: 'When a woman's married that's a job in itself and she should stay at home and look after it.'[35] The Port Augusta WEL group used the new complaints mechanism to get a Council by-law rescinded that prevented women taxi drivers from driving after dark – a by-law that considerably diminished their earnings during the winter months.[36]

In Tasmania the secretary of the EDC was a WEL member, and in this State WEL was particularly active in its use of this mechanism to try to break down employment discrimination, including the exclusion of women from work on the wharves. In this case, when lack of toilets was said to prevent the employment of women, WEL suggested that 'portaloos' be brought in – they were known at the time as 'Prendergast potties', after Helen Prendergast whose idea they were.[37] In Western Australia, the EDC investigated complaints from WEL concerning lack of promotional opportunities for female prison officers and of equal access for female prisoners to vocational training. After lengthy correspondence with the Department of Corrections more women were appointed as prison officers and a manager was appointed to reorganise prisoners' vocational training activities.[38]

The EDCs were able to solve many cases by persuasion and fulfilled an important role in officially documenting the extent of discrimination in employment at that time. There were, however, major drawbacks to their operation, largely because of their inability to impose sanctions. There were none of the educative effects that flowed from front-page reporting of high-profile cases under discrimination legislation, for example.

Meanwhile, WEL was lobbying strongly at the State level for statutory protection against discrimination. Progress was made when Australia's first Sex Discrimination Bill was introduced by Liberal David Tonkin, as a Private Member's Bill, in South Australia in 1973. It was referred to a Select Committee to determine the extent to which sex discrimination actually existed – a golden opportunity for WEL to collect glaring examples and present submissions based on evidence from more than sixty women to help persuade the Committee that discrimination did indeed exist. Banks, for instance, offered only ledger machinist jobs to a girl with top examination passes, while boys with poorer passes were allowed to become trainee tellers.[39]

The South Australian *Sex Discrimination Act* was passed by the Dunstan government in 1975 and immediately became the basis for WEL lobbying and draft Bills in other States. South Australia continued to be a trailblazer for many years. When its *Equal Opportunity Act* was introduced in 1984, WEL organised a demonstration on the steps of Parliament House to prevent the Legislative Council from watering it down. To the jubilation of WEL and other women this became the first Act to define sexual harassment as a detriment in itself – without it being necessary to prove any other employment harm. This breakthrough was successfully used by WEL in lobbying for the ACT *Discrimination Act* and then for the strengthening of the Commonwealth *Sex Discrimination Act* in the early 1990s.

In New South Wales, Labor leader Neville Wran had introduced a Sex Discrimination Bill as a Private Member's Bill while in Opposition in 1975. When Labor was elected to government the following year WEL renewed its demands for action. The NSW *Anti-Discrimination Act* was enacted in 1977, an omnibus Act despite strong lobbying by WEL member Helen Coonan. She argued that to mix sex discrimination with racial discrimination was 'like trying to mix oil and water – racial discrimination is so blatant that sex discrimination could seem trivial and less prevalent'.[40] Ironically, Coonan was later a Cabinet Minister in the Howard government which on several occasions tried to abolish specialist positions such as Sex Discrimination Commissioner in favour of positions with omnibus responsibilities.

As in other States, WEL members in New South Wales were not only instrumental in lobbying for the passage of anti-discrimination legislation (against strong opposition) but also for its subsequent strengthening. In particular this meant pressing for affirmative action, so that responsibility for removing discriminatory practices was shifted from victims to employers. Success came in 1980 when the NSW *Anti-Discrimination Act* was amended to require public sector agencies to develop EEO management plans. WEL activist Alison Ziller, who had already produced the *Affirmative Action Handbook*, brilliantly illustrated by cartoonist Patrick Cook, was appointed the first Director of Equal Opportunity in Public Employment.[41] Another WEL stalwart, Joan Bielski, successfully campaigned from both inside and outside government for the scheduling of higher education under the requirement for EEO management plans.

WEL supported test cases under the NSW Act, including the successful *Melinda Leves Case*. Leves lodged a complaint with the Anti-Discrimination Board in 1984 that she had been treated less favourably than her twin brother by the Department of Education. While her brother was able to take computer science and graphics at Canterbury Boys High, at Canterbury Girls High Leves was offered cooking and needlework. Bielski headed a WEL campaign to raise funds and other support for the case, which went as far as the Court of Appeal before the complaint was upheld in 1987.

Meanwhile WEL–Victoria had also submitted a draft anti-discrimination bill at the request of the State government. In 1977 came the Victorian Equal Opportunity Bill, on which WEL prepared a detailed critique, particularly of the exemptions and the lack of power of the Equal Opportunity Commissioner to initiate inquiries or take action on behalf of individuals or groups.[42] WEL also criticised the low level of penalties compared with the South Australian Act, and the resulting message about the seriousness of discriminatory behaviour.

Despite its weaknesses, the new Victorian Act was to achieve headlines in 1979 with the case of *Ansett Transport Industries (Operations) Pty Ltd v Wardley*. Ansett Airlines had refused to employ Deborah Wardley as a pilot, despite her qualifications and experience, purely because she was a woman. WEL played a major role in the campaign to support Wardley, from meetings with senior management to boycotting Ansett and picketing Ansett headquarters. Some believed that WEL's boycott was more feared once Business and Professional Women (BPW) joined in, for WEL members were assumed to be always more likely to travel by the government airline, TAA. Apart from direct action and consumer boycotts, WEL was at the same time seeking government funding to support future test cases. The need for such a fund, to take the pressure off victims of discrimination like Wardley, became a significant theme within WEL lobbying on anti-discrimination legislation over subsequent decades.

Western Australia had to wait for equal opportunity legislation until the election of a Labor government in 1983. WEL organised public meetings, petitions and information leaflets to drum up public support and systematically lobbied Opposition members to enable its passage through the Upper House in 1984. There was an even longer wait in Queensland, where in the 1970s the Mayor of Rockhampton had been adamant in pursuing his policy of sacking married women from Council employment. Sackings of this nature were only stopped through the use of ILO Convention 111 to insert a non-discrimination clause in the relevant award; actual legislation did not come until after a Labor government was elected in 1989.

In Tasmania WEL had been giving evidence to inquiries and working hard for legislation for six years when it had the frustration of seeing the Legislative Council send the Labor government's Equal Opportunity Bill to a select committee. The committee reported in 1980 that Tasmania had no need of anti-discrimination legislation and that employment of married women was already increasing at the expense of male and youth employment. In Darwin WEL was meeting strong resistance from the Country Liberal Party government, although somewhat encouraged by a private member's Discrimination Bill tabled by the Labor opposition.

The long pursuit of federal legislation

In Canberra the dismissal of the Whitlam government did not diminish WEL's pursuit of federal sex discrimination legislation. Members were soon lobbying the new Fraser government on the issue and the minister with responsibility for women's affairs, R.J. Ellicott, was convinced by their arguments. In 1978 he told the first meeting of the newly appointed National Women's Advisory Council that the government was considering sex discrimination legislation. Convenor of the Council, Beryl Beaurepaire, promptly organised a major conference in Melbourne in 1979 to prod the government into action. Liberal women such as Queensland Senator Kathy Martin played important roles in this conference, but battle lines were beginning to emerge on the issue. Tasmanian Liberal Senator Shirley Walters opposed sex discrimination legislation, along with Babette Francis and Jackie Butler of the newly formed Women Who Want to be Women (WWWW).

The Melbourne conference was strongly supported by WEL women, who made up about a third of the participants. Their recommendations won the support of the conference, and included provisions for affirmative action and sanctions, as well as scope to cover sexual preference as well as marital status, pregnancy and parenthood. Despite this momentum, Minister Ellicott was consistently frustrated by his Cabinet colleagues in his attempts to advance proposals for Commonwealth legislation. He attempted to legislate by press release, announcing, as Minister for the Capital Territory, the introduction of a sex discrimination ordinance for the ACT (21 December 1979). Federal Cabinet remained unconvinced, despite WEL organising supportive action by the ACT House of Assembly and the ACT Trades and Labour Council.

As Chair of the National Women's Advisory Council, Beaurepaire maintained the pressure for legislation through holding town-hall meetings around the country over a draft plan of action for the UN Decade for Women. WEL women were elected as delegates to a 1980 national conference at the Academy of Science in Canberra at which the plan was to be finalised. The plan, however, along with its commitment to sex discrimination legislation, was never approved by government, thanks again to National Party opposition.

At the Mid-Decade Conference in Copenhagen in 1980, Ellicott did manage to sign the UN Convention on the Elimination of All Forms of Discrimination against Women (CEDAW) on behalf of the Australian government, despite WWWW press representatives physically trying to prevent him. Ellicott promptly issued a joint statement with the Minister for Foreign Affairs, saying that signing the Convention was an important indication of 'Australia's policy of equality for women and the elimination of discrimination'.[43] This, however, was wishful thinking, as no further progress was made by the Fraser government towards ratification.

Meanwhile, Labor's Susan Ryan had been elected in 1975 to one of the ACT's new Senate seats. As a founding member of WEL–ACT she was firmly committed to sex discrimination legislation, and as Shadow Minister for the Status of Women she introduced the first Sex Discrimination Bill as a private senator's Bill in 1981. Chris Ronalds did the initial drafting. This was a broad-ranging Bill that subsequently gave rise to two major pieces of legislation.

The Sex Discrimination Bill became a major plank in the Labor Party's election policy, endorsed by national women's organisations never previously seen as part of Labor's constituency. The momentum seemed unstoppable. In October 1982 the Coalition government finally announced its intention to legislate, although only in relation to the ACT and Commonwealth employment, and without undue haste. The Coalition remained opposed to the use of the external affairs power to implement international treaties such as CEDAW and thus extend Commonwealth government powers in areas such as human rights.

With the election of the new Labor government in 1983 the way seemed clear for action at last. A Sex Discrimination Bill modelled on Chris Ronalds' original Bill, but without its affirmative action provisions, was introduced into Parliament in June 1983. CEDAW, which was to provide some of the constitutional basis for the Bill, was ratified in July. CEDAW obliged signatories to promote women's equal enjoyment of human rights and freedoms in all areas of life, including education and employment. The High Court had confirmed in the recent *Koowarta Case* in Queensland that the federal government was able to use its external affairs power to legislate to meet obligations under international human rights conventions.

Demonstration against the Sex Discrimination Bill, 1983.
Christine Fernon.

Yet at about this time the unpredictable occurred: a nation-wide campaign was launched against the 'Sex Bill' and against the UN Women's Convention on which it relied. The campaign was spearheaded by the Queensland co-ordinator of WWWW, Jackie Butler, who was also Chair of the Council for a Free Australia. She claimed that the Convention would lead to the banning of the Bible and the placing of Australia under the control of foreign powers. A propaganda sheet under Butler's name, which was widely circulated through church networks, claimed that changes were being made to the Bible to eliminate differences between masculine and feminine roles. Liberal Senator Shirley Walters claimed in Parliament that ratification had already led to the headmistress of a Tasmanian school removing the Bible from the school library and burning it.[44] National Party Senator Ron Boswell was confident that the women of Australia did not want legislation drafted by Mongolian public servants.[45] Elaine Nile of Festival of Light took out newspaper ads saying 'Stop the Ryan juggernaut' and arranged for busloads of Christian women to come to Canberra to demonstrate against the Bill.

As we saw in chapter 3, Pamela Denoon, the national co-ordinator of WEL, stitched together a broad coalition of women's organisations and conducted community education to help counter this highly emotive campaign. In Sydney a practical guide to the Bill was prepared by WEL members including June Williams, later to be WA Equal Opportunity Commissioner. Indeed, at the same time as the Commonwealth campaign, WEL was engaged in a similar campaign in Western Australia.

In federal parliament Susan Ryan was constantly on her feet defending the Bill, overall introducing 53 amendments to placate opponents. Apart from the spectres of communism and Bible-burning, there was opposition to intrusion on the rights of States and the rights of churches to discriminate. Trouble also sometimes came from within government. WEL members in Sydney spotted that employer liability for sexual harassment of employees had been removed from the Bill at the insistence of Attorney-General Gareth Evans. After strong protests, the liability of employers where they had not taken steps to prevent employees being harassed was reintroduced into the second Bill of late 1983, along with other changes.

There was staunch support for the Bill from some Liberal parliamentarians such as Kathy Martin and Ian Macphee, and from Australian Democrat Senator Janine Haines. More unusually, National Party member Tom McVeigh had become a convert while holding ministerial responsibility for OSW. Opponents commented that WEL would probably give them zero marks for opposing the legislation. Independent Tasmanian Senator Bruce Goodluck singled out Anne Summers, the new head of OSW, as someone who had got her 'grass-roots training' in WEL. He believed that radical feminists within WEL were responsible for the legislation and were a group of 'given-up Catholics who have something against men'.[46]

Myths and misconceptions

Perhaps this is the point at which to tackle some of the myths about the *Sex Discrimination Act*. The first is the myth that the parliamentary debate over the Sex Discrimination Bills was 'the longest in the Senate's history up to that time' or even 'the longest in the history of the Australian Parliament'.[47] Even limiting ourselves to the post-war period, the debate on the Sex Discrimination Bills was only the eleventh longest debate. The Senate Table Office maintains a statistical record of hours spent in consideration of Bills. While there were 17 hours of debate on the Sex Discrimination Bills there were almost 70 hours on the two Communist Party Dissolution Bills, almost 56 hours on the Commonwealth Bank Bills, 28 and a half hours on the Family Law Bill and 27 hours on the Customs Amendment Bill (No 2) 1979. If we go further back, in the first ten years of the federal parliament the average time spent debating each Bill was 25 hours, considerably longer than was devoted to the Sex Discrimination Bill.

A second myth that has received a wide airing is that WEL was guilty of ingratitude – attacking the Bill on the day it passed through Parliament (7 March 1984), despite having been its foremost proponent. It is said that two spokeswomen for WEL, an organisation whose 'long-standing top priority had just been enacted', appeared on the *7.30 Report* with Susan Ryan and described the *Sex Discrimination Act* as 'useless, an insulting token'.[48] This vagary of memory has been widely repeated and has even given rise to scholarly speculation as to why WEL might have behaved in such an astonishing and ungrateful way. In fact WEL had been lobbying for the Bill to be passed by International Women's Day (8 March) so that a 'WELebration' could be organised around Australia.[49] In the event, the celebration took the form of a large party held on the lawn in front of Parliament House in Canberra, attended by some 300 people including politicians and public servants.

Far from being attacked by WEL spokeswomen, Susan Ryan was cutting a purple, green and white cake in the shape of the women's symbol and being presented with flowers by the WEL national co-ordi-

 L to R, Pamela Denoon, Ian Macphee and Susan Ryan at WEL party celebrating passage of the *Sex Discrimination Act*, 8 March 1984. *Christine Fernon.*

nator. Despite the press release about the party, only the *Canberra Times* gave WEL any credit for organising it. The incoming WEL co-ordinator wrote to the *Australian* to correct its headline 'Govt marks women's day with champagne and promises'. She pointed out:

> WEL organised the party outside Parliament House. The champagne and cake were paid for by WEL members and WEL wishers including politicians. Taxpayers should be assured the celebration was not at their expense.
> Our salute to the Government and to those members of the Opposition who voted for the Bill. We know that our delight at the passing of the Bill is shared by those other national women's organisations who joined us in lobbying for the Bill.[50]

The myth conflates the passage of the *Sex Discrimination Act* with the release of the green paper on affirmative action three months later, when a new WEL co-ordinator did incur the wrath of the minister by appearing on television with her (on *Nationwide*, not the *7.30 Report*) and criticising the delay in introducing affirmative action legislation.[51] WEL described the green paper as 'a sop to business and unions' – there had been no input from women's organisations and WEL thought it would further delay the resolution of problems facing women in the workforce.[52]

WEL had been involved for a decade in lobbying for affirmative action legislation. Under anti-discrimination legislation the onus is placed on the victim of discrimination, by definition a relatively power-less person, to bring about organisational change. The legislation only comes into play after discrimination has already occurred and someone takes the risk of further victimisation by lodging a complaint. WEL argued that rather than leaving it up to the victims, any such legislation should require employers to be proactive in identifying and removing the barriers that prevented women being recruited and promoted on merit. Much discrimination stemmed from the fact that work prac-tices and career structures were geared to what was regarded as normal for a male employee. It was traditionally assumed that employees had someone else to deal with family responsibilities.

The introduction of affirmative action legislation was highly controversial, thanks to the belief propagated by opponents that it would mean quotas, or 'positive discrimination'. An affirmative action pilot program, involving 28 major companies and three higher educa-tion institutions, had been set up in 1984. It was intended to increase community acceptance but in fact the scaremongering continued unabated. By 1986 the Affirmative Action Bill was ready for passage through Parliament. The Opposition Spokesman for the Status of Women, Peter Baume, who had been on the working party overseeing the pilot program and was a WEL ally, played a major role in achieving Coalition support for the Bill, although Coalition members remained free to speak against it.

WEL's position was that this legislation would be more effective if the government included a sanction for non-compliance – that companies 'named' for non-compliance should be ineligible for government contracts or industry assistance. This had been WEL policy since its 1974 national conference, which resolved that Commonwealth and State governments should use their purchasing power to combat discrimination – in other words, that governments should only contract with employers with non-discriminatory employment practices. At the time of its dismissal the Whitlam government had been committed to establishing an Australian Purchasing Commission that would ensure such contract compliance among government suppliers.

The Leader of the Australian Democrats, Senator Janine Haines, who held the balance of power in the Senate, was readily converted to the WEL position and suggested blocking the legislation with Coalition support until the government agreed to 'put its money where its mouth was' on the issue of sanctions. With the end of the 1986 parliamentary session looming, however, and the possibility of no legislation at all, WEL reluctantly advised the Australian Democrats to let the legislation go through. In the event, the Victorian Labor government was the first to refuse government contracts to companies named under the federal legislation. In September 1992 Prime Minister Paul Keating finally announced at a conference initiated by WEL that his government would introduce the sanctions WEL had been calling for since the 1970s. This meant no industry assistance or government contracts for companies named for non-compliance with the Act.

The 1992 announcement was the culmination of work that WEL had been doing since 1989, taking advantage of a parliamentary inquiry set up to mark the fifth anniversary of the *Sex Discrimination Act*. At first the inquiry, put together quickly to take advantage of the anniversary, looked unpromising – with its all-male committee and ambiguous terms of reference. Yet with the help of inquiry secretary Jon Stanhope, WEL was able to ensure a highly participatory inquiry process. Equal opportunity commissioners came from around Australia to comment at a public forum on what worked and what didn't in their legislation, and women's units joined with the committee in sponsoring other forums.

The *Half Way to Equal* report was effectively promoted in the media by energetic committee chair Michael Lavarch and led to significant legislative improvements in two tranches – in 1992 (with the assistance of Anne Summers in the Prime Minister's office) and 1995. These included strengthening the sexual harassment provisions, making dismissal on the ground of family responsibilities unlawful and removing the exemption for industrial awards. The onus of proof was now reversed in cases of indirect discrimination, so that an employer had to demonstrate the business necessity for practices that disadvantaged women. The 'special measures' provision of the Act was also strengthened, to ward off complaints such as that the provision of women's health services was discriminatory.

Some of the improvements to the Commonwealth Act had already been trialled in the new ACT *Discrimination Act* of 1991. The work of Canberra WEL had been important in achieving both commitment to the Act and its model provisions. WEL commissioned analysis of the draft Bill from the South Australian Equal Opportunity Commissioner and from leading discrimination barrister John Basten. Their input was crucial to the final shape of the Act and the ACT Attorney-General expressed his thanks to WEL for its substantial contribution.[53]

Under the Howard government, by contrast, WEL was repeatedly in the position of trying to protect Commonwealth anti-discrimination and equal opportunity legislation. As we saw in chapter 4, one high-profile campaign was to prevent the watering down of the marital status provisions of the *Sex Discrimination Act*. WEL also campaigned against the attempt to provide an exemption for male-only teachers' scholarships, a Howard government initiative that was blocked by the Senate.

There were continuing struggles over the resourcing and structure of the Commission responsible for administering the Act. These struggles had begun under the Hawke government but were exacerbated under the Howard government, which straightaway made a 40 per cent cut to the Commission's budget. The Howard government also introduced successive Bills to remove specialist commissioners, including the Sex Discrimination Commissioner, but these were blocked in the Senate. WEL wrote repeated submissions and appeared before Senate committees to argue the deleterious effects of losing specialist expertise. WEL also campaigned over the prohibitive costs involved for complainants in the transfer of responsibility for complaints to the Federal Court. With the risk of costs being awarded against complainants, the number of complaints collapsed.

In relation to affirmative action, WEL made a major submission to the review of the Act in 1998, arguing that reporting requirements should be extended to companies with less than 100 employees, that the Affirmative Action Agency should be given powers to investigate and audit companies and that non-complying companies should be referred to the Sex Discrimination Commissioner. In the event the Agency was given none of these increased powers and its name was changed to the Equal Opportunity for Women in the Workplace Agency.[54]

WEL's policy influence up to this point had owed much to timing – the conjuncture of women's movement mobilisation and the election of reforming governments. The creation of state agencies to promote equal opportunity for women appeared a logical extension of traditions of seeing the state as a vehicle of social justice. When these traditions eroded, WEL's reliance on the state became a weakness. As Joan Bielski wrote:

> WEL was designed to influence governments and public institutions. The challenge for WEL is to redefine and modernise its role in an era of minimalist government, economic rationalism, business triumphalism, union decline, employment insecurity, time poverty, compassion fatigue, individualism, and political and social conservatism.[55]

6

ECONOMIC AND SOCIAL POLICY

While WEL had a unique role in initiating and supporting government machinery for women, it was active across a much wider area. To see the universe of WEL's policy interests we need only open its 1996 Women's Charter, which ranged from children's services and competition policy through to wage fixing and women's services, taking in gun laws and pornography on the way. WEL did not try to take a lead in every area; often members helped initiate more specialised groups and joined in advocacy coalitions with them.

Issues on which progress could be made under non-Labor governments differed from those under Labor governments, although the increased influence of neo-liberalism was to blur the distinction. Generally 'law and order' issues such as violence against women were more likely to appeal to non-Labor governments than issues like equal pay, which required labour market regulation. Symptomatically, the Australasian Council of Women and Policing was one women's organisation that was founded and flourished under the Howard government.

In terms of policy, WEL differed from many past and present women's groups in its greater focus on macro-economic policy. This owed much to Eva Cox in Sydney, whose powerful intellect and strong views helped shape WEL policy over the years. Her social policy expertise, as Director of the NSW Council of Social Service, as a staffer to a federal shadow minister and as a bureaucrat in the NSW State government, was always accompanied by a determination to challenge economic orthodoxies. In her forthright way she declared that while economics sounded scary, it was a language that had to be learnt to 'realise they're all talking bullshit'.[1] She was joined by feminist economists and others who agreed that women had first and foremost to engage with public economics if government was to be made responsive to women's needs. WEL's embrace of economic policy was reflected in its publications, where articles on the tax transfer system might jostle with lighter offerings on feminist science fiction or attitudes to housework.

From 1973 WEL eagerly seized opportunities to be part of pre-Budget consultations at different levels of government and followed up with analyses of the impact on women when budgets were handed down. The Fraser government held pre-Budget consultations with women's groups each year; the 1982 consultation was famous as the occasion when Babette Francis of Women Who Want to be Women

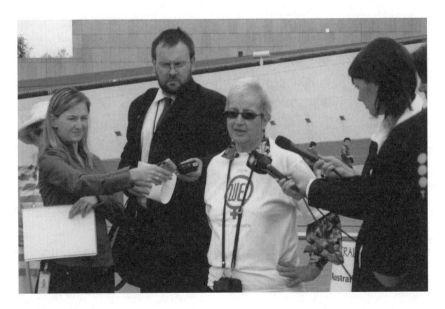

Eva Cox at the launch of WEL's 2004 federal election campaign, Canberra, September 2004. *Gail Radford.*

presented the Prime Minister with a cake reading 'To the men in the House from the women in the home'.[2] This was a performance piece borrowed from the United States, where Phyllis Shlafly's supporters had presented legislators with home-baked bread to persuade them to vote against the Equal Rights Amendment.

WEL was a child of its era, in terms of its vision of the role of the public sector in the achievement of equal opportunity. Collectively provided services such as education and child care were more important than cuts in personal income tax. Journalists sometimes expressed amazement at its pre-Budget submissions urging the deferral of tax cuts. While community services had a special significance for women as family carers and were drastically under-funded, women would generally benefit less than men from tax cuts, being lower earners.[3] The questioning of 'hip pocket' arguments became a consistent theme of WEL lobbying, frequently joined to criticism of proposed tax cuts pitched above the level of female average earnings.

WEL's presentation by Frances Davies to the Hawke government's Economic Summit in 1983 highlighted familiar themes: emphasis should be placed on provision of services in the community, rather than individual tax cuts; the individual should remain the unit of account in the tax system; and the Dependent Spouse Rebate should be abolished and the $1 billion savings used to increase family allowances.[4] On the subject of community services, WEL tried to counter the view that jobs in this sector were not 'real' jobs by pointing to the multiplier effect they had in the local economy, quite apart from improving the quality of life for women.

On superannuation WEL called for a national scheme rather than an occupationally-based one, so that Australian citizens would have adequate retirement provisions in their own right rather than as the dependant of another person. Occupationally-based superannuation inevitably discriminated against women because of their patterns of workforce participation. WEL also consistently argued for measures to address the poverty of sole parents and other social security recipients, including an increased earnings threshold so that pensions and benefits could be supplemented by earnings up to the minimum wage without penalty.

These themes were successfully promulgated at the major conferences WEL organised or co-sponsored in the 1980s – the National Women's Tax Summit, the National Agenda for Women Conference, and the National Women's Tax Convention. A wide range of groups agreed that income support for families should be shifted towards direct payments for primary carers rather than tax rebates for primary earners. Shifting the $1 billion from the dependent spouse rebate to family allowances was a popular demand, as both a more efficient way to help families and an important recognition of the role of women as carers and their need for some economic autonomy.

The argument for retaining and strengthening the individual as the unit of account in the tax system had been elaborated by WEL's leading tax expert, Meredith Edwards. Edwards had done pioneering empirical research on financial arrangements within families, showing the dangers of easy assumptions about income pooling (on which most social security policy was based). She also showed the importance women placed on having an independent source of income.[5] As Edwards and other WEL spokeswomen argued, women were made economically and socially vulnerable through the non-market work they performed, and there had to be adequate recognition of this in both the tax and transfer systems. Family unit taxation, through increasing the tax rates for secondary earners, abandoned the principle of neutrality in relation to choices, such as whether or not to participate in the paid workforce. Moreover, it provided an incentive for men to spend more time away from their families rather than sharing the earning and caring.[6]

WEL's opposition to family unit taxation brought it into conflict with powerful forces keen to put it onto the agenda, including, for a time, the Australian Council of Trade Unions (ACTU).[7] WEL always argued that increasing and indexing family allowances paid to the mother was a more efficient and equitable way of supporting families than income splitting or dependent spouse rebates which were paid regardless of whether there were children in the family. The demeaning rebate should be redirected into increased family allowances, as it was children, not wives, who reduced the earning capacity of a family. Wives, through their household work, in fact increased rather than reduced their husband's capacity to earn income outside the home.

After the repeated calls from the big women's conferences of the 1980s, the abolition of the dependent spouse rebate was finally announced in Labor's 1993 election campaign. It would be replaced by a home child-care allowance paid to the mother. This breakthrough owed much to the presence of Anne Summers in Prime Minister Keating's office, advising him on how to win electoral support from women. But while the rebate was finally cashed out and paid to mothers, the family allowance already paid to mothers had become means-tested on 'family' income six years before. The goal of increasing the economic independence of women working full-time in the home remained elusive, despite the lip-service paid to the value of such work.

As part of making macro-economic policy women-friendly, women's budget statements seemed a good way to ensure that gender analysis of spending became routine within government. WEL helped ensure this device was adopted in all Australian jurisdictions. But by the time the Howard government was elected in 1996, serious analysis of the gender implications of macro-economic policy had been largely abandoned. No analysis was done of the changes to the tax system that had increased the effective marginal tax rates on secondary earners until they became among the highest in the OECD.[8] Ironically, the changes were presented as 'increasing women's choices'.

Equal pay

From the beginning WEL was engaged in agenda-setting on equal pay. Since 1907 the Australian wage-setting system had been based on the idea of the family wage: that is, that the male wage should be sufficient to provide for a wife and children. Women's wages were set as a proportion of the male wage, initially 54 per cent but rising after World War II to around 75 per cent. There was no recognition within the wages system that women might also have dependants and so might also need a living wage. When it was acknowledged that not all men had dependants it was felt that they still required the family wage because of the need to buy in services such as laundry which would otherwise be performed by a wife.

In June 1969 the Commonwealth Conciliation and Arbitration Commission made its first equal pay for equal work decision, which meant that women who did identical work to men would now be eligible for the same pay. Unfortunately, because of the highly sex-segregated nature of the Australian workforce, this only meant increases for about 18 per cent of women in the workforce. Anger at this inequity led to Zelda D'Aprano chaining herself across the doors of the Commonwealth Building in Melbourne on 21 October that year. The case also generated the ever-popular equal pay song by Glen Tomasetti, 'Don't Be Too Polite Girls'.

The reopening of the equal pay case by the Whitlam government in 1972, with Mary Gaudron now presenting the government case, led to the adoption of a new equal pay principle, that of equal pay for work of equal value. This meant that women doing similar, but not the same work as men became eligible for the same pay. The centralised system of wage-fixing with legally enforceable awards meant that an overall rise of in women's wages of about 30 per cent flowed through the system in the mid-1970s. This did not lead to women's unemployment, as had been widely predicted by opponents of equal pay. In 1974, when WEL was founded in Port Pirie, a man signing himself 'O Tempora, O Mores' wrote to the local paper to say that 'ordinary women would lose the sole competitive advantage they had over males, in that they would do the same work for less money'. When WEL responded, 'Mr O'Mores' turned up at their next meeting to pursue his argument.[9]

One thing still missing from the federal equal pay principle was women's eligibility for the same minimum wage as men. WEL–NSW member Edna Ryan, inexplicably the only woman observer at the reopened equal pay hearing in 1972, was determined to push forward while the political opportunity existed. Ryan's long industrial experience gave her the confidence to tackle the 'industrial relations club' with all its arcane knowledge about wage-fixing principles. The tenth child in a working-class family, her university had been the Workers' Educational Association (WEA). Her first equal pay demonstration had been an International Women's Day rally organised by the Communist Party in the Sydney Domain in 1928. She soon left the Communist Party but continued in the labour movement, joining the Labor Party and holding office in local government. She had often been frustrated by male unionists' lack of commitment to wage justice for women: 'The years and years I've worked in the cause of working-class emancipation, dreamed about it, read about it, believed in it and all those years I've been saying: "I'm not a feminist BUT why don't you men support the rate for the job..."'[10] In the 1960s she had finally tossed away her girdle and said she was a feminist and proud to be a feminist. When WEL appeared it was a natural home for her.

Even after the adoption of the new equal pay principle, the *Conciliation and Arbitration Act* still enshrined the family wage in the form of a 'male minimum wage' that took account of the need of low-paid male workers to provide for families. WEL successfully lobbied in 1973 to have the Act amended to refer instead to an 'adult minimum wage'. The Opposition, which controlled the Senate, had to be persuaded to withdraw its alternative proposal to retain the male minimum wage and simply add a female one.

The amendment of the Act opened the way for WEL to argue for the payment of the full minimum wage to women in its submission to the 1974 national wage case, for which it received very extensive and sympathetic media coverage.[11] The submission pointed to the large number of women supporting families, the very low award wages earned by women, and the secondary consequences in terms of access to home ownership, insurance, superannuation and other forms of economic security.

What was needed to clinch the argument was to show the exact numbers of women responsible for supporting families. Such statistics had not previously been collected by government but the ongoing Henderson Poverty Inquiry had commissioned a survey on low-income families. In an historic coup, Edna Ryan managed to obtain the unpublished data from the acting Commonwealth Statistician. When she rose in the Commission to present the WEL case the atmosphere was electric. Mary Owen, as her 'associate', carried a concertina file bursting with the dozen exhibits. The calm presentation of the figures, which showed there were 131 700 families dependent on the mother's earning power, was the high point of the hearing. For the first time there was solid evidence of how many women were family breadwinners. The court was adjourned and Ryan was besieged by reporters.

The ACTU had supported the principle of the minimum wage for women before the Commission but had provided no evidence, on the grounds that the Henderson data was not yet available. The ACTU executive was still divided over what was seen as loss of the breadwinner loading. The government itself had been wavering. The tightly-argued WEL submission, which included costings, was the turning point. The Commission brought down its decision three months later, extending the minimum wage to some 300 000 women who had been receiving less than the male minimum. This was a huge victory – delay might have been fatal in view of the inflation and unemployment that were about to beset the Australian economy. For Ryan herself it was a source of jubilation: 'Women were doing for women what union men

Edna Ryan in the 1980s.
Diana Goldrick.

had done for men … My life seemed to have been directed towards this one event: the case for our low-paid sisters. I, who was born on the day the federal Arbitration Court was established'.[12]

While the male minimum wage had been extended to women under federal awards, this was not yet the case under most State awards. In Western Australia WEL was not allowed to intervene directly in the State wage hearing of 1973 at which the Arbitration Commission established a female minimum wage pegged at 83 per cent of the male minimum. It was not until 1975 that Yvonne Henderson was able to intervene successfully on behalf of WEL's equal pay submission. Four years later Henderson intervened on behalf of WEL in the State maternity leave case. Another WEL member, Pat Giles, appeared for the Trades and Labour Council. As elsewhere, twelve months unpaid leave was granted, although WEL had argued for a longer period of leave and for it to be available to either parent.

WEL was often given the cold shoulder by longer-standing members of the industrial relations club – its early intervention in the Arbitration Commission in support of part-time work for bank tellers was in the face of union opposition.[13] In fact, union officials had taken Mary Owen and June Williams to an expensive lunch to try to persuade them to drop that case. WEL went on to lobby for amendments to Commonwealth and State arbitration Acts to enable 'unregistered organisations' (such as WEL) to intervene in a wider range of hearings, as it could never rely on the labour movement be whole-hearted in its support for equal pay. For example, when the NSW *Anti-Discrimination Act* was amended to provide an exemption for over-award payments, the Labour Council of NSW, which had sought the exemption, accused WEL of union-bashing for its protest against allowing discrimination in over-award payments.[14]

In 1998 WEL, along with the National Pay Equity Coalition (NPEC), was closely involved in instigating and providing evidence to the ground-breaking pay equity inquiry conducted by the NSW Industrial Relations Commission, with Clare Burton presenting detailed evidence on gender bias in methods of job evaluation. The inquiry found that the undervaluation of work traditionally performed by women and historically gendered concepts of skill had resulted in a lack of pay equity in female-dominated industries and occupations. Subsequently the Commission adopted a new equal remuneration principle, intended to remove gender bias from the assessment of work, skill and responsibility.

In 2002 the NSW Commission ruled in favour of a pay equity claim comparing public sector librarians with geologists – a senior librarian at the time being paid nearly 20 per cent less than a senior geologist. The Commission found clear evidence both of undervaluation of the work of female librarians and of resistance to full recognition of librarianship as a profession. Unfortunately, the advances made in New South Wales and other States on pay equity were effectively negated through the federal *Work Choices Act* of 2005, which precluded equal remuneration cases being taken to State industrial tribunals but did little to provide an alternative.

At the federal level, in 1991 WEL was campaigning against the introduction of the enterprise bargaining principle into the industrial relations system. Led by Edna Ryan, WEL raised funds and briefed a barrister to present a case before the Industrial Relations Commission on the impact of enterprise bargaining on women, arguing that women's lack of industrial muscle and the nature of the industries in which they worked, such as human services, would make it much harder for them to establish 'productivity' increases. Women benefited from centralised wage fixing because wage increases flowed on to those who worked in smaller workplaces, were less highly unionised and performed work that was harder to quantify. The importance of the centralised system for women was underlined by the relatively rapid rise in women's wages that had followed the 1972 equal pay decision and moved Australia ahead of many other OECD countries in terms of pay equity.

In the end, the efforts of WEL and other women's organisations with which it campaigned only managed to delay the introduction of enterprise bargaining by a few months. WEL was successful, however, in persuading the Labor Minister for Industrial Relations to use Australia's ratification of ILO conventions to prevent women's gains being bargained away at enterprise level. Safeguards for equal remuneration for work of equal value and for family-friendly work provisions were inserted into the *Industrial Relations Reform Act 1993*. The campaign on the problems presented by decentralised wage bargaining, particularly for groups such as immigrant women, also resulted in the federal funding of Working Women's Centres in each State to provide advice and support. WEL participated in the management committees along with union and other representatives to help ensure continued funding from both federal and State governments.

Despite the safeguards in the Act, the introduction of enterprise bargaining had the adverse effects on the gender wage gap that WEL had feared, with female-dominated industries doing significantly worse than male-dominated ones. Moves away from centralised wage fixing and equal remuneration guarantees were taken much further by the Howard government, including a concerted push beyond enterprise bargaining, which at least involved unions, toward individual employment contracts. Together with NPEC, WEL campaigned against the proposed removal of the equal remuneration protection from the new *Workplace Relations Act* and continued to appear before the Industrial Relations Commission in the attempt to defend earlier gains. WEL also undertook a joint research project with the National Foundation for Australian Women and the Human Rights and Equal Opportunity Commission on the impact of the 2005 Work Choices arrangements on equal pay for women. Unsurprisingly, the most deleterious impact was on women in the service industries, including the loss of penalty rates and control over hours.

Child care and maternity leave

Although until the 1970s child care was largely seen as a welfare issue for working-class mothers rather than an equal opportunity issue, in the late 1960s, with women's workforce participation increasing, the

Women's Bureau in the federal Department of Labour put forward a number of proposals for intervention in the field. This advocacy, supported from outside by Marie Coleman at the Victorian Council of Social Service, contributed to the Commonwealth *Child Care Act* of 1972, enacted in the dying days of the McMahon government. The Act provided for capital and equipment grants for child-care centres and operational funding tied to the employment of qualified staff. Those eligible for funding were local government authorities or not-for-profit organisations, usually with volunteer management committees involving parents.

The Department of Labour was to have administrative responsibility for the federal child-care program, but the incoming Whitlam government controversially shifted it to the education portfolio, in effect favouring preschools. (WEL's campaign to prevent diversion of funds to preschools is described in chapter 1.) Paradoxically, it was the conservative Fraser government that ensured eventual victory. Femocrats were able to persuade Fraser that, on the needs principle, federal funding should be given to child care rather than to preschools that were not accessible to, for example, immigrant working parents. To deliver the program an Office of Childcare was set up in the Department of Social Security, headed by Marie Coleman.

The young mothers of WEL were acutely aware that access to quality child care was crucial to equal opportunity. Winsome McCaughey, who had just returned to Australia from setting up a co-operative child-care centre in New York's Greenwich Village, was allocated the child care portfolio by WEL in Melbourne. With the support and encouragement of members she led Community (Controlled) Child Care in Victoria. It obtained funding from the Myer Foundation and then the federal government, and ran a Resource and Advisory Centre from 1973 to 1980 providing advice to local councils and community groups on how to establish community-based children's services. Barbara Spalding of the Brotherhood of St Laurence set up a pilot family day-care scheme, intended to be complementary to centre-based care, and together with McCaughey helped launch campaigns for a range of children's services as well as working with Marie Coleman in Canberra on national child-care policy.[15] McCaughey and Community Child Care saw the process of developing funding submissions and establishing locally controlled centres, the steps required by the federal *Child Care Act*, as an important aspect of community development. The process ensured women did not lose control to bureaucrats or 'experts' simply because they were not full-time mothers.

In 1981 WEL mounted a successful national campaign to fend off the recommendations of the Spender Report to extend government subsidies to commercial child-care centres. The Liberal Feminist Network in Victoria, created by WEL members, was an important part of this campaign. While united on not-for-profit child care, there were other issues on which WEL women were divided. One was industry-based child care. WEL had opposed extending the government subsidy to employer-provided child care on the grounds that it gave employers too much power over their employees and made separation difficult. On the other hand, this meant a lack of child care at places of large-scale female employment.

Meanwhile criticism was emerging from Eva Cox and others in New South Wales of the submission-based model for child care on the grounds it disadvantaged the most needy groups in the community.[16] They persuaded the Labor Party, and the Hawke government elected in 1983 was firmly committed to a planning model for child care, rather than the old submission-based approach. While Victoria's Community Child Care was 'truly a daughter of WEL', WEL members elsewhere, like Cox in New South Wales, had worked closely with Labor women on child-care policy. Access to quality child care was an expensive item and WEL rarely risked relying on justice arguments alone when lobbying, bringing in 'broader' arguments including the contribution of women's skills to general economic growth and the need to invest in children's cognitive and social development.[17]

Although there were differences over submission-based or planning models, the most divisive issue was that of child care as a tax deduction. While tax deductibility was sought from the federal Treasurer during the Whitlam period, there was also recognition of its regressive character (giving greatest returns to those on the highest marginal tax rates) and the need to cater for those whose tax was too low to benefit. A Victorian Labor MP wrote to the *Australian* expressing his disappointment that WEL should press for tax deductibility after leading the push for universal access. In Sydney, Clare Krinks (Burton) urged a rethink of the policy, arguing that WEL should only support policies that either benefited all women equally or effected a redistribution of income towards the lower income-earning group.[18]

With the election of a conservative government there seemed little prospect of further expansion of child-care funding (despite the useful redirection of priorities) and Kay Johnston of Canberra WEL led a renewed campaign for tax deductibility in 1976–82. The argument for child care as a necessary expense involved in earning an income seemed a strong one – particularly as many other expenses were tax deductible, including business lunches. Johnston claimed for child-care costs on her own tax return and appeared on television and in newspapers and magazines (including the mass-circulation *Women's Weekly*) urging others to do the same. A smart WEL brochure was produced, aiming to generate a flood of child-care cases and reconsideration of existing laws. It provided advice on how to claim for child care and how to appeal against disallowance of claims.

Johnston eventually appeared before the Taxation Board of Review in 1982 over her claim for child-care expenses for the year 1978–79. She told the Board that her employer, CSIRO, assumed that she would find alternative care for her son during the hours she was employed and had told her she could not bring him to work. On the other hand, society would not allow her to leave her child unattended while she worked to earn an income to maintain him. Hence, she argued, the use of child care was not a private choice but one required by society and by her employer, and was a prerequisite to earning an income. The Tax Commissioner's case was that although the child-care expense was a prerequisite to earning an income, it was not of a business nature and the bringing up of children was a matter for private or domestic concern.[19] The all-male Board accepted the Commissioner's argument.

Although the argument for tax deductibility seemed unassailable to many women, it caused considerable controversy within WEL. The 1982 national conference resolved to circulate the arguments for and against to all WEL groups, asking for a decision within three months on whether to continue the campaign. The brochure and other materials produced by Kay Johnston were circulated, along with the papers by Ann Morrow and Eva Cox. The argument against was that priority should be given to funding an expansion of child-care services, rather than providing tax deductions that were regressive in nature and benefited those who already had access. The result of this exercise was a majority of groups favouring continuation of the campaign, although the two Territories and Western Australia opposed and other groups preferred rebates or thought provision of places was still the main priority.

The change of federal government in March 1983 brought the possibility of renewed expansion of not-for-profit children's services, and tax deductibility disappeared from WEL policy. But soon WEL was again campaigning to protect the community-based centres, this time from Labor government advocates of more market-based approaches. As we have seen, not-for-profit centres were eligible both for capital grants and for operational subsidies tied to the employment of qualified staff. Parents were eligible for means-tested fee relief. The Finance Minister, Senator Peter Walsh, believed that qualified staff were unnecessary and that the private sector should be encouraged to expand through being made eligible for fee relief. In 1985 the level of subsidy was reduced and detached from the employment of qualified staff.

After the 1990 election, the Labor government crossed the Rubicon by extending eligibility for fee relief to the commercial child-care sector. It became the subject of a classic policy muddle, with fee relief being extended to the private sector before a new accreditation system was in place to determine eligibility. It was also an indication of the inroads of market liberalism. A decade before, as we have seen, Liberal feminists, WEL and child-care advocates had together successfully beaten off similar proposals.

Although WEL was no longer campaigning for tax concessions for child care, others were taking up the cause. Both Government and Opposition took a policy of child-care tax rebates to the 1993 election, although the detail varied. With the election of the Howard government in 1996 child care moved still further away from WEL policies, with the abolition of operational subsidies for community-based child care and a greater reliance on the for-profit sector. The role of the not-for-profit sector shrank from providing the vast majority (85 per cent) of long day-care services to less than a third. The parties competed over tax rebates for child care, which, as WEL pointed out, did nothing to increase accessibility or quality of child care or the training and pay of child-care workers. Meanwhile, much of the advocacy for non-profit children's services had passed into the more specialised hands of the National Association of Community Based Children's Services, founded in 1982 as the National Association of Community Based Child Care.

In addition to child care, WEL saw paid maternity leave and family-friendly work arrangements as essential underpinnings of equal opportunity in the workplace and, from the beginning, lobbied for the public service to act as a pacesetter in the granting of such conditions. By November 1973 the federal Minister for Labour was able to provide the Opposition with the following answer on what action had been taken on a WEL submission on women in the workforce:

> On most of the issues raised in the submission significant progress has been made and considerable improvements brought about by this Government. The ILO Convention No. 111 on Discrimination (Employment and Occupation) has been ratified and we have established National and State Committees to eliminate improper discrimination and promote real equality of opportunity in employment and occupation. The Government has helped to achieve further progress towards the realisation of equal pay. The Government has also considerably extended the maternity provisions available to

Australian Government employees and removed the age barrier
to permanent employment in the Service ... I am effecting
improvements to the Commonwealth Employment Service
and vocational guidance services, planning the introduction
of a National Training Scheme, and proposing to enhance and
enlarge the functions of the Department of Labour's Women's
Bureau. I have given considerable attention to the matter of
apprenticeship training and taken steps to greatly increase the
opportunities available to all our young people.[20]

WEL was delighted at the granting of three months paid maternity
leave to Commonwealth public servants in 1973 but worried that
claims for paid maternity leave in the private sector might lead to
discrimination against female employees. WEL lobbied the Minister
for Social Security, Bill Hayden, to develop a universal scheme for three
months paid maternity leave (then the ILO standard) to be paid at the
minimum wage out of general revenue.[21] For the next thirty years WEL
consistently called for Australia to adopt the ILO standard on paid
maternity leave as a basic recognition of the rights of women to be
in the paid workforce. When talk of women's rights became unfash-
ionable, less threatening themes of the need for physical recuperation
and the establishment of breastfeeding were emphasised. WEL always
supported the payment of such maternity leave out of general revenue,
unlike recreation and sick leave, because otherwise the burden would
fall too unevenly in Australia's highly sex-segregated labour market.
Just as consistently, conservative opponents tried to drum up opposition to paid maternity leave by suggesting employers would have to
pay for it.

From the beginning of its existence in 1919 the International
Labour Organization had been concerned with the rights of women
workers; the first maternity protection convention was ILO Convention 3. Australia ratified neither this nor Convention 103, which superseded it in the 1950s. When 103 was in turn being reviewed in 1999,
Australia excelled itself by sending an all-male delegation to Geneva, a
government spokesman explaining that you didn't need to be a woman
to present a policy position.[22] WEL joined the general outrage at the

WEL–NSW supporting the campaign for paid maternity leave. L to R, Wendy Jowsie, Melinda Riches, Gina Andrews, Cate Turner, Sandy Killick, Anne Barber, International Women's Day 2002. *WEL–NSW Office.*

proposition that women were not needed at a conference on maternity protection. The new Convention 183 set an international standard of fourteen weeks paid leave, together with employment protection. Australia again turned its back on it.

WEL lobbied for the ratification of ILO Convention 183 and for the removal of Australia's reservation to Article 11 (2) (b) of CEDAW (on maternity leave with pay) in order to give the federal government the power to legislate for uniform rights to paid maternity leave around Australia.[23] Seeking to exert pressure internationally, WEL also briefed members of the CEDAW Committee, who expressed amazement at Australia's continuing failure to provide paid maternity leave despite being such a wealthy country.

Back home WEL took all opportunities to push for paid maternity leave, including the consultations over the National Agenda for

Women in the 1980s and in 2002 the inquiry by Sex Discrimination Commissioner Pru Goward. WEL also worked on the details of a paid maternity leave campaign by Democrats leader Senator Natasha Stott Despoja. By 2002 Australia was the only industrialised country apart from the United States that did not provide paid maternity leave. It was one of the signal failures of the long campaign for equal citizenship, despite skilful campaigners and widespread community support. The establishment in 2008 of a Productivity Commission inquiry into paid maternity leave by the newly elected Rudd Labor government was a welcome breakthrough, although the goal itself was yet to be reached.

Access to job creation and retraining

Early WEL successes included opening up retraining opportunities for married women under the Whitlam government's National Employment and Training Scheme (NEAT). NEAT derived from the Cochrane Report that recommended training to meet new labour market needs and saw married women as an important and underused resource. One of the scheme's objectives was 'to aid in the removal of past inequalities in employment opportunities'. Regardless of their particular talents, women had long been steered into 'gender-appropriate' jobs as secretaries or nurses before dropping out of the workforce altogether to have children. NEAT would enable them to retrain for broader vocations in a changing labour market, as well as updating disused skills. WEL was closely involved with NEAT and with issues such as the importance of child care, both for participants' children and as a skilled job for which the scheme could provide training.

While the scheme applied to both sexes, the majority of early approvals for retraining were for women.[24] The combination of opportunities under NEAT and the abolition of tertiary fees caused a revolution in many women's lives as they discovered previously unsuspected academic and professional potential. Some of the opportunities were relatively short-lived, however, for the rapid rise in unemployment due to tariff reductions led to a change in government priorities by the end of 1974. The new priorities stressing recent unemployment and primary breadwinner status, both of which tended to exclude women trying to return to the workforce after childrearing. WEL campaigned strongly for the retention of the original objective of redressing past discrimination against women, in addition to short-term relief for unemployment.

Many years later the right-wing journal *Quadrant* published a bitter editorial written by P.P. McGuinness describing NEAT as a ridiculous scheme leading to 'a large proportion of middle-class married ladies' being funded. WEL had always seen the scheme as one way out for the many women who had been consigned to poverty because of the assumption they had male providers.[25]

Despite the particular frustrations over NEAT, WEL did run successful campaigns to get married women to register at the Commonwealth Employment Service (CES) and thus become eligible for job creation and retraining schemes. Because married women (or de facto spouses) were ineligible for unemployment benefit few had previously registered. WEL also campaigned for them to be eligible for unemployment benefit. Most women could see the justice of this, querying why they should be expected to become financially dependent during periods of unemployment just because they had a heterosexual partner, but governments were unsympathetic.

The issue of job creation for women continued to be an important one for the organisation up into the 1980s. In May 1976, for example, when the male unemployment rate was 3.4 per cent, the female rate was 5.6 per cent. Moreover, as WEL pointed out in its pre-Budget submissions, in certain regional areas female unemployment was more than twice the male rate.[26] But while unemployment rates were higher for women, job creation programs consistently focused on blue-collar men – including the Whitlam government's Regional Employment Development Scheme, under which only 6 per cent of jobs went to women. Not only were women neglected in job creation, but married women were often blamed for causing unemployment in the first place, just as they had been in the 1930s. The 1978 WEL national conference condemned the 'carefully orchestrated campaign against married women workers' and the 'cynical scapegoating of women to divert the anger of the unemployed from those really responsible for their situation'.[27]

When the Fraser government initiated its Wage Pause Program, State governments came up with the usual proposals for construction and other male jobs to spend the $200 million saved from postponement of wage increases. Ian Macphee, the Commonwealth Minister for Employment, hit the headlines in January 1983 for sending State ministers away so they could come up with new proposals generating equal jobs for women. WEL member Julie Macphee was asked if she was responsible for her husband's action but assured the *Australian* that he was a feminist himself and didn't need much convincing.[28]

In the run up to the 1983 federal election WEL–Australia created a coalition of women's groups to press for formal commitments on equality in job creation and retraining. Labor leader Bob Hawke was more forthcoming than the Coalition and on achieving government honoured his commitment with the Community Employment Program – which quickly succeeded in reaching the target of equal places for women. WEL declared Tuesday 16 August 1983 National CES Registration Day in the hope the publicity would encourage women to register and thus become eligible.

Sowing the seeds of policy and law reform

In a large number of policy areas, WEL's early initiatives helped create an environment for more specialised advocacy groups to appear and flourish, often with the help of WEL stalwarts. For example, the many members who were teachers sought action to overcome the pattern of discrimination documented in the landmark Commonwealth Schools Commission report of 1975, *Girls, School and Society*, saying: 'There is now no excuse … for pursuing private prejudice using funds from the public purse'.[29] WEL members were in the forefront of initiatives such as developing non-sexist curriculum resources and resources for non-sexist career counselling, but they also helped create an organisation with a more specialised focus – the Australian Women's Education (Action) Coalition. AWEC was founded in 1974 and WEL member Joan Bielski took a leading role in its lobbying on gender bias in schooling and curriculum. In 1981 Bielski was also the founder of Women in Tertiary Institutions (WITI), of which fellow WEL member Margaret Thornton was foundation president. WITI was a cross-campus group lobbying to bring universities under legislative requirements for affirmative action. Thornton had defied the expectations of her Tasmanian high school, which had required girls to do a subject called 'Cooking, Sewing, Laundry and Home Management', to become a legal academic.

For the first WEL members generally, issues of reproductive health were a top priority. Apart from the successful campaign for the removal of sales tax from the pill, WEL groups everywhere lobbied for family planning and women's health services. In Sydney, WEL achieved a takeover of the NSW board of the Family Planning Association. Wendy McCarthy, who led this takeover, went on to become the chief executive officer of the Family Planning Association of Australia. WEL members adopted a holistic view of health and were critical of the medical approach typified by the once common prescription of tranquillisers to unhappy women in the suburbs. As Sydney member Diana Wyndham wrote, 'My doctor gives me pills to put *him* out of my misery.' Another who played an important inside/outside role in women's health policy was Stefania Siedlecky, who in 1974 became the first family planning and women's adviser in the Commonwealth Health Department. She and Wyndham co-authored a book on Australian women's struggle for birth control and contributed to *Women's Rights: Human Rights*, published by the International Alliance of Women, to which WEL was affiliated.[30]

From the beginning WEL was involved in campaigns around abortion, whether through the women's tent embassy of 1973, or warding off the recurrent threats to abortion funding. In the 1990s, abortion law reformer Jo Wainer led WEL's first attempt at a High Court intervention in the *CES v Superclinics* case, in which a woman was seeking damages because of failure to diagnose her pregnancy and hence denial of the opportunity for an abortion. A bombshell was dropped on the first day of hearing when the Australian Catholic Bishops Conference was unexpectedly granted leave to intervene. This intervention threatened all existing case law on abortion in New South Wales and Victoria, sparking action by WEL to ensure women were also represented in the case. Application for intervenor status in a High Court case was a significant challenge, even with the help of WEL barristers such as Joce-lynne Scutt and pro bono legal assistance. It was only WEL's networks that made up for the lack of financial resources. As Wainer wrote:

> Everyone we called for assistance provided it. Money, pledges, information, time, analysis, support, contacts. I do not doubt the capacity of the women's movement and their supporters to galvanise around such a symbolic issue, and seeing it in action was both exhausting and joyful.[31]

WEL's intervention highlighted to the media the potential implications for women of what had started off as a fairly obscure medical negli-gence case.[32] Ultimately it was settled out of court and WEL did not have to proceed with the application. Wainer was also part of the long campaign to make RU486 available in Australia, as a means of abor-tion of particular importance to rural women, and in 2006 WEL–ACT convenor Ros Dundas appeared before a Senate committee inquiry on RU486, despite a government senator taking exception to WEL being called to give evidence. The committee went into closed session before deciding that Dundas should be heard. Thanks to the cross-party work of women senators, the ministerial veto on the drug was finally removed.

Across Australia WEL continued to promote abortion law reform. In Western Australia Cheryl Davenport introduced a successful Private Member's Bill into the Legislative Council in 1998 while Diana Warnock, a former WEL–WA convenor, had carriage of it in the Lower House. In Tasmania in 2001 WEL was involved in lobbying for a Private Member's Bill, drafted co-operatively by all the women in Parliament, which clarified the legal status of abortion. In Canberra WEL founded a coalition of pro-choice groups, Options for Women, which successfully lobbied for the passage of two Territory Bills in 2002. One made the ACT the first jurisdiction in Australia to remove all references to abortion in its criminal code and the other repealed offensive legislation that had tried to force women considering an abortion to view photographs of foetuses.[33] The ACT legislation became the basis for a Private Member's Bill in Victoria supported by WEL. It was introduced into Parliament in 2007 but withdrawn when the Premier referred it to the Law Reform Commission with a promise of future action. The Commission delivered its final report on options for decriminalising abortion in late March 2008, to be tabled within fourteen sitting days of Parliament (probably not until June).

A more specialised advocacy network, the Australian Women's Health Network (AWHN), was established in 1986, and in the early

 Celebrating the passage of WA abortion law reform, Ruth Greble and Barbara Buick (WEL), Cait Calcutt (Abortion Law Repeal Association), Legislative Assembly. *West Australian*, 22 May 1998. *Don Palmer/Courtesy West Australian.*

1990s WEL members Manoa Renwick, Dorothy Broom, Julie McCarron-Benson and Gwen Gray worked to strengthen the fledgling organisation. Gray has been a continuing national office-bearer since that time. While AWHN became the key advocate on general women's health issues, there was also a proliferation of 'single-issue' women's health groups and a range of pro-choice groups and coalitions. At the national level the Reproductive Choice Alliance was launched in 2005 as a pro-choice lobby, joining the Australian Reproductive Health Alliance set up a decade earlier to promote reproductive health as a key form of development assistance.

WEL also played a pioneering role in rape law reform in a period before the establishment of women's legal services and the increased specialisation in feminist legal advocacy. In the 1970s WEL's focus was on broadening the definition of rape and changing the understanding of consent, arguing, for example, that submitting to sexual intercourse because of fear of force or violence could not be construed as consent. Later there was also a concern to reframe how the woman was perceived, through moving from the passive connotations of 'victim' to the more positive connotations of 'survivor'. WEL's draft bill on rape and other sexual offences, prepared by Jocelynne Scutt in 1976, became the centrepiece of WEL lobbying and rape law reform around the country. It was incorporated into a report of the NSW Attorney-General's Department in 1977 and set the agenda for a National Rape Law Reform Conference in 1980. It was influential in rape law reform in New South Wales and elsewhere in Australia, as well as contributing to rape law reform overseas.

In 1976 South Australia became the first Australian jurisdiction to broaden the definition of rape and one of the first in the world to remove the exemption in the criminal code for rape in marriage. WEL's position was that women should not be denied the protection of the law just because they had entered the state of matrimony. WEL groups campaigned hard on this issue around Australia and had a breakthrough in the Northern Territory in 1981. After a vigorous campaign WEL–Darwin was able to proclaim, 'We've had a win', and recorded the thanks of the Chief Minister for the assistance provided by WEL. Other jurisdictions were more intransigent.[34] The issue was not finally resolved until 1990, when the High Court upheld the validity of the South Australian law and rendered spousal immunity in other States invalid.

Other WEL law reform campaigns included those led by Jocelynne Scutt and Di Graham on probate and community of property in marriage. The issue of community of property led to major policy ructions within WEL, similar to the divisions over tax deductibility for child care. Eva Cox led the opposition, arguing at the 1981 national conference that it contradicted WEL's general position that individuals within marriage should have the right to independent identity. Eventually the push for community of property was abandoned. Less contentious, at least within the organisation itself, was the campaign for prostitution law reform, in which Jan Aitkin of WEL–NSW played an agenda-setting role in the 1970s.[35] Existing law was arbitrary and discriminatory, exempting clients from prosecution and encouraging police corruption. WEL campaigned for decriminalisation and for protection of sex workers, but also raised alarm bells about the trafficking of Asian women into the sex trade, a matter of rising concern over subsequent decades.

More specialised feminist legal advocacy groups were also appearing. In Sydney in 1978, WEL activists Joan Bielski and Margaret Thornton founded the Feminist Legal Action Group (which met in the boardroom of the law firm of another WEL member, Helen Coonan) to run test cases, conduct research and lobby for law reform. FLAG campaigned for the release from prison of Violet Roberts, gaoled in 1976 for killing her husband after twenty years of domestic violence. (She was released in 1981.) In 1982 the NSW criminal code was amended to change the law of provocation and recognise that provocation could build up over a number of years.

In the wake of the Australian Law Reform Commission's 1994 reports on equality before the law, WEL assisted with the creation of the National Women's Justice Coalition (NWJC). WEL auspiced the new organisation's application for funding, anticipating that NWJC would strengthen capacity to deal with complex legal issues and to lobby at the national level. As the number of women's legal centres increased in the mid-1990s, NWJC gave rise to the National Network of Women's Legal Services and the National Network of Indigenous Women's Legal Services. The introduction of amendments to the *Family Law Act*, in response to pressure from non-custodial parents, required detailed responses relating to financial issues and the safety of children.

Another policy area in which WEL was active was the portrayal of women in the media. In 1980 WEL members, including Jocelynne Scutt, were creating a stir with claims that 'the ABC would rather show a second-rate rugby match than a high-class program of women's sport' and that sexist language could be heard daily on ABC broadcasts. WEL–Victoria surveyed newspaper coverage of women's sport, finding the lack of coverage discriminatory and likely to have detrimental effects on sponsorship.[36]

The portrayal of women in advertising was another issue for WEL's media action groups, with Ann Villiers and Maria De Leo preparing *Guidelines on Non-sexist Advertising* for the Advertising Standards Council and trying to persuade the Council that sexism constituted offensiveness. Typical of the problem was Ansett Airline's award-winning full-page advertisement showing an air hostess dressed only in one end of a galley curtain. Objection was made not only to such demeaning or stereotyped portrayals of women (and in this case encouragement of harassment by male passengers), but also to the invisibility of older women except as, for example, a nagging mother-in-law placed on a spit by Barbeques Galore.

Diana Wyndham, a long-time WEL–NSW media spokeswoman, summed up the problem as: 'Ad men, subtract women: Profit without honour'.[37] In addition to writing submissions on media issues Wyndham compiled the 1986 *Sexism Complaints Checklist*, with assistance from the NSW Anti-Discrimination Board and cartoons by Christine Smith. Media work undertaken by WEL and feedback from community consultations led to federal government initiatives during the Hawke government's time in office. The Working Party on the Portrayal of Women in the Media was set up in 1988, with industry, community and government members. Its media complaints brochure was launched at the WEL national conference in January 1992. Additionally, a group including Wyndham successfully applied for seed funding for MediaSwitch, a community-based media watch organisation, inspired by MediaWatch (Canada) and aiming to achieve a media portrayal of women more compatible with women's equality.

MediaSwitch grew into the National Women's Media Centre (NWMC), established in 1994 by Helen Leonard with a small operational grant to continue the work of the now-defunct government working party. The NWMC produced an updated complaints brochure, undertook activities such as competitions for best and worst billboards, and coached women to participate in talkback radio. While Leonard was WEL executive officer the NWMC shared office space with WEL and the National Women's Justice Coalition and sometimes undertook joint submissions. Leonard produced the National Women's Media Directory there – in response to findings that despite the increase in women journalists, of those interviewed in the Australian media women still made up only 20 per cent. The assumption remained that men were the voice of authority, despite the availability of women experts.

The replacement under the Howard government of the old Advertising Standards Council by a self-regulatory system with no power to remove offending advertisements signalled a loss of government interest in the subject of women's portrayal in the media. The NWMC was defunded in 1999, ceasing operations in 2003. Many believed the portrayal of women in the media was going backwards, with demeaning images used to promote products such as whisky or men's shoes. One way in which feminists were still able to address such images was to make fun of them, for example through the feminist cartoon awards discussed in chapter 8.

One example of expert research and a well-organised campaign falling largely on stony ground was WEL's attempt to involve women more effectively in the process of Constitutional change. During the Keating government years it seemed possible there might be some Constitutional renovation and in 1996 the Howard government was elected on a promise to hold a people's convention. WEL immediately began lobbying to ensure that this time women would be equally represented in any processes of Constitution-making – a hundred years earlier, not one woman had participated in the drafting of the Constitution and it was said you had to have whiskers to be eligible. In 1996 the Australian Republican Movement was happy to agree to gender equity in its voting tickets for the Constitutional convention, but Australians for a Constitutional Monarchy were not. WEL's proposal to make gender equity a condition for registration of voting tickets was rejected by Senator Minchin, Minister in charge of the legislation, despite the efforts of Democrat Senators at amendment. All this awareness-raising did, however, contribute to women ending up with 35 per cent of the places at the convention.

Meanwhile, WEL developed an agenda-setting exercise to take place in January 1998, just before the government's Convention. The Women's Constitutional Convention was organised at Parliament House in Canberra, together with partners such as the National Women's Justice Coalition, the YWCA, the Women into Politics Coalition (founded in 1992 by Joan Bielski) and the Association of Women Lawyers. It was attended by some 300 delegates from national women's organisations and the Aboriginal and Torres Strait Islander Commission, as well as women who had been elected or appointed to the government's convention. It produced agreement on the need to tie constitutional change to the issue of gender equity, and the proceedings were made instantly available through WEL's website.

Despite an excellent campaign, spearheaded for WEL by constitutional lawyer Kim Rubenstein, and with organisation by Christina Ryan, little headway was made. Although an opportunity had been identified and resources mobilised efficiently, including networking and alliance-building, in the new conservative political environment the issue of women's equality was dismissed as an example of political correctness. Equality was either a dangerous precedent or something that could be safely assumed without needing to be mentioned. A proven agenda-setting strategy, which had been successful in relation to the Hawke government tax summit, this time brought little return, underlining the importance of the political opportunity structure.[38]

The government convention shied away from including the equality of men and women among the elements recommended for a draft Constitutional preamble. The referendums on the head of state and the preamble were eventually defeated, but even if they had succeeded there would have been no reference to the fundamental value of the equality of women. All other democracies renovating their Constitutions have introduced a commitment to the equality of men and women into either the provisions of the Constitution or a preamble. The Women's Constitutional Convention strongly supported a formulation such as that found in the preamble to the South African Constitution, which affirms the 'equality between men and women and people of all races'. Australia alone has held out against the inclusion of these basic democratic principles.

Births, deaths and marriages

WEL was always concerned that women should have the right to be themselves, rather than an appendage of somebody else. Early on this concern came up against official insistence on categorising women in accordance with their marital status. For example, government departments demanded that women identify themselves as either Miss or Mrs. 'Miss' meant being the object of pity if over a certain age, or derision as a spinster or battle-axe. 'Mrs' meant not being entitled to serious career consideration. One of the first (and highly controversial) changes sought by feminists entering government, whether at the Commonwealth or State levels, was that women should be able to choose the title by which they were addressed, and to be addressed as Ms if they didn't want to be known by their marital status or if their marital status was unknown.

WEL's concern that women should have the right to choose how they were known extended to the issue of parental choice over the family name of babies. WEL–WA campaigned on this from 1979 until finally achieving success in 1985, despite last-ditch resistance by a former Attorney-General in the Legislative Council. When WEL began its campaign the situation was that a child must be given its father's family name, unless the identity of the father was left off the registration paper – which caused other problems, including illegitimacy. WEL–WA began its campaign with an article in the *West Australian*. As a result of this it received many phone calls and letters with case studies of how the compulsory adoption of the father's family name caused hardship, difficulties and embarrassment. The most common circumstance was where the parents were unmarried and living apart and the mother and child were forced to have different family names.

The case studies were compiled in a submission to the State government in December 1979. The suggestion that the *Registration of Births, Deaths and Marriages Act* be amended to allow parents a choice of either family name or a combination of both was greeted as an 'attack on the family'. The Deputy Premier informed WEL that because the government stood firm on recognising and supporting the family unit as the basis of society he did not favour the suggestion that decisions about the family name of a child should 'rest on the whim of one or both of the parents'.[39] WEL quickly realised that progress was unlikely to be made with the existing government. Attention turned instead to the Labor Opposition and, with the assistance of feminists within the ALP, the reform was adopted as Labor policy.

Even the election of a Labor government in 1983 did not guarantee success, given Opposition control of the Legislative Council. Nonetheless, support was recruited from the new Women's Advisory Council and others and success did eventually come, after a tortuous exchange of letters with ministers and the Registrar-General of Births, Deaths and Marriages. As usual with public policy, not everything the campaigners wanted was achieved. Parental choice was still constrained under the amended Act, so that all children of 'a marriage' had to have the same family name, even if the parents wanted the daughters to have the mother's name and the sons the father's.[40] However, another change achieved by the campaign was the recording of the occupation of the mother as well as the father on birth certificates, with Western Australia becoming only the second State to do this.

The federalism foxtrot

As we saw in the last chapter, WEL had little time for the States' rights arguments used to stave off Commonwealth sex discrimination legislation, regarding women's rights as having precedence over the right of States to maintain discriminatory regimes. WEL had a longstanding commitment to an equality guarantee in the Australian Constitution, both as a symbolic statement of women's equality as citizens and as a guarantee that women's rights would be given uniform protection across the country. Similarly, WEL was a strong supporter of the Whitlam government's use of special purpose grants (s 96 grants) to fund women's services, so that women would have equal access regardless of where they lived and the money could not be diverted to pay for roads or bridges.[41]

Women's refuges, as the life-raft to enable women to leave violent relationships, were seen as the kind of essential service that should not be at the mercy of State or Territory borders. Every time 'new federalism' reared its head, the funding of women's services came under threat. There was an immediate crisis under the Fraser government caused by the refusal of premiers in Queensland and Western Australia to pass on funds, to which WEL responded nationally as well as at State level, campaigning strongly on refuge funding in the 1977 Queensland election.[42] In 1981 the issue returned, with a Commonwealth decision to transfer all funding responsibility for women's services to the States, despite continuing hostility on the part of some States. When a change of federal government was looming in 1983, WEL created a coalition of women's organisations to take advantage of the political opportunity. One of its four demands, a return to direct Commonwealth funding of women's services, was met when the Hawke government re-established direct funding through the Women's Emergency Service Program.

The federalism foxtrot was by no means over, however. In 1991, WEL was again campaigning against the proposed devolution of special-purpose payments to the States.[43] Although the threat to untie specific-purpose grants receded with a change of prime minister, another ominous development appeared. This was the trend toward inter-governmental decision making through forums such as the Council of Australian Governments, created in 1992. Decisions made in this way were increasingly presented to parliaments as a *fait accompli*, something that could not be overturned because all jurisdictions had already signed up. So even as women's parliamentary presence was gradually increasing, more decisions affecting women were being made elsewhere. The competition policy agreements of the mid-1990s were an example of this kind of policy ambush. They had major gender implications that were unexplored because of the way the decisions were reached. WEL was deeply concerned over the consequences of turning the delivery of needs-based community services into commercial transactions and the impact on the community sector.[44]

WEL's concern to keep responsibility for women's services in the hands of the Commonwealth was reflected in a paper adopted by the first meeting of the inter-governmental ministerial council on the status of women in 1991. Written by feminists inside government, the paper noted that a high proportion of specific-purpose payments made to the States were made to human-service areas and that attaching conditions to such payments was a significant means of enhancing the status of women. Conditions might include provision of specific kinds of statistical information and forms of monitoring and review, as well as directing how the payments were to be used. The position paper was critical of the argument that devolution was required to allow diversity in approach. It suggested that social policy must respond to diversity but that diversity in the lives of women, including the special needs relating to culture and ethnicity, in no way corresponded to State boundaries.[45]

On the other hand, federalism can provide opportunities such as 'forum shopping' to find the jurisdiction most amenable to innovation. A successful innovation in one jurisdiction can then be disseminated through inter-governmental meetings, such as those of women's advisers that took place from 1978 onwards. In the 1980s there were a number of inter-governmental women's advisory bodies, in portfolio areas such as employment and health, as well as the regular meetings of women's advisers to heads of government. Inter-governmental frameworks can enable momentum to be maintained in some policy areas despite the election of conservative governments at one level or another.[46] Federalism itself increases the number of points at which pressure can be applied. For example, in the 1970s when the Commonwealth Government drastically cut the budget of the Community Health Program, under which women's health centres and services were funded, most States responded positively to intensive lobbying and provided funding from their own treasuries.

Another example of federalism working in this positive way occurred in 2004. The Commonwealth Government had prepared a draft public health funding outcome agreement for the next five years that contained no reference to women's health. Because women's health centres and other women's health projects are jointly funded under these agreements, the Australian Women's Health Network devised a hasty but successful strategy that included lobbying the more sympathetic State and Territory governments, as well as the Commonwealth Government, to ensure the continued funding of services.[47]

The drive towards market-based policy solutions in the 1990s increasingly constrained WEL's policy influence as a generalist women's advocacy body tied to ideas of using the state to deliver gender equity. Public interest advocacy came under attack, with campaigns mounted by free-market think tanks to reduce the access of non-government organisations to government and to government support. NGOs such as WEL were identified as seeking to interfere with market forces in the name of equity goals rejected by 'ordinary' voters and taxpayers.

At the same time there was increasing specialisation of advocacy

bodies, including those associated with women's health and legal services, and increased demands from the state for specialised (and quan-
titative) knowledge. In the face of diminishing returns and demands
for policy expertise that were hard to meet from within their active
membership, WEL groups found themselves struggling to maintain
policy engagement.

7

NEW HORIZONS

Few who belonged to WEL in its glory days thought their lives would ever be the same again. Their ways of thinking about themselves and about the world had shifted irrevocably, and they had found a sisterhood with other women who shared their dissatisfactions. 'Exciting' and 'exhilarating' are the words most often used about the experience of being part of WEL's early years. While the impact was greatest on those who had previously thought of themselves as housewives, none were untouched by the experience of wielding influence on government and other decision-making bodies. It gave them for the first time the feeling that they had the power to change things, to have an impact on society, that they didn't have to accept the way things were for women – 'we thought we could do anything'.

For those responding to the history survey, the most common life difference that WEL had made for them was to increase their confidence. The new horizons opened up, and the new talents they were discovering, encouraged many women to embark on new careers, often re-entering education or employment. WEL also gave them good friends and mentors, and in many cases introduced them to the skills and networks necessary to achieve political and policy goals. Their new-found confidence also affected their personal relationships and their marriages. All things combined to make them feel that no-one could have been part of WEL and not been changed by it.

Growing two inches taller

All women who joined WEL were treated (at least in principle) as having a valuable contribution to make – as was said at the time, all women were experts when it came to oppression. Kath Balfour, an American-born potter who joined during a return to study in Perth, summed up the experience of many members:

> I joined WEL because WEL women inspire confidence in each other and exert tremendous energy and leadership. They offer overwhelming support and solidarity. Yet the personal experiences of women, as women, are never dismissed as trivial or irrelevant to the larger issues. On the contrary, there is an atmosphere of real caring because every woman has faced tough emotional crises on our own and we know that the political issues are all reflected in everyday life. That's what it's about, sharing pain and loss, joy and accomplishment.[1]

Being treated seriously in this way created a world of difference for women used to being put down and having their contributions ignored or trivialised. In the 1950s and 1960s Australia had become famous for the way the sexes split up at parties, the men congregating to talk about important things, leaving the women to discuss home and babies. For Pennly Attwood in Adelaide, the most radical effect of WEL occurred at her first general meeting. Deborah McCulloch was trying to get a decision on some matter under debate and went around the circle asking the opinion of everyone in turn: 'This was a revelation to me – what I said actually mattered! I went home feeling wonderful'.[2]

In Sydney one newcomer said to another member: 'You must be a professional woman.' Asked why, she replied: 'Because you talk like you expect to be listened to.'[3] For women who had been secretaries it was a revelation not to be talked down to, and WEL provided a new sense of self-worth. One commented in 1974:

> I not only feel an individual, I know people care, I have some pride in what I do. More pride than I had when I was somebody's handmaiden. I am nobody's handmaiden any more. I'm treated by my friends as an equal in my particular

field and you just don't get that in the workforce. Secretaries
are definitely second-class citizens ... I think it was the
confidence more than anything, confidence as a person. I'm not
just mother of, or wife of, any more. I'm not afraid to talk to
people.[4]

For Wendy McCarthy, a teacher who had found herself turned into just
someone's wife and someone else's mum – a common experience for
the university-educated woman of the 1960s – WEL gave a new sense
of power:

No one should ever under-estimate it. It was like you grew two
inches taller because suddenly you felt so powerful. People
listened, they wanted to know what you said. I could get a line
in a newspaper every day if I wanted to. I learned to ring up
radio stations. I didn't know until then that you could ring up
radio stations and get on the air.[5]

Working closely with other women on submissions or campaigns, and
seeing policy change as a result of such efforts, was hugely empowering. It countered the loss of self-esteem that many women experienced
on leaving the workforce to raise children, particularly those who had
higher education and had been in semi-professional jobs. Internalising
the low status accorded to 'suburban housewives', they felt isolated,
their talents unused or unrecognised. WEL gave women a break from
housework, an opportunity to talk about things other than recipes, a
feeling of 'oneness' with other women and a feeling of greater power
in confronting political systems and social organisation.[6]

Elsa Atkin, a young wife at home with a baby in nappies, described
feeling uplifted by the knowledge that other women felt the same
injustices she felt and were doing something about them:

Things were starting to happen. Politicians were actually
starting to pay attention to women's issues. Apart from the
sense of achievement we had, how much more stimulating,
interesting and invigorating such activities were than being
at home doing the never-ending washing and cooking. When
any guilt feelings overtook as either a group or an individual,

there was one woman who would constantly remind us that
no woman she knew of had, as part of her epitaph, 'she kept a
clean house'.[7]

For a member of WEL–Darwin, the organisation provided a focus for
the passion she had about the inequities in the world:

> It made me much more politically aware and gave me the
> courage to stand up for what I believed – even if it gave me a
> reputation as a 'rabid feminist'. I still view that tag as a badge
> of honour. I think that when a 66 year old is proud to declare
> herself as a feminist then some younger people might think it's
> not such a bad thing to be.[8]

For Pat Vines, a young mother in Bendigo, WEL was a means of discovering her own power and the power of women. She and her husband
had decided to swap roles and he was to stay at home with their three-
year-old while she went out to work. She couldn't get work immediately, and the story begins with her being instructed to apply for the
dole:

> I filled out the form and claimed my husband as a dependent.
> They told me I couldn't do that and that in the case of a
> married couple the husband had to go on the dole and claim
> the wife as a dependent. This seemed wrong to me and I
> went to see our local MP. He was intrigued by my case and
> promised to take it up with the Minister … to my delight and
> surprise after a couple of months, during which time we had
> moved to Melbourne and I had got a job, I received a letter
> saying the Minister had reviewed my case and was aware of
> changing values in society, a cheque was enclosed for all the
> back pay which we'd missed out on. (I had dug my heels in and
> preferred to get less dole than to be forced to be a dependent.)
> In fact the department's policy was changed because of my
> persistence.[9]

Some experienced WEL as a 'safe space' or 'halfway house' where they
gained the confidence to advance into more dangerous terrain, including Women's Liberation and various forms of local politics. A Western Australian member later described this in terms of WEL being a

Horacek image consultant cartoon.
Judy Horacek.

mother ship, providing the safety from which she could branch out to explore the ideas and campaigns of Women's Liberation and the Labor Women's Organisation.[10]

While the WEL candidate surveys described earlier were intended to have an effect on politicians, they often had an equal effect on the interviewers who found that the 'man of importance' knew little or nothing about the subject and it was they themselves who had become the competent person or the expert. They were discovering that what they looked best in was, after all, authority.

One member of WEL–WA discovered when part of an interviewing team that the Minister of Education thought that the issue of sexism in education was about providing sex education in schools. A subsequent lobbying experience was less empowering. On leaving an interview with Senator Peter Durack she was talking so vehemently to her fellow interviewer that she fell into an ornamental pool and had to catch her bus home dripping wet.[11]

Thirty years after the founding of WEL in Perth an original member, Dot Goodrick, summarised the lobbying skills that were acquired in the process of developing a repertoire of political action:

- how to prepare a press release
- how to write letters to the editor
- how to write proposals and submissions
- how to call and run public forums
- how to organise deputations to Ministers and MPs
- how to develop effective networks
- how to assess and publish the rating of MPs' current views on issues.[12]

An early Sydney and Canberra member, Meredith Hinchcliffe, remembered the lessons she learned the very first day she was involved with lobbying:

> June Surtees (Williams) and Wendy McCarthy said: 'We are going to see Clyde Cameron and he likes women to wear dresses.' So we did – there was no point antagonising him and getting him off side. He listened to us that day and took us seriously. I learned many other lobbying skills and still use them … Many of the jobs and volunteer groups I have worked in have involved advocacy and lobbying and it is due to that work I did with WEL that I have often been asked to be involved in campaigns.[13]

Rosemary Webb also learned new negotiating styles from WEL, including how to exploit biases:

> Later, in the 90s, when I worked as an organiser and industrial officer for the CPSU I never gave free points to the opposition – there were always girlie shoes and a decent jacket in the back of my car for impromptu meetings with public sector managers.[14]

In developing their lobbying skills WEL members also acquired the research skills needed to underpin submissions and practice in public speaking for a multitude of purposes – being on a delegation with someone like Clare Burton providing evidence to an Australian Senate inquiry was a learning experience in itself.[15] WEL groups ran regular courses on lobbying and media skills and in later years on use of the

Internet. The acquisition of such skills increased the sense of being able to make a difference and help make the world a better place.

Apart from more directly policy-related skills, there was also the acquisition of a general frame for interpreting the world. Helen Leonard had a background in the Nursing Mothers' Association when she was appointed to the National Women's Consultative Council in 1988. Deciding she needed to know more about women's issues than breast-feeding, she rang WEL in Sydney: 'They put me in touch with Eva Cox and I went to see her and we had this incredible three hours where I took notes and she just kept talking and that was the beginning of a wonderful friendship and mentorship.' By the next year Leonard was organising the National Women's Tax Convention co-sponsored by WEL and the Consultative Council, and making sense of her former husband's telling her not to take part-time work running self-esteem courses because it would 'mess up his tax'.[16]

WEL left its mark on members through providing them with a framework for making sense of their own and others' experience. As one founding member said of those who had departed: 'People who have dropped out of WEL have not been lost – they have gone on to study or work or the bureaucracy or business and they have all remained feminists.'[17]

Second chances

Joining WEL gave many women the confidence to embark on new careers. The abolition of tertiary fees by the Whitlam government meant the opportunity for 'second-chance' education for women origi-nally trained to be secretaries or nurses because those were 'appropri-ate' female occupations. The impetus to re-enter education or to try a new career was particularly important for the first cohort of members:

> They joined WEL, saw other women in action, learned to write
> submissions, interviewed politicians, debated issues in public
> forums and then, fired up, went out into the world. They went

back to school, to university, became councillors, journalists, researchers.[18]

Barbara Coddington, whom we have encountered working as a volunteer co-ordinator in the WEL–Sydney office, was one such woman. After she left school she worked in an office, then married and had a baby. It took two years at home to develop what she described as a 'severe attack of suburban neurosis'. She then began typing up newsletters from home for small groups such as dog obedience schools. Her work for WEL–Sydney, however, led her in a new direction. Because she had found that every time women wanted to change something they came up against the law, she went to university and became a family lawyer, as well as a member of the NSW Government's Women's Advisory Council. A handmaiden no more.[19]

The 'new career' effect was so marked that as early as 1974 Juliet Richter found that some of the original activists in Sydney were disconcerted to find WEL was becoming a 'pre-retraining scheme' rather than simply a political lobby, serving as a re-entry vehicle for suburban women who had left jobs to raise children or who were discovering aspirations to 'upgrade' or change fields.[20]

Similarly, when Ruth Martin surveyed women who had been founding members in Melbourne she found a number of self-described 'housewives' for whom WEL was a springboard into careers. 'Jo' regarded herself as an untrained housewife when she joined WEL and became involved in the media group. She became very interested in journalism and received professional support and encouragement to move into a career, becoming a full-time ABC news commentator.

'Jan' also regarded herself as an 'extraordinarily passive' wife and mother before joining. She started working in the Melbourne office and found herself becoming a referral centre for the many desperate women who contacted the organisation. At the suggestion of the police surgeon she set up the group that began the Rape Crisis Centre, and was then elected to local government, where she was a forceful speaker on the needs of women. She also became an office-bearer in the

Liberal Party and took on a position running a government-sponsored program for unemployed young people. 'Roz' was another housewife who plunged into working for WEL, changing her views of a woman's place and discovering new capabilities in the process. With her new-found confidence and experience in writing press releases and newsletters, 'Roz' was inspired to enter journalism and became the editor of a suburban newspaper.[21]

Those who worked in part-time and poorly paid jobs in WEL offices were also able to build on their experience to move into new women's sector jobs inside and outside government, or into advocacy work in feminised areas such as consumer and environmental advocacy. As WEL-NSW said at the beginning of 1975: 'The co-ordinator's job can be undertaken as an interesting experience in itself or it can be viewed as your own retraining scheme.'[22] One of the first WEL–NSW co-ordinators had moved on to be administrator of the Adelaide Women's Health Centre. In 1984, however, another NSW co-ordinator proclaimed she was not sure whether she was ready to follow the increasingly popular route into the public service and to fight the good fight from the position of femocrat.[23] If she had, she would have found both the skills and the networks gained through WEL an invaluable resource.

In the 1980s 'New Opportunities for Women' (NOW) courses were instituted at TAFE colleges for the same 'pre-retraining' purpose that WEL had so often served – restoring the self-esteem of women, for whom motherhood and absence from the workforce had meant a loss of confidence, to the point where they could tackle re-entry into education or employment. Where TAFE had previously been largely a male domain, apart from hairdressing and secretarial studies, there was suddenly an influx of feminist lecturers and mature-age women students learning to 'build on their strengths'. In Western Australia the inaugural NOW co-ordinator in 1984 was WEL member and Women's Advisory Council chair Janet Pine.

WEL women in politics

As we have seen, one result of interviewing politicians for WEL surveys was that women discovered how inadequate some of these supposed figures of authority were. With the support of other members, a number of these women went on to enter local government or to join political parties and stand for preselection. Some of the founding WEL members played important roles in local government. Carole Baker became Mayor of North Sydney, while in Melbourne Ann Morrow became Mayor of Malvern and Winsome McCaughey was later elected to the Melbourne City Council and became Lord Mayor in 1988.

Dawn McMahon, the very successful publicity officer when WEL began in South Australia, was elected to Marion City Council in 1973. Helen L'Orange (born Helen Alidenes) was already an alderman on Strathfield Council when she became active in WEL in Sydney. For others the organisation was a vital preparation for entering local government:

> I became very confident, wrote letters to the local press,
> spoke to community groups and was very surprised, after the
> local government election to be told by an older man in the
> community that he admired my election campaign, which was
> based on the methods gained from WEL. In fact no candidate
> had handed out 'how to vote' leaflets before I did in Bellingen.[24]

A 1980 survey of Melbourne women in local government found that WEL had been the single most important influence on their lives, while a follow-up survey of all Australian women politicians in 1981–82 showed that 28 per cent were current or former members.[25] When WEL–ACT rallied around to support the election of Susan Ryan to the Senate in 1975, members silk-screened hundreds of T-shirts with the message 'A Woman's Place is in the Senate'. As we have seen, Ryan became the first woman member of a federal Labor Cabinet and introduced landmark sex discrimination and affirmative action legislation, as well as being responsible for important equity initiatives in the education portfolio. She was joined in federal parliament by the other

WEL women who followed her in the Status of Women portfolio (see Appendix A7).

While ministers in general relied on (male) networks, new women ministers were able to draw on their WEL networks for appointments to their office. Margaret Reynolds, for example, had become politically active in WEL–Townsville, along with Patti Kendall and Dale Spender. She was elected to the Townsville City Council in 1979, to the Senate in 1983, became Minister for Local Government from 1987 and held the Status of Women portfolio from 1988. She appointed Kendall to her office along with policy bureaucrat Hazel Moir, also a WEL member.

From Western Australia, in particular, many members went on to important political careers. Founding convenor Pat Giles, who had been appointed to chair the WA employment discrimination committee in 1974, went on to head the ACTU women's committee from 1978. She entered the Senate in 1981 and was responsible for the creation of the ALP caucus Status of Women Committee, which maintained a watching brief over the party's commitment to women. She was one of the 'critical actors' who introduced women's movement discourse into parliamentary debate, raising the subject of domestic violence and calling for women's unpaid work to be included in the national accounts. Her electorate secretary, Cheryl Davenport, also entered politics. Davenport became a member of the WA Legislative Council in 1989, where she dedicated herself to the task of achieving abortion law reform. After a mammoth struggle she finally achieved it in 1998, with the support in the Legislative Assembly of another WEL member, Diana Warnock.

Another founding member of WEL in Perth, Wendy Fatin, was elected to the federal parliament in 1983 and held the Local Government and Status of Women portfolios from 1990. She appointed fellow member Val Marsden to head the National Women's Consultative Council. Meanwhile Senator Ruth Coleman, West Australian Senator from 1974, played an important role in helping WEL–ACT open up public bars for women. Dr Carmen Lawrence, the psychologist who worked on the 1972 WEL candidate survey, left academia to enter West Australian politics in the 1980s. She became the first woman premier in Australia in 1990, then a federal Minister for Health and the Status of Women and the first woman to be national president of the ALP. She took herself to the backbench over her opposition to aspects of party policy on asylum seekers and the Iraq War before leaving Parliament in 2007.

WEL members in the West Australian government in the 1980s included Yvonne Henderson, who had been a WA convenor and had presented WEL submissions in the State Arbitration Commission. She had startled this masculine domain by breastfeeding her six-week-old daughter while attending the equal pay case in 1975 and being accompanied by her nine-month-old son for the State maternity leave case in 1979. After entering Parliament, Henderson was to have the unusual privilege, for a backbencher, of having carriage of the government's *Equal Opportunity Act 1984*. Her second reading speech was greeted by applause from the packed public gallery and from MPs on both sides of the chamber.[26] She became a minister in 1988 and went to hold various portfolios including Labour Relations. After retirement from politics she became WA Equal Opportunity Commissioner. One of WEL–Australia's few paid workers, Ruth Webber, employed under the Community Employment Program in the mid-1980s, was fifteen years later elected as a Labor Senator for Western Australia.

In South Australia, founding member Anne Levy entered the Legislative Council for the Labor Party and became the first woman Presiding Officer in Australia in 1986 – a few hours before Joan Child became Speaker of the House of Representatives. Levy became a Minister in 1989 and held a range of portfolios, including Status of Women. There were WEL members active in all parties in South Australia, including the Australian Democrats, and they promoted many of WEL's policy priorities such as paid maternity leave.

The new profession of EEO

Many members took their commitment to social justice into the new jobs opening up for equal opportunity (EEO) or women's policy officers. In promoting new agendas for government WEL had unwittingly opened up new career opportunities for its members and for other women's movement activists – a situation which lasted until 1996.

Public choice theorists would argue that such opening up of opportunities is just another example of the inauthentic nature of equality-seeking: the real gains are made by those whose cultural capital stands them in good stead to achieve public sector jobs implementing equality legislation.[27] In fact, as journalist and WEL member Rosemary Harris commented, 'any WEL-trained bureaucrat will almost certainly have served a long and arduous apprenticeship, doing gratis what she is now fit and deserving to be paid to do'.[28] For example, in 1975 Joan Russell and another member of WEL–SA worked on a voluntary basis organising a survey of Adelaide working women to provide data for a submission to the Royal Commission on Human Relationships on work/family issues. Russell later held a range of positions in government, including Director of Human Resources for the South Australian police. But as we shall see below, it would be a mistake to believe that the change-agent jobs such women entered were a passport to an easy life.

In the 1980s, when both State and Commonwealth public service legislation required the development of EEO plans, and large private employers and universities were coming under similar obligations, many WEL members became EEO officers. Those who had helped write submissions detailing the barriers to women posed by employment practices and organisational culture now had the opportunity to put this knowledge to work in departments, agencies and companies.

Many of the founding members of WEL we encountered in chapter 1 ended up as equal opportunity commissioners or heading up EEO units in the public sector or tertiary education. To name but a few: Gail Radford became the long-serving head of the EEO Bureau in the Australian Public Service. She also played an important role in developing EEO guidelines for the private sector, through a tripartite body, the National Labour Consultative Council. The Council had a cluster of WEL members, including Pat Giles for the ACTU and Kerry Lovering, who for a time was executive officer, and Helen Prendergast, of the Tasmanian portaloos. Lovering had been impelled into a career of activism when she discovered that in her first job as a geologist she was to be paid only 70 per cent of the male rate. She went on to become Director of the Women's Bureau in the Department of Employment, a senior adviser in the EEO Bureau and then EEO Manager in the State Electricity Commission of Victoria and then at Melbourne City Council. Also in Victoria, founding member Jan Harper became EEO officer for the University of Melbourne (1985–95), after a decade with the Women's Movement Children's Literature Co-operative, producing non-sexist *Sugar and Snails* books.

June Williams, one of the founders of Sydney WEL, became the inaugural Equal Opportunity Commissioner in Western Australia, a role she filled for almost 20 years until she was replaced by former minister and WEL activist Yvonne Henderson. Barbara Wertheim, at whose house WEL–Brisbane was founded, later held women's policy and equal opportunity positions in New South Wales before becoming Equal Opportunity Commissioner in Victoria in 1987. Pamela O'Neil, a founding member in Darwin, was elected to the Legislative Assembly and then became the first Commonwealth Sex Discrimination Commissioner. In New South Wales, WEL activists who took on important statutory roles included Carmel Niland, who after being Women's Adviser to the Premier became Counsellor for Equal Opportunity and then President of the NSW Anti-Discrimination Board. Alison Ziller, who had been the convenor of an action group, became Director of Equal Opportunity in Public Employment and was responsible for the first legislated equal opportunity programs. Her *Affirmative Action Handbook*, illustrated by cartoonist Patrick Cook, became a classic for the emerging occupational group of EEO co-ordinators in the 1980s. It also showed the importance of humour in making palatable the kind of challenges EEO presented to hidebound institutional practices.

The career of Clare Burton illustrates the kind of lifelong commitment that gives the lie to charges that EEO is just a form of 'rent-seeking'. She was a prominent participant in WEL debates in Sydney in the 1970s but it was her academic research on work value and perform-

 Gail Wilenski (Radford), Wendy McCarthy and June Surtees (Williams), WEL business, Sydney 1972. *Wendy McCarthy.*

ance appraisal that provided the intellectual firepower for many equal opportunity and pay equity initiatives. Her monograph *Redefining Merit* became the bible of EEO practitioners while another book, *The Promise and the Price*, reflected on organisational resistance to reform. She became the second Director of Equal Opportunity in Public Employment in New South Wales in 1989 and then Commissioner for Public Sector Equity in Queensland.

Burton had an uncompromising commitment to social justice, always hoping for more than these positions were able to deliver. She left Brisbane in 1993 to work as an independent researcher and consultant, exercising far-reaching influence on university equity programs as well as conducting trailblazing studies of the integration of women in the Australian and New Zealand defence forces. Regularly starting work before dawn, she conducted about a dozen equity reviews at universities around Australia, leading to new and revamped programs. She also provided crucial evidence on 'managing for diversity' to the Karpin Report. She returned to WEL in Canberra and did much of the work on submissions to the review of the Affirmative Action Agency and on the new Public Service Bill. She succeeded in having her definition of 'merit' adopted by the Howard government, although her critical assessment of performance pay was rejected.[29]

Apart from those named, many other members took on equal opportunity positions in the public service, in statutory agencies and universities, WEL networks often providing moral support for those occupying these challenging positions.

From feminists to femocrats and back

But not all WEL members moving into government became EEO officers dealing with public sector employment issues. Others played a crucial role in the development of women's policy machinery at all levels of government – both from outside and inside. Founding members became the first women's advisers in Tasmania, South Australia and New South Wales and sometimes played a role in more than one jurisdiction. For example, Deborah McCulloch of South Australia helped set up the WA machinery and Helen L'Orange, the second women's adviser in New South Wales, became the head of the federal Office for the Status of Women in 1988 – *The Age* headline read 'Orange among the mandarins'.[30]

Moving into women's policy units provided feminists with opportunities to apply the insights they had gained in WEL to policy analysis. It meant being in reach of policy power and being able to develop new policy addressing women's needs, for example for safety in the home. From within government it was possible to make resources available to support the community-based women's movement and equality work in the community at large. Funding programs were introduced to assist groups such as Indigenous and migrant women, and women with disabilities, to have a seat at the policy table and a voice in public debate. It was possible to support feminist research and service innovation as well as consultation and policy advocacy.

Many members derived a great deal of satisfaction from what they were able to achieve in dismantling legislative and policy barriers to equal opportunity and in promoting the community services needed by women returning to paid work. Val Marsden gained confidence from WEL–Gold Coast and when she moved to Western Australia became part of the long WEL campaign there for women's services and women's policy machinery, founding co-ordinator of the Women's Information and Referral Exchange (WIRE) and later an EEO practitioner. Appropriately, she became a member and convenor of the National Women's Consultative Committee at the time it was promoting the ratification of ILO Convention 156 on equal opportunity for workers with family responsibilities. Other members played key roles in the promotion of women's health policy and programs, and in the campaigns against domestic violence which became such a feature of the 1980s.

But work as change-agents also tended to lead to burnout. While critics saw WEL members and feminists more generally as having created cosy jobs for themselves within the public sector, these jobs involved all the strain of trying to turn around entrenched organisational cultures and of raising issues that antagonised those who held organisational power.[31] Drawing attention to the deleterious effects on women of the prescriptions of government economic advisers was enough to raise the hackles of many in the upper echelons. Femocrats were also working against the grain of established policy practice. This was particularly the case when it came to democratising the policy development process to give a greater role to the intended beneficiaries of the policy – as with the exemplary process adopted in 1987–88 for the development of the national women's health policy.

Despite the hours involved, WEL members quite often worked from both inside and outside government, some senior public servants using different names or remaining anonymous in the minutes while doing WEL work, others drafting material to appear under a co-ordi-nator's name. Women's policy agencies were sometimes more relaxed about their staff having roles with WEL. In New South Wales, Joan Bielski pushed from both outside and inside in lobbying for and then heading the Social Development Unit of the NSW Ministry of Educa-tion (1977–84). From this position she campaigned successfully for the inclusion of higher education under the NSW public sector require-ment for equal opportunity plans and also launched campaigns to get women into apprenticeships and mathematics. Her apprenticeship program for girls, initiated in 1979, was to become a national program under the Hawke government, with financial incentives for taking on women apprentices and 'Tradeswomen on the Move' buses visiting schools. The opening up of trades to women followed years of work by WEL: only two years before the NSW program was launched, WEL had lambasted the Public Transport Commission's headline news that two new female apprentices had been accepted – along with 800 males.[32]

In 2001–03 Sandy Killick and Sarah Maddison combined very public roles as respectively National Chair and NSW Spokeswoman for WEL with their work for the NSW Department for Women. While the head of the department (herself a former member) was somewhat nerv-ous about their media profile, there was no attempt to interfere with it. Sandy Pitcher, a co-convenor of WEL–ACT in 2000–02, was also a senior policy officer in the federal Office of the Status of Women. While some were worried on her behalf, she reassured them her WEL work was concerned with the ACT rather than the government she worked for. She went on to positions in the Equal Opportunity for Women in the Workplace Agency and the British Commission for Racial Equality before becoming Director of the South Australian Office for Women in January 2006.

WEL might be viewed as a conduit for careers for many of its members, and certainly in the Hawke-Keating years some may have joined as a useful piece of preparation before applying for women's policy jobs in government. For others, membership is unlikely to have been purely instrumental in nature. For example, Yvonne Carnahan, an early national co-ordinator, had spent time in a women's refuge at the time of her marriage break-up and wanted to give something back to the women's movement that had given her support when she needed it.

A number of those who did go into important women's policy jobs in government, such as Deborah McCulloch as SA Women's Adviser, and Ann Wentworth as ACT Women's Adviser, pushed very hard to bring their experience with democratic service provision into the way government delivered programs. As we saw in chapter 5, their initiatives included the creation of the Women's Information Service in South Australia and the 24-hour Domestic Violence Intervention Service in the ACT. After departing from their public service jobs McCulloch and Wentworth returned to pushing from outside – McCulloch as convenor of WEL–SA, Wentworth as WEL national co-ordinator. This was also true of Helen L'Orange who, after her spells as Women's Adviser in the NSW and Commonwealth governments and other public service work, returned to an active role in WEL–NSW. Kerry Lovering had been part of the WEL–Victoria group drafting the Victorian *Equal Opportunity Act* in the 1970s. Thirty years later, after a career as a femocrat and equal opportunity practitioner in Canberra and Melbourne, and a time in Adelaide, she returned to be Convenor of WEL–Victoria. Together with Barbara Cameron she revived the group through a new website and email communications.

In New South Wales the career of Juliet Richter had a similar trajectory. Activism in WEL in the 1970s led to her appointment to the NSW Women's Advisory Council and then as first Research Co-ordinator for the NSW Anti-Discrimination Board. From 1980 she worked on equity and diversity reforms in the State public service and in 1984 became head of the women's directorate in the Department of Industrial Relations. She lasted six years in this position before moving into a 'mainstream' area, exhausted by the prolonged struggles to save the women's policy unit during successive restructures. She took early retirement and rejoined WEL in 1994, taking over the role of industrial relations spokeswoman from Edna Ryan. She became a member of the National Pay Equity Coalition (NPEC) and appeared before State and federal industrial tribunals, being one of the few women in NPEC who did not have a job that silenced them in public. She continued as WEL spokeswoman until 1997, dealing with the first phases of the Howard government's workplace reforms, before handing over to Suzanne Hammond.

Friendship

Quite apart from the acquisition of skills and confidence and the possibility of new careers, WEL provided the emotional satisfactions of sisterhood, of solidarity and support from other women. There was the feeling of 'oneness', of community, which is such an important part of social movements. It gave rise to friendships that helped sustain the organisation beyond the initial burst of high levels of political energy and political engagement. Members repeatedly told researchers that 'WEL gave me the best friends I ever had'. For a Melbourne woman:

> WEL women and our friends are my tribe. When I wonder how
> I fit into my community I know the existence of these women,
> highlighted at the annual Mary Owen dinner, means there is
> a place for me and I can draw on these women for friendship,
> skills, networking and strategic thinking.[33]

Although there were some damaging conflicts, as in any organisation with powerful personalities, for many members WEL has been a source of lifelong friendships. As early as 1975, the survey of national conference participants found that 'friendship/companionship' was ranked first of the benefits derived from membership, closely followed by 'self-confidence'.[34] A 1981 survey of early members in Melbourne also found that although a question about friendship had not been included, it was uppermost in many interviewees' thoughts. The 2002–03 history survey again confirmed the importance of WEL as a source of friendships, particularly for the early members, but also through the Fraser and Hawke-Keating periods.

Friendship often began with the discovery and mutual validation of attitudes and values. A number of the early members had been feminists before their time and rejoiced at suddenly finding large numbers of like-minded women. Joan Bielski, for example, was a teacher who had been describing herself as a feminist since writing to the *Sydney Morning Herald* about equal pay in the 1950s. Along with another future member, Dorothy Simons, she had participated in Madge Dawson's pioneering adult education women's studies course at the University of Sydney and in the project that gave rise to Dawson's book charting the fate of women graduates, *Graduate and Married* (1965). But it was WEL that provided her with a large crowd of sisters. For Di Graham as well, born in late 1909, it was like 'coming home' to find in WEL so many women who thought the same way as she did, after decades feeling that she was alone in a fight against inequality and the putting down of women.[35]

Edwina Doe, a market researcher who had migrated to Sydney from the United Kingdom, joined on the night of the 1972 candidate meeting in Mosman. Like Graham she found it provided affirmation of her own attitudes, although in Doe's case it also affirmed her unmarried and independent life:

> All my life I had wondered why I was out of step with other
> people and now I realised it was because I was a feminist and I

was not alone. I was one of the lucky ones: I had not married in desperation or been left with children I didn't really want.[36]

For the next 20 years Doe was a member of the team that produced *WEL–Informed* and part of a close feminist community.

The camaraderie and emotional support network provided by WEL was a source of renewed energy for young mothers experiencing isolation and loss of self-esteem. Finding 'it's not just me' was very important for these women. For one young Sydney member who had suffered anxiety and depression while at home with three children, the best thing about WEL was 'unquestionably finding people who are on the same wavelength as oneself about non-acceptance of traditional roles – not having to explain yourself if you don't agree with the current view. Support, it boils down to that one word support'.[37]

There was the feeling of belonging and being part of a sisterhood. For Joyce Nicholson in Melbourne, who had taken over her father's publishing business at the age of 49 but felt guilty that she wasn't content just to be a wife and mother, this was particularly important. She had read Germaine Greer's *Female Eunuch* and felt a burden roll off her back – women didn't have to enjoy being wives and mothers. It was a joy to 'find you have joined a huge sisterhood'.[38] Another Melbourne member admitted feeling embarrassed when typing and editing the *Broadsheet* and finishing off 'yours in sisterhood'. Despite the embarrassment, sisterhood was really what she felt: 'I enjoyed being a woman, there was always the warmth of support of the educated women, sisterhood was the main way to describe it'.[39]

This story about what WEL meant to women who suffered guilt from not being content just to be a wife and mother is one repeated many times. In another version:

> I'd always believed all those myths ... I hadn't ever heard any mother express anything but the most momentary exasperation about her motherly role ... one would have seen oneself as admitting total failure, to say that one couldn't stand staying home with the children. There was no other public acknowledgment of women.[40]

 Dinner to celebrate Joan Bielski's AM. L to R, Jan Aitkin, Joan Bielski, Mary Gaudron, Sydney 1988. *Diana Goldrick.*

For Joyce Nicholson, what stood out was meeting through WEL hundreds of women who had experienced the doubts, worries and guilt she had suffered over dissatisfaction with full-time domesticity:

> The happiness that the Women's Movement brought to
> me cannot be described ... After all those years of feeling I
> was swimming against the stream, I found the strength of
> sisterhood, of women swimming beside me towards the goal of
> achieving more equality for women ... I was a different person,
> and through the years since then it has been the same – here
> are so many more women one meets all the time to share one's
> problems, to encourage and praise.[41]

In Perth a member recalled having read Germaine Greer with a growing sense of recognition and then attending a talk given by Pat Giles: 'I eagerly attended and knew at once I had found a home ... Attending WEL meetings in the seventies was incredibly exciting – new ideas every time, big questions to think over, a gradual accumulation of facts and figures about the situation of women, consciousness raising, activism and an inspiring sisterhood ...' When she became a foundation staff member of Murdoch University in 1975 she put forward a proposal for the first women's studies course in Western Australia. Her background in WEL convinced her that any women's studies course needed strong grassroots links and she persuaded activists such as Pat Giles and Irene Greenwood to contribute to the lectures.[42]

This aspect of WEL, bringing together women with shared values and providing them with a sense of sisterhood, is well evoked by Joan Bielski, despite her belief there were 'always a few hoods among the sisterhood'. After more than 30 years of membership in Sydney, she says:

> WEL–NSW (and nationally) became a network of like-minded women from which many life-long friendships were formed, friendships based on having a common world view and on work for the women's movement. WEL became the public face of late 20th century feminism, a contact point for women wanting to involve themselves in the feminist cause. It provides a place where numerous women are confirmed in their feminist consciousness, where they gained the insights, the confidence, the communication, political and organisational skills which have enabled them not only to be successful advocates of women's causes but which also has enabled them to advance their careers in public administration, the professions, business, community organisations and politics. Many of the founding members became national figures in their fields.[43]

Pat Richardson's *Belle the Bushie* radio broadcasts in Sydney in the early 1990s also give a good insight into the emotional significance of WEL for members for whom it was the 'single most important organisation' they had ever belonged to. She talks of the exhilaration of being able to discuss and share ideas with other women and the way that 'if you get a few WEL members together the conversation never flags'.[44] At a 25th anniversary lunch in Sydney talk drowned out the choir that had been organised for the occasion. WEL women could be relied on to enjoy 'tales from the trenches' and jokes at the expense of a sexist world. Not only did they share indignation at injustice but their lives became intertwined in many other ways, from passing on Christmas trees to supporting each other through illness.

Marriage

Like any other life-changing experience, but particularly due to the challenge to traditional sex roles, WEL membership sometimes put a strain on marriage. Increased confidence and aspirations on the part of women were not necessarily appreciated by husbands who had expected a full-time wife and mother. The bride who had gone demurely down the aisle might become unrecognisable after reading Friedan and Greer and joining WEL. She found she didn't have to regard herself as selfish or neurotic for wanting goals of her own, beyond husband and children. When her attitudes changed, often her husband found it difficult to cope with his 'new' wife.

The greatest change was in those women who had classified themselves as 'housewives' but were no longer willing to make themselves available for this role on a full-time basis. Some marriages did not survive the shock. For one working-class woman interviewed in 1974, membership had altered her irrevocably by giving her more confidence. Her husband had been unable to adjust to the change and regarded WEL as the destroyer of their relationship. She commented: 'I had been not only dependent economically, but for companionship, socially, in every part of the marriage.'[45] Another husband described WEL as the co-respondent in his divorce. His wife said he had got it wrong – her involvement in WEL was a step towards increasing independence, but it was her studies at Macquarie University that were the real turning point.[46]

While increased self-esteem led some women to leave destructive marriages, other husbands were more positive towards WEL's influence and helped with newsletters and other tasks. For one senior public servant there wasn't much time to do anything but 'attend the odd meeting and pass messages through the telephone tree' but he felt his contribution was made through the public service arena.[47] National co-ordinator Pamela Denoon (1982–84) proposed a dinner to thank husbands for their support.

Overall, participation in WEL meant that women's lives took new and often unexpected directions. Not only did women grow two inches in height, they no longer accepted the kind of social expectations they had grown up with. With their new-found confidence and support networks they re-entered education and changed careers. Many had the satisfaction of entering the new equity-related jobs that were opening up in the public and private sectors as a result of WEL's advocacy. While jobs promoting equity tended to be a rocky road, there was at least the comfort of good friends gained through WEL. The impact of all these changes on WEL as an organisation is examined further in the next chapter, where we also look at the kind of trajectory expected of social movements and whether women's movements conform to it.

8

PART OF A CONTINUOUS
WOMEN'S MOVEMENT?

Was WEL part of a continuous women's movement that had ebbed and flowed during the previous century, or was it part of something new, the eruption of middle-class radicalism in the 1960s? Those who have written about the 'new' social movements tend to stress the timing of their appearance – when basic material concerns were satisfied and the increased number of university-educated young people could turn their attention to 'post-materialist' issues. The angry women's movements of the late 1960s and early 1970s emerged from anti-war and student movements and at first were slow to identify with their polite predecessors, as exemplified by an article in the 1974 collection of WEL papers, *From the Gilded Cage*, which confidently began: 'The women's movement in Australia is now a full two years old'.[1]

It is possible that every new wave of feminist protest starts out with sharp critique – not just of male-dominated society but also of preceding feminist organisations – and there may be stronger criticism of a mother's generation than of earlier generations.[2] Looking back, however, the succeeding waves of the women's movement seem remarkably similar. The rationale for women needing separate political space, free of the tutelage of men, remains consistent over generations of feminist activism: women wanted to be able to organise in their own way and identify their own political priorities. Even at the beginning of the new wave these continuities were felt quite strongly in some places, such as Perth, where Irene Greenwood of the previous generation of feminists taught the younger women how to set out chairs for a meeting. 'In a circle dears,' she said. 'Not in rows. Feminists don't sit in rows to talk, they sit facing each other'.[3]

The 'new' women's movement increasingly identified with and appropriated at least the more heroic moments and symbols of the movement's earlier history.[4] One of the clearest manifestations of the shift to identifying with a continuing women's movement came with the change in the political colours used by the 'second wave'. While at first red was often used, signifying closeness to other radical movements, from 1975 the International Women's Day marches in the major Australian cities were appropriating the purple, green and white used by the Women's Social and Political Union (WSPU) in the big London suffrage demonstrations before World War I.

Although the WSPU colours were originally adopted in another country, and for the purpose of distinguishing organisations within the suffrage movement from each other rather than unifying them, in public memory they had come to have much broader significations of sisterhood and feminist identity. Women who wore these colours, or even just purple, felt they showed that their wearers were part of a continuing struggle to achieve equality. Wearing the colours gave a sense of pride and identity, a feeling of 'connection with our foremothers' and of being 'part of herstory' (even though purple, green and white had not been adopted until 1908, when the struggle for the vote in Australia was largely over).[5]

The theorists of the 'new' social movements of the 1960s, particularly those in North America, tended to define social movements in terms of engagement in non-institutionalised and disruptive forms of action and hence to assume that movements had quite a limited lifespan. These theories were usually based on the experience of male-led movements. By contrast, the idea of 'abeyance', introduced by Verta Taylor, throws useful light on the trajectories of WEL and its predecessors.[6] Abeyance theory helps us to see the women's movement as persistent over time, with periods of intense activity interspersed with more unobtrusive activity, including the celebration of anniversaries and commemorative events. Viewed through this lens, WEL was part of a continuous movement stretching back over time, not simply part of the phenomenon of new social movements.

Women's movements have always operated at different levels and used diverse modes of action to a greater extent than can be captured by a singular focus on disruptive protest events. While 'dissent events' have been important[7], as for other social movements, in attracting media attention and getting a message out to a broader public, empirical evidence suggests that disruptive protests are not the primary defining feature of women's movements. In countries such as Australia, Canada and New Zealand, the first wave of the women's movement

WEL–Victoria 20th anniversary celebration, L to R, Katy Richmond, Jan Harper, Jocelyn Mitchell, Iola Mathews, Val Byth (co-ordinator), Joyce Nicholson, Beatrice Faust. *The Age*, 2 December 1992, p. 18. *Joe Sabljak/Courtesy The Age.*

rarely engaged in disruptive action as understood by today's social movement theorists. The fact that the first wave was 'polite' would disqualify it as a real social movement for some theorists, despite the challenge it represented to dominant norms and attitudes.

For over a hundred years the Australian women's movement engaged in advocacy, conducted through deputations, submissions and conferences, and only from time to time engaged in direct action. There has been continuity in terms of constituting woman as a political subject and seeking to remove the barriers to equal citizenship – but if we stayed with the definition of social movement as entailing disruptive or direct action, we should have to disregard women's advocacy as an indication of the presence of a movement. This, however, appears counter-intuitive and suggests that we need to look beyond such a definition if we are to adequately account for women's political history.

Another problem with defining social movements by reference to the use of disruptive forms of action relates to the interpretation of the relationship between social movements and the state. For some writers, disappearance off the streets and into public institutions is a sign that a movement is over because it has succeeded – bringing new people and new perspectives to the policy process. For others it is a sign of co-option, of buying off revolutionary potential. But social movements do not just disappear into existing public institutions. They may be responsible for creating a new constellation of institutions reflecting a movement's values and perspectives – for example, the institutionalising of women's movement values in services such as domestic violence refuges.[8] The absorption of activists into running women's services might deplete the numbers available for political action, but it provides the opportunity to model women's movement values for the ever-larger numbers of women seeking help.

Perhaps, instead of focusing on non-institutionalised and disruptive forms of action, we should focus more on the kind of elements highlighted in European social movement theories – the mobilising of collective identity and the sustaining of challenging discourses. When women's movements were in abeyance, this oppositional discourse only occasionally broke the surface of public life, continuing in a subterranean fashion through roneoed newsletters and correspondence, while the lack of acknowledgment of women's political history in schools and universities, and the absence of feminist publishing, further restricted public awareness. Nonetheless, women's advocacy groups preserved feminist norms and perspectives through decades that were unreceptive to such claims-making and were there to welcome the resurgence of feminist energy at the beginning of the 1970s.

WEL's predecessors

The early winning of the vote in Australia by no means signalled an end to women's movement organisations. In the post-suffrage era the 'non-party idea' took on renewed forms in all States, with the goal of getting women to use their vote effectively. One early example was the Women's Political Association, created by Vida Goldstein in Melbourne, which supported her various campaigns for federal parliament and in 1913 circulated a questionnaire to all Victorian candidates for federal parliament seeking their views on equal pay, equal opportunity for women in the new Commonwealth public service, equality in family law and protection of women from trafficking.

The non-party organisations proclaimed the need for women to stand together, regardless of class or party, to achieve equal citizenship and to protect the interests of women, children and the home. Their platforms generally included equal pay and equal opportunity, equal divorce laws and guardianship rights, and the right of married women to retain their nationality. There were also welfare-oriented demands relating to juvenile justice and child protection and the appointment of women as police, prison officers, jurors, Justices of the Peace and magistrates. There was advocacy on behalf of Aboriginal women[9], although many demands were couched in the dominant discourse of 'Britishness'.

The idea that women must use their new political rights in order to become equal citizens became part of the continuity of the women's movement. Equal citizenship meant equality of opportunity, responsibility and reward.[10] The idea that women had the responsibility as well as the right to contribute to public life appears in various forms in WEL's statements of aims – for example: 'WEL Australia is an independent organisation dedicated to creating a society where women's participation and potential are unrestricted, acknowledged and respected and where women and men share equally in society's responsibilities and rewards' (1998). This understanding framed the long campaign by the non-party associations and continued by WEL to ensure that women served on juries on an equal basis.

WEL's most obvious predecessor was the Australian Federation of Women Voters (AFWV), founded in 1921 by Bessie Rischbieth of the WA Women's Service Guilds and active for 60 years. It was Australia's first national women's advocacy body, and the conduit for emerging international norms of equal citizenship through its affiliation to the International Alliance of Women (IAW).[11] At its height the AFWV included twelve affiliated bodies from around Australia and played an important role in strengthening the international connections of Australian feminists. Some of its State-based affiliates, the Leagues of Women Voters and the Women's Service Guilds, outlasted it.

The establishment of a Women's Bureau to monitor women's employment was something the International Alliance urged on all its national affiliates, and the AFWV engaged in decades of lobbying before this was achieved in the 1960s.[12] It persisted with rating parliamentary candidates on their attitudes to equal pay and equal opportunity, and in 1966 its long-standing goal of the abolition of the Commonwealth marriage bar was finally achieved. In 1969 the AFWV was one of three women's organisations granted leave to intervene in the equal pay case before the Arbitration Commission. It had been involved in earlier national wage cases – for example, intervening in the early 1950s when employers applied to reduce women's wages from 75 to 60 per cent of the male basic wage.

The rating of candidates on equality issues by first-wave women's organisations was continued up until, and in some countries beyond, the arrival of Women's Liberation. The Swedish affiliate of the IAW, the Frederika Bremer Association (founded in 1884), was still interviewing party leaders about their position on women's issues in the 1960s. The Swedish association also regularly analysed party manifestoes for what they offered women. In Sydney, the United Associations of Women wrote to candidates in the 1972 federal election seeking their views on equal pay, ILO Convention ratification, family planning clinics and child-care centres. As their historian noted somewhat tartly, they were already administering their questionnaire while WEL was still constructing its election campaign.[13]

But by the 1970s, after so many decades of maintaining feminist advocacy through hard times, the AFWV membership was ageing and dwindling. Already in 1966 the head of the Women's Section in the Department of Labour had written to the departmental secretary that the AFWV was 'very strongly feminist in the narrower sense of the word – its methods and policies are those of fifty years ago'.[14] At its 1972 congress the AFWV's president, Mrs R.D. Collman, was reported as saying: 'Perhaps over the years we have not been forceful enough to achieve our aims ... We have been working for women's rights for a long time and are only too happy to see the emergence of keen young organisations with similar aims'.[15] She invited representatives of Women's Liberation and WEL to the triennial congress, and the AFWV joined in the lobbying on issues such as the sales tax on oral contraceptives.

Despite the welcome extended to the new generation, the older organisations were sometimes put out by how promptly they were eclipsed by WEL's high media profile. An activist from the Victorian League of Women Voters complained that the *National Times* appeared to think that WEL was the only women's organisation in Australia, instead of simply the newest.[16] Indeed, through lack of historical background, WEL was sometimes guilty of behaving as if it had invented an issue long the province of older women's organisations. A good example was the campaign by WEL–Tasmania to ensure equality in jury service (defeated by the Legislative Council in 1974 and not achieved until 1996).

In South Australia the League of Women Voters advised WEL on methods, including its own long-standing use of carefully prepared candidate questionnaires. When Ellinor Walker gave the valedictory address at the last meeting of the League in 1979, it was in the expectation that WEL could carry on the League's work, and a donation was provided for this purpose.[17] Walker had been a member and office-bearer of the League since 1914. She had wanted to join immediately after hearing an inspirational lecture on feminism by Vida Goldstein in 1912, but promised her father she would wait until she turned twenty-one. Viv Szekeres, a member of both WEL and Women's Liberation, has written about her delight in encountering League women at a meeting on prostitution law reform. The League women were probably well into their eighties, but their ideas were radical and they presented them with confidence:

> I came away feeling quite optimistic about our future as women. After all we would one day inevitably find ourselves the same age as the women from the League. For me to find a group of much older women who defied society's expectations for them to be either invisible or silent was reassuring. These women were still in the public arena fighting for what they believed to be right.[18]

The continuity between WEL and first-wave women's political advocacy was even more evident in Western Australia and was epitomised in Irene Greenwood. Greenwood was a hereditary feminist whose suffragist and pacifist mother, Mary Driver, had been a president of the Woman's Christian Temperance Union in Western Australia and an office bearer in the AFWV. During World War I Driver had climbed aboard a naval ship anchored at Albany to ask the Minister for Defence to close the hotels when the New Zealand troops were in town.[19] Her daughter inherited the feminism and pacifism but as a grown woman enjoyed a vermouth bianco. As a child in Albany, Greenwood had watched her parents writing up minutes by oil lamp and she too became an organisation woman. She became a professional radio broadcaster in the 1930s, encouraged by journalist and broadcaster Linda Littlejohn of the United Associations in Sydney and, like her mother, became an AFWV office-holder. She represented the AFWV on the National Advisory Committee for International Women's Year and spoke at the Women and Politics Conference in 1975. While she was in Canberra she addressed over 100 women at a WEL meeting on her life in the women's movement – emphasising the continuity of endeavour over the century.

The Perth-based Women's Service Guilds (founded 1909) had been a political home for Greenwood and her temperance mother. At about the time that WEL was being established in the eastern States, the Guilds were trying to recruit young blood. They called a meeting of daughters of members and out of this in March 1972 came the Harvest Guild, with Wendy Fatin as its president. She in turn helped recruit women politicised by the anti-Vietnam War movement and Women's Liberation.

But when the young women of the Harvest Guild heard that on the other side of Australia WEL had been created, they decided they should be part of it. Four of them, together with Pat Giles from Women's Liberation, travelled to Canberra for WEL's national conference in January 1973. They returned to set up the new organisation in Perth, using their Women's Liberation and Guild networks. WEL meetings were held in the Guilds' headquarters in Harvest Terrace, opposite Parliament House, and its establishment sounded the death knell for the Guilds' hopes of recruiting younger members.

Issues of sexual morality continued to mark a dividing line between the older and newer women's organisations. The older organisations had promoted sexual restraint for both sexes and had been deeply opposed to the regulation of prostitution, which they saw as directed only to making it safe for men. By contrast, WEL was campaigning for prostitution law reform and the rights of sex workers. The AFWV and its affiliates continued to be wary of moves to legalise prostitution, and hopeful that as equality between the sexes increased prostitution would decrease.[20]

Talks in the late 1970s, mediated by Greenwood and Giles, led to

IAW Congress, Sri Lanka, September 2002. L to R, Pat Richardson (WEL/IAW Membership Secretary), Priscilla Todd (WEL/IAW Secretary), Irene Dunsmuir (Union of Australian Women, Victoria), Chandrika Bandaranaike (President of Sri Lanka), Pat Giles (WEL/IAW President), Una Ellis (IAW hon. member), Pat Goble (League of Women Voters, Victoria). *Pat Richardson.*

the AFWV taking the decision to wind itself up in 1982 and pass on its international role to WEL. WEL inherited the role of the national affiliate of the IAW, benefiting from the latter's status with a plethora of international bodies including the ILO and diverse UN agencies. WEL members Pat Giles and Pat Richardson joined the IAW Board and in 1989 WEL, together with the Victorian League of Women Voters, hosted an IAW congress in Melbourne. In 1996 Giles became world president of the IAW and went on to serve three terms running up to its centenary in 2004.

One continuing concern of the IAW from the earliest days was the trafficking of women. This re-emerged as a major issue in the 1990s, again illustrating the continuity between the goals and actions of the women's movement from the past into the present, even though the issue of sex work had itself become divisive. The earlier generations of feminist activists had seen prostitution as incompatible with the dignity and worth of the human person, or with improvement in the status of women. This position was maintained by AFWV through the 1970s and continues in the IAW, strongly backed by its Scandinavian affiliates. In Sweden law reform in 1999 criminalised the buying of sex while decriminalising its sale, resulting in a significant decrease both in prostitution and trafficking.

Back in Australia, despite the differences over prostitution, the Women's Service Guilds supported WEL's campaign for women's policy machinery and equal opportunity legislation. But the Guilds' membership dwindled to become a single Guild before finally dissolving in 1997, after almost 90 years of lobbying for women's equality.[21] The League of Women Voters in Victoria is the last AFWV affiliate still in existence. In late 2004 Kerry Lovering took over both as League President and as Convenor of WEL, and in 2007 was helping plan the celebration of the forthcoming centenary of women's suffrage in Victoria.

In hindsight it seems obvious that WEL was part of a long tradition of women's non-party advocacy. At the beginning, however, the generation gap and the lack of media coverage of the older organisations meant that few WEL members had any idea of what they had been doing. An article in the 1980 *WEL Papers* was unable to name any forerunners of WEL apart from Catherine Helen Spence, the 19th century reformer and suffragist, although it did say that historians were now attempting to fill these gaps in knowledge.[22] The subsequent flourishing of the discipline of feminist history helped to strengthen the sense of being part of a continuous movement rather than a new one, and counterbalanced the tendency of young activists to believe that they had invented feminism.

Did reformism kill the women's movement?

WEL has sometimes been blamed for placing too much emphasis on 'moving into government'. It has been pointed out that without an effective women's movement working on the outside, it will not be long before a government will decide it is 'politically safe to purge itself of the demands of the women's movement'.[23] From this perspective, the Australian women's movement came to place too much reliance on Labor governments as a vehicle for achieving reforms:

> Many activists went from the streets into government bodies, universities and non-government organisations and, in the case of Women's Liberationists, into services for women. The dependence on an ALP government for funding then took its toll on many who previously had fought the system from without. The ensuing demobilisation left the movement ill-equipped to challenge the attacks that came during the 1980s and '90s from both ALP and Coalition governments.[24]

WEL members did seize opportunities to influence policy from the inside, which did mean that fewer women with political and policy skills were available for community-based politics. While women within government were able to direct resources to women in the community and enable more diverse groups to organise, dependence on public resources rendered these groups vulnerable to political change. The ebbing of the community-based women's movement in turn deprived feminists within government of their political base, for there was no longer a visible presence in the community for politicians to appease. Beyond women's services, whose policy advocacy and community education became increasingly constrained by competitive tendering and under-resourcing, there was little ongoing community activity to enlist support for change.

While it is widely accepted that feminist policy interventions within government cannot succeed without an outside political base[25], what is less clear is what determines the life-cycle of protest movements. In general the direct action phase of women's movements around the world did not seem to last much beyond five years, regardless of engagement or otherwise with the state. There is the natural phenomenon of burnout among those actively engaged in promoting social and policy change. As Iola Mathews observed as early as 1977, many dropped out simply because they could not stand the pace for long: 'With a few members and a shoe-string budget, it has always been difficult for anyone to be actively involved for long without being over-burdened with work'.[26]

It can be argued that the ebb and flow of the women's movement in the late 20th century was very similar to the cycle that had affected earlier manifestations of the movement. Reflecting this cycle, the word 'feminism' itself dropped in and out of fashion. In the 1930s, a long-time feminist activist in the United Kingdom observed the strong hostility shown by young women to the word and all it was assumed to connote. She pointed out that these young women were themselves products of the women's movement and the difficult and confusing conditions in which they lived were in part due to the changeover from old to new conceptions of women's place in society.[27]

In Australia too, 'feminism' came to connote something old-fashioned. An article published in the *Bulletin* in 1965, not long before the arrival of the 'second wave', pointed out there were no folk-songs for feminism and that feminists had been made to seem ridiculous soon after the achievement of political rights. The Feminist Club in King Street in Sydney was described as a 'pleasant backwater', while 'hard-core feminists' clustered around the League of Women Voters. The League, like the other affiliates of the AFWV, engaged in polite lobbying through letter-writing to ministers and other authorities. The Business and Professional Women's Association, with its engagement with equal pay, was seen as the most active and effective feminist organisation.[28] This image of feminism made it perhaps unsurprising that even when the second wave arrived, young women wanted to be seen as liberationists, not as feminists.

The term 'feminist' became important for WEL members as they rediscovered the continuity of the women's movement. The 1980 *WEL Papers* began with a period woodcut and a 1915 definition:

Mother, what is a feminist?

A feminist, my daughter,
Is any woman now who cares

To think about her own affairs
As men don't think she oughter.[29]

The term was to fall out of favour again among young women, however, and become a flashpoint for the inter-generational tensions of the 1990s. The pressures of combining work and family would be seen as the ambivalent legacy of feminism to the new generation. Moreover, for WEL, the media images of feminism, such as 'ugly, hairy legs, separatists, man-hating, fat', were a barrier to the recruitment of young women.[30] While these images were different from the scrawny, bespectacled and beaky-nosed images of the suffragists, they were just as hostile. The setting up of 'Young WEL' groups in the 1990s was not, in the long term, sufficient to overcome these problems, despite recruitment drives during university orientation weeks and a successful Young Feminism conference in Melbourne.

Quite apart from the limited lifespan of direct action and generational conflicts, there is also the more general phenomenon of youth disengagement from politics, at least as that term has traditionally been understood. In all Western democracies youth are now much less likely to join political parties or advocacy organisations, or even to vote, than the baby-boomer generation. The problem of how to engage young women who are not already politically engaged is a difficult one. As Eva Cox has commented:

> The younger generation is much more cynical about the political process – and it is very hard to find an argument as to why they should be involved. There is a sense in which it is all happening 'out there', it is all global. It is all elsewhere, it is all too hard.[31]

To some young women, including those doing gender studies at university, the increased salience of 'diversity' meant that a politics based on an assumed sisterhood appeared hopelessly simplistic. They saw the transfer of energies into micro-politics or 'small acts of disruption' as an indication that broader social movement solidarity was no longer possible in a world where diversity rather than sisterhood had taken centre stage. While feminist activism was still possible in different locations, the women's movement as such was seen to be over.[32] For others, however, identification with the struggles of the past and the linkage to the struggles of the present were strong enough to constitute evidence of its continuity. While they might not turn out to a demonstration to defend the community-based child-care program, the industrial relations system or gender-neutral tax principles, they could be relied on to protest against threats to abortion rights.

The emotional life of movements

Questions about the emotional life of social movements were not prominent when the new wave first appeared, but more recent research has emphasised not only the emotions that bring recruits into social movements, such as anger at injustices, but also the emotions that keep them there. While it may be hard to 'maintain the rage', the satisfactions of friendship can sustain continuing connection with a movement. This is particularly important when political opportunities contract and there are no longer the immediate payoffs that made participation so rewarding. Verta Taylor has pointed out how central the emotional life of movements is to their survival in hard times.[33] WEL was like other movement organisations insofar as the intense activity of the early days created enduring bonds. Lives as well as campaigns were shared and groups were often sustained by personal friendships.[34] On the negative side, these emotional ties could lead to organisational exit when ties were severed or when feelings were hurt, and serve as a barrier to the recruitment of younger women.

Only a decade after its founding, Kate White predicted that for the rising generation WEL would seem as middle-aged as the League of Women's Voters and the AFWV had seemed to WEL. While WEL had been youthful and slim in the 1970s, by the 1980s it was already 'a little thicker around the waistline'.[35] Attention turned in the 1990s to initiatives to attract young women, but they reported feeling patronised by more experienced older members. However, the existence of strong emotional bonds between long-standing members of social movement organisations has a positive as well as a negative side. While they may be an obstacle to organisational renewal, they may also enable organisational survival through long periods of abeyance.

One of the common features of both waves of the women's movement is the importance of newsletters as a means of maintaining community. In 1981 the editor of *Equality*, published for more than a quarter of a century by the NSW League of Women Voters, attended the celebration of the 100th issue of *WEL–Informed*, the most important and long-lasting of the WEL newsletters. In the 1970s and 1980s *WEL–Informed* was put together by a group led by Dorothy Simons and including Jan Aitkin, Edwina Doe, Diana Wyndham and cartoonist Chris Smith. Rosemary Webb, a member of the group in the late 1970s–early 1980s, describes the experience:

> The editorial group was a self-contained, supportive, inclusive women's collective. Those years were pre-desktop publishing and producing a print-ready journal meant literally cutting and pasting copy to fit a predetermined number of pages. Because of this the monthly meetings were at Ashleigh Gallagher's publishing business in Artarmon, with the collective arguing layout and pasting up content around a large worktable while sharing feminist perspectives and trading updates on WEL campaigning. The work and the range of expertise in the collective meant we could all contribute to and pick up technical skills in media and layout, as well as honing our negotiating skills through being just one remove from policy action. People were dedicated – most managed to turn up every month. In retrospect this was impressive, given that we all had work and carer commitments. And paste-up couldn't start 'til early evening when the room was free, so someone would bring snacks along, usually borrowing Diana's gleeful line 'I bought it myself'.[36]

Newsletters were produced by all WEL groups, with names such as *Broadsheet*, *WEL–Read*, *Alive and WEL*, *Ink–WEL*, *WEL–Spoken*, *WEL–ACTivist* and even at one stage *SWELter* (in Darwin). They provided gender analysis of the news of the day and often reproduced articles by feminist journalists such as Yvonne Preston, Adele Horin or Anne Summers. In Cairns, the newsletter produced for decades by Joan Trewerne provided a feisty dialogue with North Queensland sexism and the *Cairns Post*.

Humour was an important part of the newsletters, which featured feminist cartoons such as those by Judy Horacek. They also drew on the cartoons entered in the national awards for feminist cartoons run by WEL–WA in the 1990s.[37] An ever-popular feature was the 'pig pen' item, with sexist remarks of the month – for example, Justice John Gallop saying in an ACT custody case: 'Despite some serious errors of judgement in the past – such as taking the children to peace rallies and demonstrations – she had emerged as the parent who was more emotionally mature'.[38] Also popular were Sir Charles Court's remarks on retiring as Premier of Western Australia: 'My wife has played an important role in my career. She always packed my bag, sometimes at a moment's notice. She also brought up our five sons practically single handed ... There is nothing as beautiful as family life.'[39]

Building on such traditions of exposing the sexist remarks (and assumptions) of public figures were the Ernie Awards in Sydney, with which many WEL members were involved. The Ernies, instigated in 1993 by Meredith Burgmann, a Labor parliamentarian who became President of the NSW Legislative Council, were awarded for the most sexist or unhelpful comments made by public figures during the year and came in different categories including 'repeat offender', won by John Howard in 2003 for his comment that paid maternity leave as a solution to balancing work and family was 'intellectually insubstantial'. As many women as could be fitted into the parliamentary dining room (about 400) attended the annual dinners, where the awards were decided by the volume of booing, refereed by 'boo monitors'.

Inspired by the Ernies, in Canberra WEL launched the Gregs in 1999, named after Greg Cornwall, Speaker of the Legislative Assembly, who had suggested women's poor performance in the ACT election might have reflected men's resentment at the 'special treatment of women'. Comments were put up on a 'wall of shame' on the WEL–ACT website during the year and there was a boo-off, often at the Canberra café Tilley's, to decide the winner. Subversive activities of this kind help keep feminist discourses alive and maintain community. Laughing at sexism is just one aspect of how feminism gets handed on, along with the newsletters and e-lists that preserve feminism as a living language, waiting for its revitalisation by new speakers.

Characteristic of the 'second wave' and also an important part of its emotional life was the flowering of a feminist subculture, with feminist books, film, video, art and music. It was no longer true (if it ever were) that there were no folk songs for feminism. In earlier chapters we encountered the importance of songs such as 'I Am Woman, Hear Me Roar' and 'Don't Be Too Polite Girls'. Also popular was Robyn Archer's 'Menstruation Blues', an energetic blues treatment of a formerly taboo topic, and Judy Small's 'A Heroine of Mine' (about Jessie Street). The songbook prepared for the 1975 national WEL conference included some raunchy numbers but also 'Domestic Service', a version of 'Waltzing Matilda' written by Edna Ryan and including the lines:

> And her ghost may be heard as you pass by that billabong,
> Matilda won't make any more morning tea.

The changing character of International Women's Day

While feminist culture had continuing vitality, street marches, street theatre, sit-ins and other forms of direct action by the women's movement became less common after the 1970s. In the West, the period of radical political action of the women's movement is generally seen as ending in about 1979. One striking illustration of the movement's changing repertoire is the trajectory of International Women's Day (IWD) celebrations. From 1928 the Communist Party organised IWD rallies and marches in Australia with men forming the majority of participants. In the 1950s and 1960s the Communist-inspired Union of Australian Women (UAW) attempted to revive IWD.[40] Street rallies were hard to organise, due to the attitude of State and local authorities, but UAW members sometimes engaged in peace walks with slogans printed on aprons or shopping bags to get around the ban on placards. Closely watched by ASIO, other IWD functions featured international themes and included luncheons, concerts, folk dancing and even an exhibition of Russian dolls.[41]

Then suddenly, in 1972, the big street marches of Women's Liberation arrived, and new open-ended collectives took over IWD, displacing the UAW stalwarts. Women's Liberation, WEL and union women tussled with young Trotskyists on the organising committees and a full range of activities took place on the day, from rallies and marches to street theatre, feminist songs and women's dances in the evening. In 1972 the street theatre held after the march was 'The Stages of a Woman's Life', portraying each stage of acquiring womanhood and marriage up to addiction to Bex powders.

By the 1990s, however, IWD marches had shrivelled and were again being replaced by a range of less disruptive events. These ranged from large United Nations Development Fund for Women (UNIFEM) fund-raising breakfasts and lunches (for example, with over 1000 women present in Sydney), to government and university functions and forums and even 'corporate networking events'. Women's units and information services put out extensive calendars of events sponsored by local councils and other agencies, but they were celebratory rather than claims-making like the street marches of the 1970s. In Sydney in 2008 Anne Barber of WEL, together with Beth Eldridge of the Older Women's Network, tried to revive IWD. With the help of the City of Sydney they organised for almost 200 handsome purple, green and white banners to be flown in the Central Business District, with sponsors including the Office for Women and the YWCA, and donations from unions. This provided a striking visual backdrop for the 100th anniversary of an event begun by socialist women in New York. Like the IWD banners flying outside the ACT Legislative Assembly (initiated by former WEL–ACT Convenor, Judy Downey, when advising the Chief Minister), they helped illustrate the shift to commemoration rather than contestation.

 Reclaim the Night march, Sydney, mid-1990s. *WEL–NSW office.*

It was not only IWD that changed its character as the women's movement moved into a different phase. Reclaim the Night marches had been held in Australia since 1978 and provided a symbolic statement of the right of women to go out at night safely, without a male protector. They were dramatic occasions with candles, drums and whistles, and sometimes firesticks and other elements of street theatre. At their height they attracted about 6000 marchers in both Melbourne and Sydney as well as thousands in other cities. The events were usually organised by a collective and women's services were often involved. In Perth and Sydney, WEL played a particularly important role.

Reclaim the Night dwindled in the capital cities in the late 1990s and was largely ignored in the mainstream media. In 2006 the Sydney march was organised by young women from the Sydney University women's collective, who upset some of the older participants by being unaware of the tradition that men should not be included among the marchers – an issue increasingly the subject of dispute.[42] In Adelaide, however, Reclaim the Night was being revived that year by the Office for Women headed by former WEL–ACT Co-Convenor Sandy Pitcher, and involving more groups like Filipina women.

Meanwhile, White Ribbon Day on 25 November had gained increased media visibility. Initiated by Canadian men in 1991, in the aftermath of the Montreal massacre of women engineering students, it was subsequently endorsed by the United Nations as a statement of men's commitment to stop the violence against women. With its Saatchi & Saatchi ads and footballer sponsors, the White Ribbon campaigns, co-ordinated by UNIFEM with the Australian Federal Police and other partners, gradually displaced the more contentious repertoire of Reclaim the Night.

Protests over rape in war also changed their character. In the early 1980s, hundreds of women, including WEL women, were involved in Anzac Day actions. Sixty-one women were arrested in Canberra in 1981 and the following year 750 women laid a wreath before the official march began and then stood on the hill above the War Memorial holding their banner 'In memory of all women raped in all wars' so that all could see it during the official ceremony.[43] However, while the visible actions around Anzac Day disappeared, in the 1990s Australian feminist lawyers were helping establish new international norms whereby rape was defined as a war crime. Hence the change in political repertoire did not necessarily mean an end to political engagement, although it might now be taking place in more distant forums such as those provided by multilateral bodies.

Remembering the past

What is the role of 'memory work' in sustaining social movements once the initial period of intense engagement and direct action is over? In the United Kingdom, the achievement of the vote was followed by the creation of groups such as the Suffragette Fellowship, which focused on preserving the memory of the heroic days of the women's movement through setting up archives and getting banners returned from the police. Later, when they had succeeded in having a statue of Mrs Pankhurst put up at Westminster, there were annual ceremonies in front of it.

These activities enshrined a particular narrative of sisterhood and of women's collective agency – the 'sisterhood is powerful' theme that was to re-emerge in the second wave. As we have seen, Pankhurst symbols, such as the purple, white and green of the WSPU, took on new life in the 1970s as a symbol of the women's movement in general. The same cycle, from militant protests to commemorative activities, can be perceived in the more recent wave. The Women's Peace Camp at Greenham Common, for example, famous in the 1980s, was formally closed after almost 20 years to make way for a commemorative and historic site, which includes a nearly two-metre high sculpture of a campfire within a circle of seven Welsh standing stones, and a spiral sculpture with the words 'You can't kill the spirit'.

In Australia, the ageing membership of first-wave women's non-party organisations became increasingly absorbed in commemorative activities. For example, by the 1980s the League of Women Voters in Victoria was conducting annual events celebrating the proclamation of women's suffrage and of women being able to stand for Parliament. In recent years these have included annual young women's leadership seminars at Parliament House. The League also organised memorials for suffragist Vida Goldstein, including a plaque in the grounds of Parliament House, on which flowers were placed as part of its annual commemorations. The cultivation of public memory of women's political achievements is an important function of commemorative activities and is often linked in this way to encouraging more women into political activity.

After the initial burst in the 1970s and 1980s, many WEL members were unable to continue with such intense policy engagement, but still enjoyed the community provided by commemorative activities. The confidence-building they had experienced tended to lead to full-time careers, and where women continued to be active it was often through more specialised vocational bodies. The same patterns within

WEL–New Zealand led to its disbanding as a national organisation in 2004. But while few were available anymore for submission-writing, hundreds of women could be gathered for milestone commemorative events such as celebrating the 20th and 30th anniversaries of different groups, and the writing of their histories.

In Perth, the centenary of women's suffrage provided outstanding commemorative opportunities. In 1997 WEL successfully applied for funding for a 'mile-long' suffrage banner to commemorate a famous WCTU suffrage petition of the 1890s. WCTU members had collected signatures on sheets of foolscap, which were pasted onto a 'mile-long' length of cloth and rolled up for presentation to Parliament.[44] The commemorative banner consisted of 220 panels prepared by women's groups and schools, celebrating women's diversity and struggles over the century, and featured panels by continuing WCTU groups with their white ribbons, as well as panels by Indigenous women and women's units in government. Hundreds of women carried it in the IWD march in 1999 and it was again displayed at the launch of the suffrage precinct in Kings Park. The following year WEL made a CD-ROM to record the artwork and history of the project.

In Sydney the Anne Conlon Memorial Lecture, inaugurated by the Women's Advisory Council after Conlon's early death in 1979, was to be important feminist gathering for the next 20 years. Conlon had been a founding member of WEL and contributed to major submissions on industrial and poverty issues before joining the Women's Co-ordination Unit in the Premier's Department. In Melbourne the Mary Owen Dinner, in honour of another leading WEL member, became a major event in feminist calendars. Inaugurated in 1986 to mark Owen's retirement as co-ordinator of the Working Women's Centre, the dinner was also held annually for 20 years, attracting around 600 women and featuring prominent feminist speakers. In Canberra the ongoing Pamela Denoon Lecture was inaugurated in 1989 in memory of the former co-ordinator and regularly attracts an audience of around 300 for speakers ranging from politicians to judges and cultural figures, including Aboriginal activists.

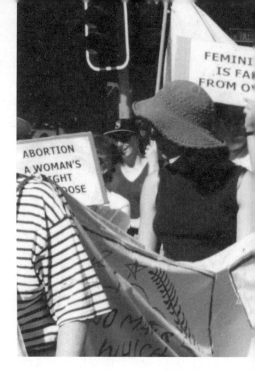

Carrying the suffrage
banner on International
Women's Day, Perth
1999. *WEL–WA CD-ROM*.

The election of an avowedly conservative federal government in 1996 had a significant impact on WEL. In the face of the unreceptive attitude of the Coalition government to policy advocacy on gender equity, there was a search for 'good news' stories that might sustain WEL values in a hostile environment. One such story was the 30th anniversary in 1996 of the abolition of the Commonwealth marriage bar, which had for so long cost married women their jobs. A forum was organised and a history prepared, documenting the feminist struggles against the bar and the manoeuvres of the Menzies government to ward off reform. In 1961, for example, a federal election year, the Menzies Cabinet decided not to lift the bar, but also not to reveal the decision, 'so as not to provoke the feminists'.[45] The 'feminists' undoubtedly included the AFWV, whose election questionnaire that year had included the issue.

WEL's celebratory forum, and the launch of the documentary history by the Public Service Commissioner, Peter Shergold, resulted in a meeting room in the Public Service Commission in Canberra being named in honour of Merle Thornton for her role in the campaign. Another Canberra initiative was Women's History Month, devised by WEL executive officer Helen Leonard and launched in 2000. In her life

before WEL, in the Nursing Mothers' Association, Leonard had established Breast-feeding Awareness Month. Women's History Month was a response to the conservative political environment and the need to find projects that were unthreatening but kept alive feminist values. WEL had lost its operational funding and there was a desperate need to find a 'safe' project that might attract future funding from a very conservative federal government. So unlike the other commemorative projects described here, Women's History Month had the subtext of trying to generate funds that could support WEL's ongoing policy and advocacy work (for example, through paying the rent for the national office).

Women's History Month became popular with Commonwealth and State libraries and collecting institutions and became a major event each March. It did not serve its intended purpose of helping shore up WEL's financial position, however. After Leonard's sudden death in October 2001, Women's History Month was taken over by the National Foundation of Australian Women and has continued to flourish. The NFAW has initiated other successful commemorative activities, including the Australian Women's Archive Project and the 30-year celebration of International Women's Year.

Both the NFAW Archives Project and the Jessie Street National Women's Library reflected the determination of second-wave activists that this time around knowledge of women's contribution to history would not be lost. The Jessie Street Library was in part the brainchild of Lenore Coltheart, originally active in WEL in Darwin and subsequently a political scientist and biographer of Jessie Street. The Library has flourished, despite frequent changes of location in its early years – it moved into the Ultimo Community Centre in late 2005. It is staffed by volunteers and relies on fund-raising events and talks, including those organised for Women's History Month. In 2006 the Chair of the Library Board was Jozefa Sobski, also Convenor of WEL–NSW. Meanwhile the National Library of Australia has been assiduous in recording feminist activists for its oral history collection, both as interviewers and interviewees, so that the joy as well as the heartbreak of 1970s feminism might be conveyed to later generations.

Another commemorative project honouring a feminist active in WEL, both in Sydney and Canberra, is the annual Clare Burton Lecture, initiated in 1999 after her sudden death from cancer. The lectures involve collaboration between a number of universities, State women's advisers and surviving gender equity agencies and are delivered in each capital city, helping raise funds for a memorial scholarship to support research in gender equity. Meanwhile, in Sydney, the annual Edna Awards were founded by WEL in 1998 to honour Edna Ryan's life and tireless campaigning. When she died in 1997 at the age of 92, all the major broadsheets and tabloids ran stories and obituaries with headlines such as 'a fighter to the finish'.[46] The Ednas honour feminists in a range of categories, including 'Grand Stirrer', awarded in 2006 to Tegan Wagner, the 14-year old victim of group rape who identified herself to encourage other victims to speak out. In 2001 WEL–Victoria followed this trend by establishing the Vida Goldstein Awards to provide recognition of feminist endeavour.

But while feminist memory is being well preserved, one of the failings of the recent women's movement may be the failure to develop or maintain popular publications. Feminist newsletters and websites provide resources for the already converted rather than making feminist insights available to a broader audience. Joan Bielski suggests that feminist writers and academics now tend to talk to one another and have difficulty in sharing their ideas or inspiring others – unlike Betty Friedan or Germaine Greer a generation or so ago.[47] Feminist blogs, sharing insights, frustrations and commentary, may be a partial exception for a younger generation.

 Still marching! Jenny Forster and Rhianna Keen carrying the WEL banner, International Women's Day, Sydney 2006. *Gail Radford.*

Conclusion

WEL has become part of the continuing history of the Australian women's movement, and its own organisational history has reproduced some of the patterns of earlier phases of the women's movement, from which at first it seemed so different. WEL, like its predecessors, has an outstanding record of policy engagement and women's advocacy. It shared much of their repertoire while giving the women's movement a new professionalism and media visibility. Unlike many of its predecessors, WEL was initially blessed by a favourable political environment that enabled it to make some rapid changes to the political agenda.

Against the odds, WEL made discrimination against women visible to politicians and persuaded them of the need for legislative remedies. To remove the onus from the victim to bring about change, WEL pressed on to make organisations responsible for identifying and removing the stumbling blocks for women, and brought issues from women's lives, such as child care and domestic violence, onto the centre stage of electoral politics. It also finally disposed of the formal barriers to equal pay, if not the gender bias in work evaluation. It introduced, at least for a time, an understanding into government that policy was likely to have a different impact on men and women and thus that it was important to subject policy proposals to expert gender analysis.

WEL not only helped to bring about these large changes for women in the policy environment, it also touched the lives of a generation of women who became caught up in its activities. It gave many a new confidence that things did not have to go on being more of the same; that women could shape their own future. It produced the joy of being taken seriously, of making policy not the tea. Seeing change coming out of a Gestetner machine was an empowering experience and few looked back. Thanks to WEL, women even began to appear in political science textbooks.

From the 1990s, however, shifts in the political landscape and the increased dominance of the language of the market made it more and more difficult for equity arguments to be heard. WEL was reduced to having to argue for domestic violence prevention in terms of the cost to the economy of lost working days and the use of emergency services, not in terms of women's rights. Nevertheless, like its predecessors, WEL continued to commemorate and affirm feminist values and to spin off feminist endeavours in a range of unexpected locations and vocations – even feminist firefighters.

To see WEL as part of an ongoing women's movement that has taken different forms over time, some more visible than others, helps situate it in relation to whatever the future holds. Ultimately WEL was unable to prevent the whole series of market-oriented 'reforms' that undid so much of what it was trying to achieve in terms of employment equity and social provision. But while the immediate successor generation may be able to see WEL's failures more clearly than its achievements, that is not the end of the story. The records of WEL have been stored up for the future, to inspire women with the idea that there is such a thing as sisterhood, and that it can be powerful. It is an idea that will come around again.

APPENDIX

A1 Issues for those attending the 1975 WEL national conference

Issue	%
All women's issues	42
Education	29
Discrimination	27
Employment/equal rights	19
Childcare/children	19
Abortion/contraception	13
Women in politics	10

SOURCE Doe, Report on the Survey of WEL Members at the 1975 National Conference, Table 8. N = 221

A2 WEL national conferences

Year	Conference title	Venue and date
1973	1st national conference *The future of WEL*	Burgmann College, ANU, Canberra 19–21 January
1974	2nd national conference	La Trobe University, Melbourne 18–20 January
1975	3rd national conference *The future and future action by WEL*	Women's College, University of Sydney 24–27 January
1976	4th national conference	WA Secondary Teachers College, Perth 24–26 January
1977	5th national conference *Women in isolation*	Mt Gravatt CAE 6–8 May

Year	Conference title	Venue and date
1978	6th national conference	Burgmann College, ANU, Canberra 17–19 February
1979	7th national conference	Lincoln College, Adelaide 16–18 February
1980	8th national conference *Women and power*	London Hotel, Melbourne 25–27 April
1981	9th national conference *Strategies, action programs and ideas for the 1980s*	University of NSW, Sydney 4–5 July
1982	10th national conference *WEL beyond the patriarchy— Strategies for the 80s*	Turner Primary School, Canberra 2–4 October
1983	11th national conference	Murdoch University, Perth 22–23 October
1987	12th national conference *Federal election strategies*	Swinburne Institute of Technology, Melbourne 14–15 July
1992	13th national conference *Looking back—Moving forwards*	ANU, Canberra 25–27 January
1996	14th national conference *Women's rights—Human rights*	University of Technology, Sydney 26–28 January
1999	15th national conference *Women: Staking our claim*	Point Walter Conference Centre, Perth 16–18 April
2000	16th national conference *Making it WEL for women*	ANU, Canberra 1–3 December
2004	17th national conference *Is Australian democracy working for women?*	Sydney Mechanics' School of Arts 12–13 June

A3 WEL National Co-ordinators*

Aug 1978–Feb 79	Maria De Leo
Feb 79–Sept 82	Yvonne Carnahan
Oct 82–March 84	Pamela Denoon
March–Sept 1984	Lorelle Thompson
Oct 84–Dec 84	Jo Morgan
Jan–Feb 1985	Lynne Gallagher (a/g)
March 85–July 86	Jane Elix
Sept 86–March 87	Lynn Lee
May–Sept 1987	Glenys Rogers
Sept 87–Feb 88	Lynn Lee
March–Nov 1988	Joy Taylor
Dec 88–April 89	Nooshin Guitoo
June 89–Feb 91	Anne-Marie Mioche
March 91–Dec 94	Ann Wentworth
June–Aug 1992	Julie McCarron-Benson (a/g)
Jan 95–April 96	Ingrid McKenzie
April 96–Jan 97	Rivera Morton-Radovsky
April 97–Sept 98	Lyn Peryman
Sept 98–April 2000	Helen Leonard
June 2000–Aug 01	Erica Lewis (a/g)
Sept 2001–Oct 03	Sandy Killick

* The national co-ordinator position began in 1978 as national communication officer, turned into national co-ordinator in 1982, into executive officer in 1997 and then into unpaid chairperson.

A4 Founding of selected second-wave women's organisations

1969	Council of Single Mothers and their Children (later NCSMC)
1969–70	Women's Liberation groups
1972–73	WEL
1974	Australian Women's Education Coalition
1975	Women's Action Alliance
1979	Women Who Want to be Women (later Endeavour Forum)
1982	National Association of Community-Based Children's Services
1986	Association of Non-English Speaking Background Women of Australia
	Australian Women's Health Network

1989	National Foundation for Australian Women
1992	Women into Politics
1992	CAPOW!
1992	WESNET (Women's Services Network)
1993	Australian Women in Agriculture
1995	Women with Disabilities Australia

A5 Mentions of **WEL** in Federal Parliament 1981–2005

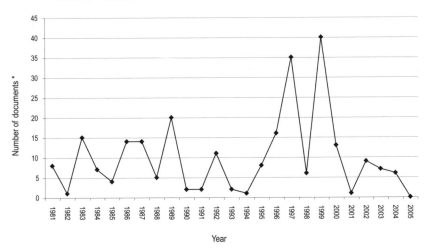

SOURCE House of Representatives, Senate and Committee Hansards

A6 Appointment of **Women's** Advisers in States and Territories

Jurisdiction	Year
Tasmania	1976*
Victoria	1976
South Australia	1976
NSW	1977
NT	1982
WA	1983
ACT	1985
Queensland	1990

* Abolished 1982, reinstated 1989

A7 Ministers Assisting the Prime Minister for the Status of Women, Hawke and Keating governments

1983–88	Senator Susan Ryan
1988–90	Senator Margaret Reynolds
1990–93	Wendy Fatin MP
1993	Senator Rosemary Crowley
1993–94	Ros Kelly MP
1994–96	Dr Carmen Lawrence MP

NOTES

Introduction

1   Fasteau & Lobel, 'Rating the candidates', p. 78.
2   Anderson, 'The MPs who care and the MPs who don't', p. 1.
3   Henry Mayer, 'Politics and the egghead', *Australian*, 14 May 1974.
4   Katy Richmond, Memo to WEL groups throughout Australia, 'Circulation of reports/submissions/kits etc', 18 August 1973.
5   WEL–NSW in *WEL Reports 1973–74*, p. 4.
6   Grahame, 'Researching WEL'.

Chapter 1

1   *Sun*, 22 January 1973, pp. 7, 8, 32.
2   'Women plan for greater role', *Mercury*, 22 January 1973, p. 2.
3   Ryan, Autobiographical writing, p. 2.
4   Lake, *Getting Equal*, p. 221.
5   Fasteau & Lobel, 'Rating the candidates'.
6   Nicholson, 'Destination uncertain', in Grimshaw & Strahan, *The Half Open Door*, pp. 152–153.
7   Aitkin et al, 'The World of WEL (NSW)', p. 186; McCarron-Benson, *WELWomen*, p. 27.
8   DeBats, 'Reminiscing about WEL', p. 9.
9   Glezer et al., 'WEL strategy, 1972', p. 178.
10 'The dilemma of a woman voter', *Daily Telegraph*, 30 November 1972.
11 Sally White, *Age Women Voters' Guide*, 20 November 1972, p. 4.
12 *National Times*, 20 November 1972; *Age*, 23 November 1972; *New York Times*, 26 November 1972.
13 Reid, 'Creating a policy for women', p. 145.
14 'It's all very WEL to woo women voters', *Sunday Telegraph*, 19 November 1972, p. 23.
15 Information from Deborah McCulloch and Karla Tan, who provided the authorisation.
16 Telegrams to Gail Wilenski, 10 & 11 November 1972.
17 Hooper, 'The emergence of contemporary feminist groups in Australia', Appendix 1.
18 Letter from Beatrice Faust to Biff McDougall (Ward), 3 April 1972.
19 'Women want the answers', *Advertiser*, 18 July 1972; '13 "angry" SA women to lobby MPs, unions', *Sunday Mail,* 22 July 1972. In its 20th anniversary history, WEL–South Australia was able to list 1000 past and present members (Sloniec, *WEL*, pp. 43–48).
20 ASIO files on WEL (1972–73), National Archives of Australia, Series No. A6122, Accession No. 2004/00686598.
21 Robinson in Preddy, *The WEL Herstory*, p. 4.
22 Degens, *From Canberra to Coffs Harbour*, p. 134.
23 'Canberra: City of unemployable wives', *Australian*, 30 June 1972.

24 Helen Bell & Susan Smith, 'The socio-economic and political characteristics of the members of WEL', 1973 survey quoted in Martin, 'The Women in WEL', p. 12.
25 'The march of Women's Lib gathers strength', *Advertiser*, 30 July.
26 Attwood, 'Rescue and a gift', p. 19.
27 Survey of WEL membership, *Broadsheet* 2 (3), 1974.
28 Luck, 'Not a dinner party', p. 103.
29 Jones, 'Rebel of God's police'. Cf Doe, 'Report on the Survey of WEL members at the 1975 WEL National Conference'.
30 Eatock, 'There's a snake in my caravan', p. 25.
31 Letter from Patricia Jones, Secretary WEL–Tasmania to Miss EM Backhouse, Acting General Secretary, Tasmanian Teachers' Federation, 29 May 1974.
32 Maureen Worsley, Letter, *WEL–ACT Newsletter* 17, 11 June 1974, p. 7.
33 DeBats, 'Reminiscing about WEL', p. 10; cf Ryan, Autobiographical writing, p. 35.
34 McCarthy, *Don't Fence Me In*, p. 102.
35 Ryan, Autobiographical writing, p. 33.
36 McCulloch, 'Twenty-one years old!'
37 Kate Basham, Letter to family in the UK, 6 September 1973.
38 Meredith Ardlie (Stokes), WEL history survey.
39 Don Aitkin, 'Women, it's time to change tactics – be single-minded', *National Times*, 16–21 April 1973, p. 3.
40 'WEL is a Feminist, Non-Party Political Lobby Group', WEL–Sydney, c. 1977; see also 'What is WEL?', WEL–ACT nd (c. 1973).
41 Preddy, *The WEL Herstory*, p. 6.
42 Katy Richmond, Letter to *The Age*, 4 November 1972.
43 Iola Mathews, 'Contraception: Most women fear and dislike the pill', *National Times*, 4 June 1977.
44 Doe, 'Report on the Survey of WEL Members at the 1975 WEL National Conference', p. 2.
45 Hooper, 'The emergence of contemporary feminist groups in Australia', p. 14.
46 'All's well', *Bulletin*, 13 January 1973, p. 11.
47 Bernie McWilliams, 'Sexist Discrimination in Employment', *WEL–Brisbane Newsletter*, May 1975, reprinted *WEL–ACT Newsletter*, 31 October 1975, p. 12.
48 Helen Glezer interview by Gail Radford, 16 February 2002.
49 'Minister on women's side over unfair pay scales', *Sydney Morning Herald*, 24 May 1973; 'WEL wants Government to ratify equal pay convention', *Australian*, 24 May 1973; 'A word to give 500 000 women a rise', *Australian*, 26 May 1973.
50 Bielski, 'Women in the workforce', p. 75. (Paper presented at the first WEL–NSW State conference.)
51 'Women's rights', *Australian*, 21 November 1973, p. 5; Geraldine Pascall, 'For conduct unbecoming of WEL's seal of disapproval', *Australian*, 17 November 1973.
52 In the WEL history survey 32 per cent of the respondents from WEL–ACT had a Women's Liberation background, compared with 24 per cent of those from elsewhere.
53 The other organisation involved was ALRA.
54 *Commonwealth of Australia Parliamentary Debates*, House of Representatives, Vol. 83, p. 1968, 10 May 1973.
55 Allan Barnes, 'Conscience yields to muscle', *Age*, 11 May 1973.
56 *WEL–NSW Newsletter*, 20 June 1974, p. 15.
57 Sawer, 'Wearing your politics on your sleeve'.
58 WEL–ACT, Minutes, 6 March 1973.
59 Reade, 'Struggling to be heard', p. 213; Castley & Daniels, 'WEL and sex roles', p. 6.
60 Cohen, *The Sisterhood*, pp. 250–51; Rhode, 'Media images, feminist issues', p. 695.
61 Comment by Enid Conochie, WEL history survey.

62   Pamela Thornley, Letter to the Editor, *Age*, 28 June 1972.
63   Nicholson, 'The Women's Electoral Lobby and women's employment', pp. 47–8.
64   Union secretary quoted in Hooper, 'The emergence of contemporary feminist groups in Australia', p. 21; 'Women drive for equality', *Herald*, 25 August 1973.
65   Hilary Freeman & Diana Gribble, 'Our say: Let women man trains and trams', *Herald*, 5 April 1974, p. 4.
66   Canberra Women's Liberation Newsletter, August 1972, p. 3; Megan Stoyles, 'Women's Electoral Lobby slates sales tax, custom duty on the pill', *Australian Financial Review*, 26 July 1972, p. 3.
67   McCarthy, *Don't Fence Me In*, p. 102.
68   For example, Tilly, *Social Movements*.
69   'Candidates quizzed by Tas. women', *The Examiner*, 24 November 1972, p. 12; Noel Rait, 'Women label the Federal hopefuls', *Advertiser*, 9 November 1972; Anne Summers 'Women out to rock the vote', *National Times*, 1–6 May 1972, p. 7.
70   WEL activist Eve Mahlab had been an unsuccessful contender for Liberal preselection in Higgins.
71   'WEL survey shows candidates "paternal"', *Courier-Mail*, 27 November 1974.
72   Kristine Neill, 'Hell for women and horses', *Sydney Morning Herald*, 7 October 1980; Helen Dash, 'Canberra kit ensures survival', *Courier-Mail*, 15 October 1980.
73   Edna Ryan, Autobiographical writing, p. 24; Anne Levy in Sloniec, *WEL*, p. 3.
74   WEL member Anne Conlon happened to be standing as a Labor candidate in this safe Liberal seat, as had Edna Ryan almost twenty years before.
75   Sloniec, *WEL*, p. 3.
76   *WEL–Victoria Broadsheet* 1 (10), November 1972, p. 14.
77   Cited in WEL–ACT Submission to the Attorney-General's Department, 'Human Rights for Women', 19 November 1973, p. 2. See also Scutt, 'Legislating for the right to be equal', pp. 230–31.
78   'End this bias against women now – Cameron', *Sydney Morning Herald*, 16 November 1972.
79   'Minister asked to upgrade the status of women', *Canberra Times*, 24 May 1973.
80   'What women want from their adviser', *Sydney Morning Herald*, 12 April 1973.
81   Mungo MacCallum, 'The women who govern Labor', *Nation Review*, 9 August 1973.
82   For more detail see Sawer & Groves, *Working from Inside*.
83   *WEL–Victoria Broadsheet* 3 (26), April 1974, pp. 5–6.
84   Ryan, *Catching the Waves*, pp. 151–2.
85   Summers, 'Women', pp. 194–5. Cf 'Women's delegation gets PM's ear on women's issues', *Age*, 10 May 1973.

Chapter 2

1   Sawer, *The Ethical State?*
2   Gail Wilenski & Margo Snyder, 'The relationship between WEL and Women's Lib', *Canberra Times*, 21 February 1973; Graham, 'Borrowing from each other', p. 4.
3   Reade, 'Struggling to be heard', p. 199. For the comment on Sydney see Graham, 'Borrowing from each other', p. 3.
4   Mercer, *The Other Half*, Editor's note. The authors' names were provided in the 1977 reprint.
5   Mercer, 'The History of WEL', p. 395.
6   Mercer & Miller, 'Liberation – Reform or revolution', p. 457.
7   Radicals control women's shelters', *Courier-Mail*, 2 September 1976.
8   'Radical feminists run Canberra', *News Weekly*, 19 May 1982, p. 5. *News Weekly* is a publication of the National Civic Council. The Labor leader was Robyn Walmsley.

9   Taylor, 'Readers writing *The First Stone* media event', p. 83.
10   Liz Conor, 'Letter to the Daughters of Feminism', Posted to Ausfem-Polnet, 26
     November 2004. See also Campo, 'Childless but not by choice'.
11   'Middle class on the march', *Australian*, 10 October 1973; Doe, 'Report on the
     Survey of WEL Members at the 1975 WEL National Conference', Table 26.
12   Bielski, 'Women in the workforce', p. 66.
13   Ryan, Autobiographical writing, p. 42.
14   Martin, 'The Women in WEL', pp. 13–5.
15   Ibid, pp. 16–7.
16   *WEL–Reports 1973–74*, pp. 7–8.
17   Atkin, 'In retrospect', pp. 95–6.
18   Sloniec, *WEL*, p. 28.
19   Martin, 'The women in WEL', p. 17.See also Faust interview in *WEL Papers
     1973/74*, p . 10.
20   Humphreys, 'Conform you little bastards or else', p. 15.
21   Sloniec, *WEL*, pp. 17; 23.
22   Atkin, 'In retrospect', p. 96.
23   Henderson, *Marking Feminist Times*, p. 178.
24   O'Shane, 'Is there any relevance in the women's movement for Aboriginal
     women?'; Burgmann, 'Black sisterhood'; Reade, 'Limited gestures'.
25   Letter from WEL–Townsville to WEL–Australia, 15 August 1974; WEL–Port
     Augusta at WEL national conference 1974.
26   Buchanan, 'Aborigines and the W.E.L. Conference', p. 6; WEL national conference
     resolutions, 1976; 'New WEL group', *Sydney Morning Herald*, 28 January 1976.
27   *WEL–WA Broadsheet* 3 (12), 1976, cited in Brankovich, 'Burning down the house', p.
     54.
28   'Special needs of migrant women', *Age*, 21 July 1973; 'Jobless women's plea on
     compo', *Sun*, 23 July 1973.
29   'Child-care needs', *Sydney Morning Herald*, 17 August 1976. See also Philida Hoy,
     'Child-care priorities', Letter to Editor for WEL Children's Services Group, *Canberra
     Times*, 7 September 1976.
30   Cooper, 'The Australian Disability Rights Movement', pp. 93; 96–97.
31   *WEL–NSW, Supplementary Newsletter* 3, October 1972, p. 3.
32   The WEL members were Chris Hollis and Margery Webster. 'WEL gears up for
     State poll', *Chronicle-Dispatch* (Wangaratta), 5 March 1973.
33   'A short history of WEL Gold Coast', *WEL–NSW Newsletter*, 23, June 1974, p. 21.
34   'WEL formed in Warrnambool', *Standard* (Warrnambool), 21 April 1973.
35   Gunn, 'Women's political mobilisation in rural Victoria'.
36   Ibid, p. 2.
37   Richmond, 'Notes on my first year and a half', p. 67.
38   Shirley Suggate-Jones, WEL history survey.
39   Margaret Boetcher, WEL history survey.
40   Pam Casey, 'What country women are up against', WEL, *The WEL Papers*, p. 56.
41   Roberts & Stewart, *We're Not Ladies, We're Women*, p. 9.
42   'All's not WEL in country', *Age*, 15 April 1978; 'Country cousins battle on', *Age*, 26
     February 1982.
43   Betty McLean, WEL history survey.
44   Bulbeck, *Living Feminism*, p. 141.
45   *Cairnsweek*, 30 July 1978. For more detail on the WEL–Cairns campaign see
     Cockburn, 'Towards a feminine manifesto', Ch. 3.
46   Degens, *From Canberra to Coffs Harbour*, p. 134.
47   NSW Women's Advisory Council to the Premier, *A Decade of Change*, pp. 190–92.
48   Katy Richmond, Letter to the *Age*, 4 November 1972.
49   'W.E.L. displays its colours', *News Weekly*, 30 November 1983; *News Weekly*, 18

January 1984; 'Unfair rebuke', Letter from Val Byth, WEL–Victoria, to the *Age*, 29 March 1984.

50   For example, *Ink-WEL* 3, Sept–Oct. 1990, p. 5.

51   'Labor Women top women's poll quiz', *Courier Mail*, 19 November 1972.

52   'WEL will take only equal pay and opportunity', *Australian*, 28 November 1973.

53   *WEL–ACT Newsletter* 31, October 1975, p. 4.

54   Kay Johnston, 'Lobbying: The past, the present and the future', WEL national conference, 1979, p. 2.

55   Owen, 'The political participation of women', p. 153.

56   'Female rights stand: Issue of jobs is raised', *Mercury*, 23 June 1973.

57   Margo Kingston, 'Just call me chairman', *Sydney Morning Herald*, 21 May 1996, p. 9.

58   'The battle for a vote in running women's shelter', *Examiner*, 6 August 1976; 'Shelter haggle', *Examiner*, 10 August 1976.

59   *Alive and WEL!* 153, September 1985, p. 7; Anna Grutzner, 'Howard says maternity leave may have to go', *Canberra Times*, 4 September 1986. In the end paid maternity leave stayed for public servants, although privatisation threatened its loss in agencies such as Telstra.

60   Pilita Clark, 'Liberal women reject "conscript" image', *Sydney Morning Herald*, 13 December 1989; 'The Liberal face of feminism', *WEL–Informed*, 205, October 1990, pp. 26–30.

61   WEL–SA, 'The Future of Women's Electoral Lobby as seen by the South Australian Group', paper for WEL national conference, 1973, p. 1.

62   Survey of WEL Membership, *Broadsheet* 2 (3), 1974.

63   Doe, 'Report on the Survey of WEL Members at the 1975 WEL National Conference', Table 12.

64   Martin, 'The women in WEL', p. 12.

65   Ibid, p. 24.

66   Dahlerup, *Comparing the Effect of the New Women's Movement in Various Countries*, p. 7.

67   Gracia Baylor MLC, quoted by Stephanie Bunbury in 'The Liberal who is at home in the House and the kitchen', *Age*, 22 February 1985.

68   Pauline Toner, *Australian Women's Weekly*, 19 May 1982, in Stephen Murray-Smith (ed.), *The Dictionary of Australian Quotations*, Melbourne, Heinemann, 1984, p. 263.

69   Sawer et al, *Representing Women in Parliament*, Introduction.

70   Haines, 'The political pathway', p. 18.

71   Cashmore, 'Two decades of determination', p. 20.

72   Bashevkin, *Women on the Defensive*; Sawer & Hindess, *Us and Them*.

73   Peter Walsh, quoted in Des Keegan, 'The telephone-book guide – to cutting govt spending', *Weekend Australian*', 18–9 April 1987, p. 17.

74   Peter Walsh, 'New class is just more of the same', *Australian Financial Review*, 28 August 1990, p. 13.

75   Mark Latham, 'The truth is out there, somewhere,' *Daily Telegraph*, 25 June 2001; 'ABC's exercise in symbolism,' *Daily Telegraph*, 9 July 2001.

76   M Ward, Convener of the Men's Confraternity Incorporated, submission to Review of the *Affirmative Action Act*, 1998.

77   John Howard, Transcript of radio interview with Alan Jones, 2UE, 16 March 1998.

78   Francis, 'Some more equal'.

79   'WEL aims to lessen discrimination', *Mercury*, 22 June 1973.

80   Mary Owen, 'Women unite for a better deal', Letter to the Editor, *Age*, 9 August 1979.

81   Ronda Fienberg, WEL history survey.

82   *WEL–NSW Newsletter* 26, September 1974, p. 6; 27, October 1974, p. 15.

83   'Sees need for help against "pills"', *Courier-Mail*, 6 December 1973.

84   Martin, 'The women in WEL', p. 40.

85   Lake, *Getting Equal*, p. 91ff.

86   *WEL–NSW Newsletter*, 20 (special conference edn), March 1974, pp. 2, 3, 20.

87   *WEL National Bulletin,* March 1984.

88   Graham, 'Through life in pursuit of equality', pp. 183–4; Smith, *Taxing Popularity*, pp.85–8.

89   'WEL backs change in Family Law Bill', *Australian*, 15 August 1974, p. 3.

90   'Women put Family Court in the dock', *Sydney Morning Herald*, 26 June 1978; 'Breakdown only grounds for divorce: WEL', *Age*, 12 January 1979; Jane Richardson, 'Women's group wants property rights for wives', *Australian*, 12 March 1981; 'Women's Electoral Lobby paper: Law not judges should decide distribution', *Canberra Times*, 14 March 1981.

91   Letter from WEL–ACT to the Parliamentary Counsel Office, *WEL–ACT Newsletter,* 17, 11 June 1974, p. 11.

92   Bruce Juddery, 'Women campaign to amend Superannuation Bill', *Canberra Times*, 23 April 1976.

93   Letter from Meredith Edwards to the Treasurer, on behalf of WEL–ACT, 22 August 1975.

94   *WEL National Bulletin*, October 1984.

95   MacKenzie, *Women in Australia*, pp. 60–78; Helen Hughes, 'The third sex', *Outlook*, 7 (1), February 1963, pp. 17–8; Encel, MacKenzie & Tebbutt, *Women and Society*.

96   Helen Wilson, 'Thirty years of MIA: A commemorative editorial', *MIA* 119, May 2006.

97   Dudley & Palmieri, 'Can ladies work here too Nanna?'

98   Warhurst, 'In defence of single-issue interest groups', pp. 389–90.

99   Phillips, 'New social movements in Canadian politics: On fighting and starting fires', p. 194; see also Dobrolowsky, 'Interest, identity and women's constitutional activism in Canada', p. 716.

100 McAllister & Studlar, 'Gender and representation among electoral candidates in Australia', p. 393.

101 WEL–Sydney, *Working WEL 1977*, p. 3.

102 'Women's preferences', *Mercury*, 14 June 1973; *WEL–ACT Newsletter* 19, 20 August 1974, p. 5.

Chapter 3

1   John Hamilton, 'What's behind the purple door at No. 16?', *Herald*, 7 March 1974.

2   Sawer, *Sisters in Suits*, p. 203.

3   Cited by Brankovich, 'Burning down the house', p. 209.

4   Jo Freeman [Joreen], 'The Tyranny of Structurelessness', reprinted by Words for Women, Glebe, NSW, 1972, p. 3.

5   McCarron Benson, *WEL Women*, Memorabilia 9; Summers, *Ducks on the Pond*, p. 277.

6   Dot Goodrick, 'Some reflections on early WEL Perth days', *Broadsheet*, March 2003, pp. 3, 7.

7   'The future of Women's Electoral Lobby as seen by the New South Wales Group', paper for WEL national conference, January 1973.

8   'Synopsis of WEL ACT Paper on Organisation', WEL national conference, January 1973; Sloniec, *WEL*, p. 30.

9   Summers, 'Where's the women's movement moving to?' pp. 410-11, and Hooper, 'Reform or revolution' pp. 84–6.

10   Sloniec, *WEL*, p. 34.

11   Robyn Greer & Jan Plummer, 'Administering an Unstructured Organisation – The Problems Thereof', WEL national conference, 1975.

12   *WEL–NSW Newsletter* 27, October 1974, p. 4; cf. *WEL–ACT Newsletter* 22,

November 1974, pp. 4–6.

13 Ryan, Autobiographical writing, p. 50.

14 Katy Richmond, Memo to WEL groups throughout Australia, 'Circulation of reports/submissions/kits etc', 18 August 1973.

15 *WEL–NSW Newsletter* 28, November 1974, p. 7.

16 *WEL–ACT Newsletter* 32, November 1975, pp. 1–2.

17 Costain, 'Representing Women', p. 23.

18 *WEL-NSW Newsletter*, February 1975, p. 10.

19 The selection committee consisted of Eva Cox, Sara Dowse, Carmel Niland, Gail Radford and Priscilla Todd.

20 Jane Elix, 'Who Should Speak Publicly for WEL?', paper presented to WEL national conference April 1987.

21 Lyons, 'Advocacy for low income Australians', p. 11.

22 Val Pitty, 'Green light for WEL?', *WEL–Informed* 204, September 1990, pp. 3–12.

23 *WEL–NSW Newsletter* 23, June 1974, p. 1; *WEL–NSW Newsletter* 26, September 1974, p. 1.

24 Barbara Coddington, 'The WEL office: Time for reconstruction', *WEL-NSW Newsletter* 23, June 1974, p. 5; Bielski, 'The history, organisation and achievements of WEL–NSW', p. 2.

25 Brankovich, 'Burning down the house', p. 78.

26 *Herald Sun*, 2 August 1995.

27 Letters to and from Cardinal Clancy, *WEL–Informed* 259, August 1995, p. 19–20.

28 'WEL fights Government, but gets favoured treatment', *News Weekly*, 19 August 1981, p. 5.

29 Sawer, 'Governing for the mainstream'.

30 'How bishops' IVF bid galvanised feminism', front page, *Weekend Australian*, 28–29 October 2000.

31 Freeman, 'The Tyranny of Structurelessness', p. 3.

32 These sections draw heavily on Sawer & Groves, 'The women's lobby'.

33 Taylor, 'Social movement continuity', p. 768.

34 'The fight will continue', *Sun-Pictorial*, 17 August 1978.

35 Marian Sawer chaired the organising committee.

36 For example, 'A peak organisation is what women need', *Canberra Times*, 11 February 2000.

37 O'Neil, 'A national women's organisation? Which way?', *Refractory Girl* 33, pp. 29–30.

38 'Don't shoot the messenger: WEL', *Australian Financial Review*, 30 July 1997; Sawer, 'Shooting the messenger'.

39 Figure from Listowner, Lin MacQueen, 1 December 2003.

40 Eveline, 'The politics of advantage', p. 140.

41 Lyons, 'Advocacy for low income Australians', p. 11.

42 *WEL–Informed* 262, November 1995, p. 35.

Chapter 4

1 Rhode, 'Media images, feminist issues', p. 691.

2 Suellen O'Grady, 'The state of half the nation', *Bulletin*, 11 September 1976.

3 John Sorell, 'A woman's guide to the poll: Full form on all the runners', *Herald*, 21 April 1972. Cf Trimble & Sampert, 'Who's in the game?'

4 Suzanne Baker, 'Resigned in disgust', *Bulletin*, 25 August 1973.

5 *Canberra Times*, 24 October 1972.

6 'WEL, it's girl talk', *Australian*, 17 January 1973.

7 *Herald*, 21 August 1973.

8 Van Gelder, 'The truth about bra-burners', p. 81.

9 Maximilian Walsh, 'The girls who take politics seriously', *Sun-Herald*, 9 October

1972, pp. 15, 20.

10   'Don't burn your bras: Poll talk to women', *Daily Telegraph*, 17 October 1972.

11   'No bras burnt – but women make a point', *Sunday Mail*, 9 March 1975.

12   Gloria Steinem, Letter to *Time* magazine, 9 October 2000; *Child Care (National Children's Services Program) Amendment Bill 1989*.

13   Martin, 'The women in WEL', p. 47.

14   Maddison & Scalmer, *Activist Wisdom*, pp. 217–8.

15   Lake, 'A republic for women?', pp. 1–2; *Saturday Evening Mercury*, 6 May 1972, p. 19; *Saturday Evening Mercury*, 12 August 1972, pp. 13.

16   *Canberra Times*, 2 January 1975.

17   See 'Rough for widows', Letter from Di Graham of WEL–NSW, *Sun-Herald*, 16 February 1975.

18   John Sorell, 'A woman's guide to the poll: Full form on all the runners', *Herald*, 21 April 1972. Cf Trimble & Sampert, 'Who's in the game?'

19   Preddy, *The WEL Herstory*, p. 8–11.

20   Yvonne Preston, 'Even the redoubtable WEL hasn't yet won over the Senate', *National Times*, 13 May 1974.

21   'For example, 'Candidates under fire from women', *Armidale Express*, 18 September 1972; '300 women will grill 4 poll candidates', *Daily Mirror*, 25 September 1972, p. 8; 'Women quiz candidates', *Tribune*, 24–30 October 1972; Candidates "grilled" in lobby poll', *Daily Mirror*, 9 November 1972; 'Candidates quizzed by Tas. Women', *Examiner*, 24 November 1972, p. 12; 'Abortion: Major parties quizzed', *Daily Telegraph*, 27 November 1972; 'State men to be quizzed by women', *Age*, 30 April 1973.

22   Anderson, 'A description and analysis of aspects of the Women's Electoral Lobby (Victorian Branch)', p. 55. Some 250 WEL members were involved in the local government surveys.

23   'Candidates face trial by women', *Examiner*, 28 November 1975; 'Leaders escape at early grilling', *West Australian*, 18 January 1989.

24   Tom Aikens, quoted in Reynolds, 'Changing feminisms', p. 209; Reynolds, *Living Politics*, pp. 90–94.

25   ABC-TV, *This Day Tonight*, 20 March 1974; Penrose, 'Women's Electoral Lobby', pp. 103–05.

26   'Victorian lawyer alleges media blackout', *Journalist*, August 1973, p. 2; 'WEL reminder for Hamer', *Australian Financial Review*, 12 June 1973.

27   *PM* transcript, ABC Radio, 1 August 1974.

28   'Balloons, crisps and icecreams to show they care', *Sydney Morning Herald*, 2 August 1974, p. 4.

29   Dowse, 'The women's movement's fandango with the State', p. 219.

30   'Hodgman hits back at WEL', *Mercury*, 23 June 1976.

31   'Keep top women's post, WEL tells PM', *Australian*, 6 October 1975, p. 1.

32   *Australian*, 8 October 1975.

33   *Herald*, 4 October 1975.

34   Naomi Mapstone, 'Women's lobby hits at erosion of rights', *Canberra Times*, 27 October 1997; Sue Monk, 'Govt eroding women's rights', *Courier-Mail*, 1 November 1997.

35   *WEL Broadsheet* 10 (10), 1983, p. 4. Quoted in Jasmina Brankovich, 'Burning down the House', Chapter 2.

36   Neil Swancott, 'Women launch attack on job training inequality', *Australian Financial Review*, 29 January 1974, pp. 3–4.

37   For example, Lyndsay Connors, 'WEL: Boost family allowances', *Age*, 23 January 1980; 'Income splitting does not recognise the needs of families with children', *Age*, 30 March 1981; 'Women opposed to income splitting', *Canberra Times*, 7 April 1981; 'System fair to women?', *Australian Women's Weekly*, 1 July 1981.

38   'Tyre man's humour was not deflated', *Advertiser*, 28 February 1974.

39   'Women plan strike protest', *Advertiser*, 9 September 1974.

40   'Silent vigil over Lords' rape ruling', *Sydney Morning Herald*, 12 May 1975.

41   Glezer & Mercer, 'Blueprint for a lobby', p. 172.

42   Anderson, 'A description and analysis of aspects of the Women's Electoral Lobby ', pp. 75–82.

43   Wendy Faulkes, WEL history survey.

44   Richmond, 'Notes on my first year and a half', p. 67.

45   Radio Adelaide, 'A History of Community Broadcasting', <http://www.radio. adelaide.edu.au/intro/history_com-radio.pdf> accessed 22 August 2006.

46   For example, 'Women's air talks are untuned', *Sunday Mail*, 9 November 1975, p. 16.

47   Richardson, *Belle on a Broomstick*, p. 177; *Belle the Bushie*, p. 141.

48   Karen Kissane, 'Whatever happened to WEL?', *Age*, 26 May 1982; 'Women's group "no" to tax cuts', *Age*, 5 October 1982.

49   For example, Lyndsay Connors, 'WEL: Boost family allowances', *Age*, 23 January 1980; 'Income splitting does not recognise the needs of families with children', *Age*, 30 March 1981; 'Women opposed to income splitting', *Canberra Times*, 7 April 1981; 'System fair to women?', *Australian Women's Weekly*, 1 July 1981. See also Sawer, *Sisters in Suits*, p. 58.

50   For example, 'Abortion bill: WEL hits out', *Mercury*, 13 March 1979; 'WEL seeks abortion support', *Northern Territory News*, 20 March 1979.

51   'Fund to fight abortion bill', *Canberra Times*, 3 May 1980.

52   *WEL National Bulletin* No. 2, 1979, p. 2.

53   For example, 'Women's groups support UN Convention', *Mercury*, 9 June 1983; 'Pact on women support', *Courier-Mail*, 23 July 1983; 'Women's groups support sex discrimination bill', *Canberra Times* 12 September 1983.

54   For example, 'Just a sop says lobby', *West Australian*, 6 June 1984; 'Women's lobby doubts value of action paper', *Australian Financial Review*, 7 June 1984'.

55   For example, 'Men still chain women to the kitchen sink', *Sydney Morning Herald*, 1 May 1992; 'Official: Men still more equal than women', *Canberra Times*, 1 May 1992.

56   For example, 'Battle of the sexes looms on tax', *Australian*, 11 April 1985; 'The taxing of families', *Age*, 22 May 1985; 'Home truths lined up for the July tax summit', *Australian*, 14 June 1985.

57   For example, Sue Neales, 'Three million voices take the tax fight to Canberra', *Australian Financial Review*, 21 February 1989; Rosemary West, 'Fixing the family injustices to close the gender gap', *Age*, 6 March 1989; Women's groups have say on tax reforms', *Sydney Morning Herald*, 6 March 1989.

58   Glenn Milne, 'Courting the ladies' favour', *Australian*, 8 May 1992; Tom Connors, 'Libs admit flop on fightback: Women find 90pc of prices up', *Canberra Times*, 6 May 1992, p. 1; Greg Roberts, 'Basics would cost more with GST', *Sydney Morning Herald*, 6 May 1992, p. 3; Ed Southorn, 'Warning on GST price rises: Most household items to cost more: survey', *Courier-Mail*, 5 May 1992, p. 3; Wallace Brown, 'Coalition moves to counter damaging survey on prices', *Courier-Mail*, 6 May 1992; Wallace Brown, 'From Senate flaw to supermarket floor', *Courier-Mail*, 9 May 1992.

59   Queensland Legislative Assembly Parliamentary Debates, 6 May 1992, p. 4986.

60   Margaret Carroll, WEL history survey.

61   For example, 'Buyer beware new wages bargaining', *Age*, 13 May 1992; 'Women's lobby critical of new industrial rules', *Courier-Mail*, 23 November 1992.

62   Interview with Dr Michael Wooldridge, *PM*, ABC Radio National, 22 January 2000; 'Minister says tampon campaign contrived', *AM*, ABC Radio National, 26 January 2000.

63   Michaela Kronemann, 'Taxing Australia's Women', <http://www.aeufederal.org. au/Women/Taxingaustwom.html>

64   'It's a bloody shame', *Feminist Wire*, 28 June 2000, <http://www.msmagazine.com/ news/uswirestory.asp?id=6140>

65   Australian Catholic Bishops Conference & Anor, Ex parte – Justice Sundberg C22/2000.

66   Chappell, *Gendering Government*, Chapter 5.

67   Sian Powell, 'Crossing the IVF line', *Australian*, 30 April 2001, p. 13.

68   Sian Powell, 'How bishops' IVF bid galvanised feminism', front page, *Weekend Australian*, 28–29 October 2000; 'IVF row before the High Court: Women's lobby challenges the church', *Canberra Times*, 30 April 2001, p. 2.

69   For example, 'PM should look beyond 1950s cardigan catalogues', WEL Media Release, 23 April 2002.

70   ABC-TV, *7.30 Report*, 14 August 2001.

71   Google search using the using the search terms Women's Electoral Lobby + IVF + High Court, 21 September 2006.

72   For example, 'High Court Ruling: EMILY's List congratulates Women's Electoral Lobby', 18 April 2002 <http://www.emilyslist.org.au/news/editorial.asp?id=111>

73   Press release posted on Ausfem-Polnet, 14 August 2000.

74   Denise Hussain, 'Essay on the development of the women's movement in Australia', 1975.

75   'Corporate Woman' was reinstated in 2004.

76   *Commonwealth of Australia Parliamentary Debates*, House of Representatives, 6 November 1973.

77   *Commonwealth of Australia Parliamentary Debates*, Senate, 30 March 1976; 7 October 1976; 4 October 1977.

78   *Commonwealth of Australia Parliamentary Debates*, Senate, 2 March 1978; 5 April 1978; 26 May 1977.

79   Leonard Radic, 'Suffragettes of the '70s', 'The female ranks divide', 'Liberation a battle on many fronts', *Age*, 22, 23, 24 September 1976. See also Barbara Hooks, 'Women and liberty', *Age*, 9 January 1976.

80   David Elias, 'Women at war', *Age*, 30 July 1979.

81   Yvonne Preston, 'Women's rights: How the shout of the '70s became just a whimper', *Sydney Morning Herald*, 6 October 1981.

82   Piers Akerman, 'Dissension in the ranks', *Telegraph Mirror*, 27 June 1995.

Chapter 5

1   Sawer, 'Gender equality in an era of governing for the mainstream'.

2   Taperell et al, *Sexism in Public Service*, pp. 79–80.

3   WEL–ACT, 'Comments on *Sexism in Public Service*', submitted to RCAGA, December 1975; WEL, '1975 Election Statement' (undated).

4   For example, Niki Savva, 'Help for women on way', *Sun-Pictorial*, 8 September 1976; 'Fraser paves way for women's advisory council', *Sydney Morning Herald*, 8 September 1976.

5   Ramsay, 'Policy activism on a "wicked issue"', pp. 259–60.

6   Sawer, 'Femocrats and ecorats'; Chappell, *Gendering Government*.

7   *Australian*, 3 October 1975.

8   EG Whitlam to Gail Wilenski, 4 November 1975.

9   Letter from Margaret L Bearlin and Elizabeth Blom for WEL–ACT to The Hon. EG Whitlam, 7 October 1975, published in *WEL–ACT Newsletter*, 31 October 1975, pp. 2–3.

10   For example, 'Women to protest over Govt cuts', *West Australian*, 27 January 1976; 'WEL set for big protest on Govt cuts', *Courier-Mail*, 28 January 1976; 'Women want guarantees on welfare', *Advertiser*, 28 January 1976; 'Keep benefits going

– women', *Advertiser*, 30 January 1976; 'Women get the chop: WEL', *Sun*, 30 January 1976.

11   For example, 'WEL joins fight to save Legal Aid service', *Mercury*, 4 May 1978; 'Legal Aid must keep doors open', *Mercury*, 12 June 1978; 'WEL blasts cutbacks in guidelines for legal aid', *Mercury*, 3 November 1978.

12   Sawer, 'Australia'.

13   'Lack of action criticised', *Canberra Times*, 17 November 1973; 'WEL wants law to prohibit discrimination in PS', *Canberra Times*, 5 August 1976.

14   For details of this campaign see Sawer, 'Life after Block'.

15   Deborah Hope, 'Women's job status in PS a farce, says lobby group', *Sydney Morning Herald*, 28 November 1991.

16   *Mercury,* 21 May 1975; *WEL–Tasmania Broadsheet*, June 1975.

17   Toni Jupe, 'Women's groups on attack', *Mercury*, 3 November 1983.

18   Niland, 'Women's Policy', pp. 184–5, 188.

19   'Women call for top advisor', *Northern Territory News*, 6 April 1979; 'Face up to issue – Women', *Northern Territory News*, 1 May 1979.

20   'Women back bid for adviser', *Northern Territory News*, 10 October 1979; 'Battle ahead for women's adviser', *Northern Territory News*, 24 October 1979.

21   'New call for women's adviser: WEL still fighting', *Northern Territory News*, 8 November 1979.

22   'WEL wants action on domestic violence', *Northern Territory News*, 27 February 1982.

23   Marsden, 'White knuckles and strong women', p. 137.

24   'Candidates know women's issues', *Courier-Mail*, 21 October 1983.

25   Marian Sawer, 'Feminism and the State workshop' and 'Feminism and the State: Five dilemmas', *WEL National Bulletin* 11 (12), Nov–Dec 1989.

26   Sawer et al, *Representing Women in Parliament*, Introduction.

27   Toni Jupe, 'Women's groups on attack', *Mercury*, 3 November 1983.

28   Judith Whelan, 'How the Libs are looking after women', *Sydney Morning Herald*, 4 May 1988; Balfour, 'Reclaiming power', pp. 107–8.

29   Meredith Doig for WEL–Victoria, Letter to the Prime Minister 29 May 1997, in *WEL–Informed* 279, June 1997, pp. 21–2.

30   Catherine Cusack, 'How an Electoral Lobby Failed in its Role', *Sydney Morning Herald*, 26 April 2004.

31   Jan Roberts, Posting on WEL-members e-list 17 December 2007.

32   *WEL–ACT Newsletter*, No. 17, 11 June 1974, p. 3.

33   Sawer, *Sisters in Suits*, p. 192.

34   Women's Information Service, *Women's Information – Women's Power*, p. 4.

35   'Getting married? So get moving', *Australian*, 3 November 1973. See also, 'Discrimination alleged in Pt Pirie Council', *Advertiser*, 31 October 1973.

36   *WEL–SA Newsletter* No. 28, May 1975, p. 13.

37   'WEL complains on job issue', *Mercury*, 13 August 1974.

38   Burnett, *History of WEL Perth*, p. 23.

39   'Response to WEL call', *Advertiser*, 28 November 1973; Parliament of South Australia, *Report of the Select Committee of the House of Assembly on the Sex Discrimination Bill, 1973–1974*, 16 October 1977, p. 2.

40   'The battle for rights', *Sydney Morning Herald*, 2 September 1976.

41   In 1989 another WEL activist, Clare Burton, succeeded Ziller as Director of Equal Opportunity in Public Employment.

42   Rita Erlich, '"Don't expect too much from equality bill"… but it's a start', *Sun-Pictorial*, 9 March 1977; Barbara Hooks, 'Equal opportunity bill "discriminatory"', *Age*, 8 March 1977.

43   *Australian Foreign Affairs Record*, July 1980, p. 240.

44   Senator Shirley Walters, Senate Hansard, 8 November 1983.

45 Senator Ron Boswell, Senate Hansard, 29 November 1983.
46 '"Radical feminists" attacked over Bill', *Canberra Times*, 21 February 1984.
47 Ryan, *Catching the Waves*, p. 242. See also Summers, Introduction, 2nd rev. edn, *Damned Whores and God's Police*, p. 17.
48 Ryan, *Catching the Waves*, p. 243; Magarey, 'The Sex Discrimination Act 1984'.
49 'Sex Discrimination Bill', *WEL National Bulletin* 7 (1), February 1984, pp. 6–7.
50 *Australian*, 22 March 1984.
51 Transcript of *Nationwide*, 5 June 1984, Senator the Hon. Susan Ryan and Lorelle Thompson (WEL).
52 Deborah Snow, 'Women's lobby doubts value of "action" paper', *Australian Financial Review*, 7 June 1984.
53 See Terry Connolly MLA to Marian Sawer, 11 March 1992, and Michael Lavarch MP to Marian Sawer, 25 February 1992.
54 Jane Dargaville, 'Agency to lose "affirmative action" name', *Canberra Times*, 18 December 1998.
55 Bielski, 'WEL NSW 1972–1997', p. 4.

Chapter 6

1 Quoted in Rosemary Neill, 'Women plan to tax the Treasurer', *Bulletin*, 7 March 1989.
2 Marsali MacKinnon, 'Squabbles mar push for better deal: Divided women's groups fight for a slice of the Budget', *Australian*, 27 March 1982.
3 'WEL wants welfare funds, not tax cuts', *Canberra Times*, 26 March 1982; 'WEL sets priorities', *NT News*, 12 May 1982; 'Women's group "no" to tax cuts', *Age*, 5 October 1982.
4 'WEL-defined portrayal of the distaff disadvantaged', *Canberra Times*, 16 April 1983.
5 Edwards, *Financial Arrangements within Families*.
6 WEL–Australia, 'Policy for Parents' brochure, 1980.
7 *WEL–ACT Newsletter* no. 22, November 1974, p. 6; 'WEL's anti-family tax policy', *News Weekly*, 26 September 1979; Ian Wilson, 'The case for income-splitting', *Bulletin*, 11 December 1979; Nancy Dexter, 'Flaws in tax proposed – Little help for needy', *Age*, 26 January 1980.
8 Apps, 'The high taxation of working families'.
9 *WEL Reports 1973–74*, p. 11.
10 Ryan, Autobiographical writing, p. 3.
11 'Minimum wage for all – WEL', *Sydney Morning Herald*, 28 February 1974. Those who worked with Ryan on the submission included Anne Conlon and Joan Willson (employed on the *Manufacturers' Monthly*).
12 Ryan, Autobiographical writing, p. 70; Ryan & Conlon, *Gentle Invaders*, p.169ff; Lyndall Ryan, 'Women's Electoral Lobby celebrates 30th anniversary of the adult minimum wage'.
13 The right to part-time work was won, but not the pro rata pay and conditions WEL had sought.
14 'Amendments worry WEL', *Sydney Morning Herald*, 25 November 1982.
15 Email from Winsome McCaughey, 19 December 2007.
16 Brennan, *The Politics of Australian Child Care*, 116–18.
17 *WEL–NSW Newsletter* 26, September 1974, p. 9.
18 Tom Roper MLA, Letter to *Australian*, 20 July 1974; *WEL–NSW Newsletter* 26, September 1974, p. 16.
19 Crispin Hull, 'Child-care expenses basis of tax appeal', *Canberra Times*, 6 July 1982.
20 *Commonwealth of Australia Parliamentary Debates*, House of Representatives, Vol. 86, p. 2873, 6 November 1973.
21 Submission on paid maternity leave adopted by WEL Sydney, 11 March 1973. Circularised to all WEL groups for endorsement and action.

22 Jackie Dent, 'Motherhood – too important to leave to women', *Sydney Morning Herald*, 4 October 1999.

23 Rachel Wynd, 'ILO – Maternity Protection', welmembers e-list, 10 September 1999.

24 Niland, 'NEAT and women', p. 40.

25 Editorial, *Quadrant*, December 2001; Eve Mahlab, 'Women are worst-hit of poor in Australia', *Age*, 10 May 1976.

26 '9pc female jobless rate, WEL says', *Canberra Times*, 6 July 1976, p. 3.

27 Press release from WEL Fifth National Conference, 19 February 1978.

28 *Australian*, 23 February 1983.

29 'Fund programs to fight sexism, Govt told', *Sydney Morning Herald*, 20 February 1978; 'WEL calls for end to school sexism', *Canberra Times*, 20 February 1978; 'Call to act on schools sexism', *Age*, 20 February 1978.

30 Wyndham, 'My doctor gives me pills to put *him* out of my misery'; Siedlecky & Wyndham, 'Women and abortion in Australia'.

31 Wainer, 'Abortion before the High Court', p. 138.

32 For example, 'Women's group fights to limit abortion test case', *Weekend Australian*, 14 September 1996, p. 5.

33 Merri Andrew, 'WEL–ACT', *Inkwel*, 4, October 2002, pp.17–18.

34 'Rape and the law', *Star*, 23 May 1981; *WEL–Darwin Newsletter*, September 1981. Cf 'Urgent need to alter rape laws', *Mercury*, 8 August 1983; 'Women hit delay on rape law', *Mercury*, 12 August 1983; Lisa McKee, 'WEL seeks wife rape law change', *Courier-Mail*, 20 December 1983.

35 See Frances & Gray, 'Unsatisfactory, discriminatory, unjust and inviting corruption'.

36 'ABC favours 2nd-rate male sport', *Canberra Times*, 11 July 1980; 'ABC inquiry told of sexist discrimination', *Sydney Morning Herald*, 11 July 1980; Elizabeth Lopez, 'Not enough women's sport in *Age*: Lobby', *Age*, 25 April 1992.

37 Wyndham, 'Ad men, subtract women'.

38 For more detail on this campaign see Sawer, 'Engendering Constitutional debate'.

39 Letter from Deputy Premier of WA to Robyn Murphy, WEL, 16 January 1980, CSD 73/63.

40 This account relies heavily on Robyn Murphy, who was a leader of the campaign to give parents name choice. See also *West Australian*, 24 October 1985; 31 October 1985.

41 Gwen Gray, 'New federalism spells doom for society's poor', *Canberra Times*, 18 October 1991.

42 For example, 'WEL fights for refuges', *Sun-Pictorial*, 22 July 1977; 'Women's shelters supported: WEL poll results', *Courier-Mail*, 9 November 1977.

43 'New federalism a bad deal: Women's groups', *Canberra Times*, 20 March 1991; Gwen Gray, 'New federalism won't attract the votes of women', *Canberra Times*, 14 June 1991.

44 See the section on competition policy and community services in WEL's 1996 'Women's Charter', *Ink–WEL*, No 1/2, 1996, pp.15–6.

45 Australia, Commonwealth/State Ministers' Conference on the Status of Women, 'Women's Interests Paper'.

46 Chappell, 'Federalism and social policy'; Gray, 'Women, federalism and women-friendly policies'.

47 Gray, 'Institutional, incremental and enduring'.

Chapter 7

1 Balfour, 'Reclaiming power', p. 107.

2 Sloniec, *WEL*, p. 20.

3 Richter, 'Political Participation and Political Change', p. 17.

4 Richter, 'Political Participation and Political Change', p. 30.

5   Wendy McCarthy, in Bowen, *Feminists Fatale*, p. 82.
6   Survey of reasons for being in WEL, *WEL-Newsletter*, November 1973, p. 3, cited in Burgmann, *Power and Protest*, p. 94.
7   Atkin, 'In retrospect', p. 96.
8   Lesley Wyer, WEL history survey.
9   Pat Vines (Kendall), WEL history survey.
10   Janet Grace Pine, 'WEL (Perth) as mothership', *Broadsheet*, April 2003, pp. 8-9. See also Richter, 'Reflections on WEL's Third National Conference', p. 35; Graham, 'Borrowing from each other', p. 3.
11   Enid Conochie, WEL history survey.
12   Dot Goodrick, 'Some reflections on early WEL Perth days', *Broadsheet*, March 2003, p. 7.
13   Meredith Hinchliffe, WEL history survey.
14   Rosemary Webb, personal communication, 4 February 2008.
15   Elizabeth Dawson, WEL history survey.
16   Helen Leonard, in Bowen, *Fabulous Fifties*, pp. 109, 111.
17   Iola Mathews, 'WEL's first half decade', *National Times*, 3-8 October 1977.
18   Martin, 'The Women in WEL', p. 49.
19   Sonia Humphrey, 'Barbara willing and able to ask why not?', *Australian*, 4 October 1984.
20   Richter, 'Political Participation and Political Change', p. 36.
21   Martin, 'The Women in WEL', pp. 34-8.
22   *WEL-NSW Newsletter*, February 1975, p. 11.
23   Sonia Humphrey, 'Feminist movement with a liberal touch', *Australian*, 19 April 1984.
24   Mary Anderson, WEL history survey.
25   Kate White, 'Is the women's movement turning inwards?', *National Times*, 20 May 1983.
26   Mark Skulley, 'MPs' applause greets anti-bias Bill', *West Australian*, 21 September 1984.
27   Friedman, *Free to Choose*.
28   Harris, *Women's Electoral Lobby*, p. 9.
29   See obituaries by Marian Sawer and Philippa Hall at <http://www.users.bigpond.com/rj_gj/clare/tributes.htm>
30   'Orange among the mandarins', *Age*, 7 October 1988.
31   Dowse, 'The plight of the femocrat', *National Times*, 22 April 1983.
32   WEL-Sydney, *Working WEL 1977*, p. 9.
33   Jo Wainer, WEL history survey.
34   Doe, 'Report on the Survey of WEL Members at the 1975 WEL National Conference', Table 30.
35   Graham, 'Through life in pursuit of equality', pp. 183-4.
36   Doe, 'Not according to the rules', p. 202.
37   Richter, 'Political Participation and Political Change', p. 18.
38   Nicholson, 'Sisterhood is powerful'.
39   Martin, 'The Women in WEL', pp. 30-33.
40   Richter, 'Political Participation and Political Change', p. 16.
41   Nicholson, 'Women must keep talking', p. 192.
42   Frances Rowland, WEL history survey.
43   Bielski, 'History, organisation and achievements of WEL NSW', p. 7.
44   Richardson, *Belle the Bushie*, p. 178.
45   Richter, 'Political Participation and Political Change', p. 7.
46   Bettina Arndt, 'Degrees of strain', *Sydney Morning Herald*, 14 October 1997.
47   John Woodrow, WEL history survey.

Chapter 8

1   WEL, *From the Gilded Cage*, p. 43.
2   Dahlerup, 'Continuity and waves in the feminist movement'; Sawer et al, 'Generations of advocacy'.
3   Quoted in Wendy Fatin, 'Celebrating WEL's 30th birthday: From the Guilds to WEL', *Broadsheet*, 1973.
4   Dahlerup, 'Continuity and waves in the women's movement'.
5   Sawer, 'Wearing your politics on your sleeve', p. 53; Maddison & Scalmer, *Activist Wisdom*, p. 232.
6   Taylor, 'Social movement continuity'.
7   Scalmer, *Dissent Events*.
8   Bagguley, 'Contemporary British feminism'.
9   Rischbieth, *March of Australian Women*; Paisley, 'Federalising the Aborigines?' pp. 248–66.
10   Martin, 'Polite lobbying', p. 206.
11   The IAW was formally constituted as the International Woman Suffrage Alliance in Berlin in 1904, became the International Women's Alliance in 1926 and took on its current name in 1946.
12   Eileen Powell, Report to the AFWV 14th Triennial Conference 1966; Russell & Sawer, 'The rise and fall of the Australian Women's Bureau'.
13   Mitchell, *50 Years of Feminist Achievement*, p. 76.
14   Alison Stephen to Henry Bland, 21 September 1966, National Archives of Australia MP 1143/1/0, 62/4100/74.
15   'So what's new about Women's Lib?', *Sun*, 11 September 1972.
16   Louise Mackay, Letter to Editor, *National Times*, 24 November 1975.
17   Jones, *In Her Own Name*, pp. 227–8; 333–4.
18   Szekeres, 'Out of the limelight'.
19   Murray, *Voice for Peace*, p. 1.
20   The NSW League of Women Voters, *Equality*, no. 225, December 1978, Dawn Section, pp. 3–4.
21   For the history of the Women's Service Guilds see Davidson, *Women on the Warpath*.
22   Cameron, 'WEL's ancestors', p. 5; Curthoys, 'Australian feminism since 1970', p. 15.
23   Szramka, 'The interrelationship between interest groups and social movement organisations', p. 107.
24   Margaret Allum, '… and ain't I a woman', *Green Left Weekly* 416, 16 August 2000.
25   For example, Outshoorn & Kantola, *Changing State Feminism*.
26   Iola Mathews, 'WEL's first half decade', *National Times*, 8 October 1977.
27   Strachey, Introduction, p. 10.
28   Patricia Rolfe, 'Whatever happened to feminism?', *Bulletin*, 4 December 1965, pp. 18–22.
29   *WEL Papers: 1980: A New Era for Women*, p. 2.
30   Sarah Maddison, convenor of Young WEL in NSW, 'Why feminism is a dirty word', Interview with Jan Bowen, *Sydney Morning Herald*, 9 June 1998.
31   Eva Cox in Bowen, *Feminists Fatale*, p. 134.
32   Nash, 'A movement moves', pp. 325–6.
33   Taylor, 'Social movement continuity'.
34   Martin, 'The Women in WEL', p. 8.
35   Kate White, 'Is the women's movement turning inward?' *National Times*, 20 May 1983; Harris, *Women's Electoral Lobby*, p. 1.
36   Rosemary Webb, personal communication, 4 February 2008.
37   Goldflam et al, *Hysterical Women* and *Hysterical Women '96*.
38   Justice John Gallop in *Canberra Times*, 24 December 1988; *WEL National Bulletin*,

February 1989; *WEL–Informed*, March 1989.

39   *WEL–Darwin Newsletter*, August 1982, p. 1.

40   Curthoys & McDonald, *More Than a Hat and Glove Brigade*.

41   Stevens, *A History of International Women's Day*, p. 23.

42   Information from Lucy Honan, 13 August 2007.

43   Dowse & Giles, 'Australia'.

44   Ross, 'Votes for women in Western Australia', p. 47.

45   Cabinet Decision 1667, 24 October 1961; EJ Bunting, Advice to the Prime Minister on 'Married Women in Public Service', 3 April 1962, in Sawer, *Removal of the Commonwealth Marriage Bar*, pp. 16, 17.

46   For example, 'Fighter for women until the very end', *Herald Sun*, 11 February 1997; 'Feminist fought the good fight', *Daily Telegraph*, 11 February 1997; 'Feminist godmother Ryan a fighter to the finish', *Australian*, 11 February 1997.

47   Bielski, 'Australian feminism 2004'.

REFERENCES

Books and articles

Aitkin, Jan, Julie Boyce, Caroline Graham, Wendy McCarthy & June Surtees (1973). 'The world of WEL (NSW)'. In Henry Mayer (ed.) *Labor to Power: Australia's 1972 election*, Sydney: Angus & Robertson, pp. 184–91.

Anderson, Doris (1972). 'The MPs who care and the MPs who don't'. *Chatelaine*, 45 (5), May.

Apps, Patricia (2004). 'The high taxation of working families'. *Australian Review of Public Affairs*, 5 (1): 1–24.

ASIO files on WEL (1972–73). Series Number A6122, Series Accession Number 2004/00686598, Canberra: National Archives of Australia.

Atkin, Elsa (1987). 'In retrospect'. In Jocelynne Scutt (ed.), *Different Lives*. Ringwood: Penguin, pp. 92–100.

Attwood, Pennly (1993). 'Rescue and a gift'. In Elizabeth Sloniec (ed.) *WEL: 21 years in South Australia*, Adelaide: WEL–SA, pp. 18–19.

Bagguley, Paul (2002). 'Contemporary British feminism: A social movement in abeyance?' *Social Movement Studies*, 1 (2): 169–85.

Baldock, Cora & Bettina Cass (eds) (1983; 1988). *Women, Social Welfare and the State*. Sydney: Allen & Unwin.

Balfour, Kath (1993). 'Reclaiming power'. In Jocelynne Scutt (ed.), *Glorious Age*. Melbourne: Artemis, pp. 99–108.

Bashevkin, Sylvia (1998). *Women on the Defensive: Living through conservative times*. Toronto: University of Toronto Press.

Bielski, Joan (1973). 'Women in the workforce: The State as employer'. *Australian Quarterly*, 45 (3): 66–77.

—— (2005). 'The history, organisation and achievements of WEL NSW', WEL–NSW <http://www.comcen.com.au>

—— (2005). 'Australian feminism 2004: Gains, losses, countervailing forces, some failures and sobering thoughts', *Social Alternatives*, 24 (2): 6–10.

Bowen, Jan (1998). *Feminists Fatale*. Sydney: HarperCollins.

—— (1995). *Fabulous Fifties*. Melbourne: Angus & Robertson.

Brennan, Deborah (1994). *The Politics of Australian Child Care*. Melbourne: Cambridge University Press.

Buchanan, Betsy (1976). 'Aborigines and the WEL conference'. *Aboriginal and Islander Forum*, 2 (1): p. 6.

Bulbeck, Chilla (1997). *Living Feminism*. Melbourne: Cambridge University Press.

Burgmann, Meredith (1982). 'Black sisterhood: The situation of urban Aboriginal women and their relationship to the white women's movement', *Politics* 17 (2): 259–72.

Burgmann, Verity (1993). *Power and Protest: Movements for change in Australian society*. Sydney: Allen & Unwin.

Burnett, Pat (1985). *History of Women's Electoral Lobby, Perth, Western Australia, 1973–1984*. Perth: WEL–WA.

Caine, Barbara, Moira Gatens, Emma Grahame, Jan Larbalestier, Sophie Watson &

Elizabeth Webby (eds), (1998). *Australian Feminism: A companion*. Melbourne: Oxford University Press.

Cameron, Barbara (1980). 'WEL's Ancestors'. In *WEL Papers*.

Campo, Natasha (2004). '"Childless but not by choice" or "24-hour women having it all?" Remembering Australian feminism.' *Lilith* 13: 106–16.

Cashmore, Jennifer (1993). 'Two decades of determination'. In Elizabeth Sloniec (ed.). *WEL: 21 years in South Australia*. Adelaide: WEL–SA, pp. 20–21.

Castley, Shirley & Kay Daniels (1974). 'WEL and sex roles'. *The WEL Papers*, 4–6.

Chappell, Louise (2001). 'Federalism and social policy: The case of domestic violence'. *Australian Journal of Public Administration*, 60 (1): 59–69.

—— 2002. *Gendering Government: Feminist engagement with the state in Australia and Canada*. Vancouver: University of British Columbia Press.

Coddington, Barbara (1974). 'The WEL office: time for reconstruction'. *WEL–NSW Newsletter* 23, June, 4–6.

Cohen, Marcia (1988). *The Sisterhood: The true story of the women who changed the world*. New York: Simon & Schuster.

Costain, Anne M. (1982). 'Representing women: The transition from social movement to interest group'. In Ellen M Boneparth (ed.). *Women, Power and Policy*, New York: Pergamon.

Curthoys, Ann (1994). 'Australian feminism since 1970'. In Norma Grieve & Ailsa Burns, *Australian Women: Contemporary feminist thought*. Melbourne: Oxford University Press.

Curthoys, Barbara & Audrey McDonald (1996). *More Than a Hat and Glove Brigade: The story of the Union of Australian Women*. Sydney: UAW.

Dahlerup, Drude (1990). *Comparing the Effect of the New Women's Movement in Various Countries*. Aarhus: Institute of Political Science, University of Aarhus.

—— (1993). 'From movement protest to state feminism: The women's movement and unemployment policy in Denmark.' *NORA. Nordic Journal of Women's Studies* 1: 4–21.

—— (2004). 'Continuity and waves in the feminist movement: A challenge to social movement theory.' In Hilda Rømer Christensen, Beatrice Halsaa & Aino Saarinen (eds). *Crossing Borders: Re-mapping women's movements at the turn of the 21st century*. Odense: University Press of Southern Denmark, 59–78.

Davidson, Dianne (1997). *Women on the Warpath: Feminists of the first wave*. Nedlands: University of Western Australia Press.

DeBats, Rosanne (1993). 'Reminiscing about WEL'. In Elizabeth Sloniec (ed.) *WEL: 21 years in South Australia*. Adelaide: WEL–SA, pp. 9–10.

Degens, Patricia A. (1999). *From Canberra to Coffs Harbour*. Coffs Harbour: Patricia Degens.

Dobrolowsky, Alexandra (1998). 'Interest, identity and women's constitutional activism in Canada'. *Canadian Journal of Political Science* 31: 707–42.

Doe, Edwina (1976). Report on the Survey of WEL Members at the WEL National Conference held in Sydney, January 1975.

—— (1995). 'Not according to the rules'. In Jocelynne Scutt (ed.) *Singular Women: Reclaiming spinsterhood*. Melbourne: Artemis.

Dowse, Sara (1983; 1988). 'The women's movement's fandango with the State: The movement's role in public policy since 1972.' In Cora Baldock & Bettina Cass (eds) *Women, Social Welfare and the State*. Sydney: Allen & Unwin, pp. 205–26.

Dowse, Sara & Pat Giles (1985). 'Australia: Women in a warrior society.' In Robin Morgan (comp.) *Sisterhood is Global*. Harmondsworth: Penguin.

Dudley, Janice & Sonia Palmieri (1999; 2003). 'Can Ladies Work Here Too Nanna? Gender and Australasian Politics Textbooks.' APSA Website <http://auspsa.anu.edu.au/about/wcaucus.htm#Reviews>

Eatock, Pat (1973). 'A small but stinging twig: Reflections of a black campaigner'.

In Henry Mayer (ed.) *Labor to Power: Australia's 1972 election*. Sydney: Angus & Robertson, pp. 152–4.

—— (1987). 'There's a snake in my caravan.' In Jocelynne Scutt (ed.), *Different Lives*. Ringwood: Penguin, pp. 22–31.

Edwards, Meredith (1981). *Financial Arrangements within Families: A Research Report for the National Women's Advisory Council*. Canberra: NWAC.

Elysee, Anne (1977). 'Women in party politics – Papers from the Women's Electoral Lobby Seminar, Sydney, July 1977'. *Australian Quarterly* 49 (3): 3–66.

Encel, Sol, Norman Mackenzie & Margaret Tebbutt (1974). *Women and Society: An Australian study*. Melbourne: Cheshire.

Eveline, Joan (1992). Survey of social characteristics of WEL–WA members. Perth: WEL WA.

—— (1994). 'The politics of advantage'. *Australian Feminist Studies* 19: 129–54.

Fasteau, Brenda Feigen & Bonnie Lobel (1972). 'Rating the candidates: Feminists vote the rascals in or out'. *Ms*. magazine, January.

Four Corners (1972). *The Hand that Rocks the Ballot Box*. 17-minute story on WEL. Shown on ABC television 7 October.

Frances, Raelene & Alicia Gray (2007). '"Unsatisfactory, discriminatory, unjust and inviting corruption": Feminists and the decriminalisation of street prostitution in New South Wales.' *Australian Feminist Studies* 22 (53): 307–25.

Francis, Babette (1994). 'Some more equal', Endeavour Forum (previously Women Who Want to be Women) website <http://www.endeavourforum.org.au>

Freeman, Jo [Joreen] (1972). 'The tyranny of structurelessness'. Reprinted from *The Second Wave* 2 (1), Glebe, NSW: Words for Women.

Friedan, Betty (1963). *The Feminine Mystique*. New York: WW Norton.

Friedman, Milton & Rose Friedman (1980). *Free to Choose*. London: Secker & Warburg.

Glezer, Helen & Jan Mercer (1973). 'Blueprint for a lobby: The birth of WEL as a social movement'. In Henry Mayer (ed.). *Labor to Power: Australia's 1972 election*. Sydney: Angus & Robertson, pp. 169–76.

Glezer, Helen, Jan Mercer & Pat Strong (1973). 'WEL strategy, 1972: The methods of a protest lobby'. In Henry Mayer (ed.). *Labor to Power: Australia's 1972 election*. Sydney: Angus & Robertson, 177–80.

Goldflam, Annie, Denise Morgan & Ruth Greble (eds) (1993). *Hysterical Women: A collection of 100 Australian feminist cartoons*. Perth: Women's Electoral Lobby (WA) Inc.

Goldflam, Annie, Elaine Murphy, Lorraine Hayden & Lorraine Ruth Greble (eds) (1996). *Hysterical Women: A collection of 100 Australian feminist cartoons*. Women's Electoral Lobby (WA) Inc.

Goodwin, Jeff, James M. Jasper & Francesca Polletta (eds) (2001). *Passionate Politics: Emotions and social movements*. Chicago: Chicago University Press.

Graham, Caroline (1974). 'Borrowing from each other: WEL and Women's Liberation.' In *The WEL Papers* 3–4; and in Jan Mercer (ed.) (1975; 1977), *The Other Half: Women in Australian society*. Ringwood, Vic: Penguin, 421–26.

Graham, Di (1987). 'Through life in pursuit of equality.' In Jocelynne Scutt, *Different Lives*. Ringwood: Penguin, 179–87.

Grahame, Emma (1998). 'Researching WEL'. In Barbara Caine et al (eds), *Australian Feminism: A Companion*. Melbourne: Oxford University Press.

Gray, Gwendolyn (2006). 'Women, federalism and women friendly policies.' *Australian Journal of Public Administration* 65 (1): 25–45.

—— (2008). 'Institutional, incremental and enduring: Women's health action in Australia and Canada'. In Sandra Grey & Marian Sawer (eds), *Women's Movements: Flourishing or in abeyance?* London & New York: Routledge.

Greer, Germaine (1970). *The Female Eunuch*, London: MacGibbon & Kee.

Grimshaw, Patricia & Lynne Strahan (1982). *The Half-Open Door: Sixteen modern Australian women look at professional life and achievement*. Sydney: Hale & Iremonger.

Gunn, Heather (1999). 'Women's Political Mobilisation in Rural Victoria: The 1970s Remembered.' Oral History Association of Australia National Conference, State Library of Victoria, 2–5 September.

Haines, Janine (1993). 'The political pathway'. In Elizabeth Sloniec (ed.) *WEL: 21 Years in South Australia*. Adelaide: WEL SA, 17–19.

Harris, Rosemary (1983). *Women's Electoral Lobby: An essay*, Canberra: WEL-Australia.

Henderson, Margaret (2006). *Marking Feminist Times: Remembering the longest revolution in Australia*. Bern: Peter Lang AG.

Hughes, Kate Pritchard (ed.) (1994). *Contemporary Australian Feminism*. Melbourne: Longman Cheshire.

Humphreys, Dany (1974). 'Conform you little bastards or else'. In *The WEL Papers*. Mentone, Victoria: WEL, 14–16.

Jones, Helen (1986). *In Her Own Name: A history of women in South Australia from 1836*. Adelaide: Wakefield Press.

Lake, Marilyn (1999). 'A Republic for Women?' Pamela Denoon Lecture, Canberra, 9 March <http://www.wel.org.au/announce/denoon/99mlake.htm>

—— (1999). *Getting Equal: The history of Australian feminism*. Sydney: Allen & Unwin.

Lake, Marilyn & Farley Kelly (eds) (1985). *Double Time: Women in Victoria—150 Years*. Ringwood: Penguin.

Luck, Marjorie (1987). 'Not a dinner party'. In Jocelynne Scutt, *Different Lives*, Ringwood: Penguin, pp. 102–7.

Lyons, Mark (1995). 'Advocacy for Low Income Australians: The ACOSS Experience.' Paper presented to the Independent Sector Spring Research Forum, Alexandria, Virginia, 23–24 March.

McAllister, Ian & Donley Studlar (1992). 'Gender and representation among legislative candidates in Australia.' *Comparative Political Studies* 25 (3): 388–411.

McCarron Benson, Julie (1991). *WEL women: Recollections of some of the first WEL–ACT women*. Canberra: WEL ACT.

McCarthy, Wendy (2000). *Don't Fence Me In*. Sydney: Random House.

McCulloch, Deborah (1993). 'Twenty-one years old!' In *WEL: 21 Years in South Australia 1972–1993*. Adelaide: Women's Suffrage Centenary.

MacKenzie, Norman (1962). *Women in Australia*. Melbourne: Cheshire.

Maddison, Sarah & Sean Scalmer (2006). *Activist Wisdom: Practical knowledge and creative tension in social movements*. Sydney: UNSW Press.

Magarey, Susan (1977). 'And now we are six: A plea for women's liberation.' *Refractory Girl* 4.

—— (2004). 'The Sex Discrimination Act'. *Australian Feminist Law Journal* 20: 127–34.

Marsden, Val (1996). 'White Knuckles and Strong Women'. In Jocelynne Scutt, *Living Generously: Women mentoring women*, Melbourne: Artemis, 130–43.

Martin, Elaine Wilson (1999). '"Polite lobbying": The Australian Federation of Women Voters and its allies in the Australian post-war women's movement.' In Joy Damousi & Katherine Ellinghaus (eds), *Citizenship, Women and Social Justice*. History Department, University of Melbourne, 204–16.

Mayer, Henry (ed.) (1973). *Labor to Power: Australia's 1972 Election*. Sydney: Angus & Robertson.

Mercer, Jan (ed.) (1975; 1977). *The Other Half: Women in Australian society*. Ringwood, Vic: Penguin.

—— (1975). 'The history of the Women's Electoral Lobby.' In Jan Mercer, *The Other Half: Women in Australian society*. Ringwood, Vic: Penguin, 395–404.

Mercer, Jan & Don Miller (1975). 'Liberation – reform or revolution?' In Jan Mercer, *The Other Half: Women in Australian society*. Ringwood, Vic: Penguin, 447–73.

Mitchell, Winifred (1979). *50 Years of Feminist Achievement: A History of the United Associations of Women*. Sydney: United Associations of Women.

Morgan, Robin (comp.) (1985). *Sisterhood is Global*. Harmondsworth: Penguin.

Murray, Kaye (2005). *Voice for Peace: The spirit of social activist Irene Greenwood 1898–1992.* Bayswater, WA: Kaye Murray.

Nash, Kate (2002). 'A women's movement moves … Is there a women's movement in England today?' *European Journal of Women's Studies* 9 (3): 311–28.

Nicholson, Joyce (1982). 'Destination uncertain'. In Patricia Grimshaw & Lynne Strahan (eds). *The Half-Open Door: Sixteen modern Australian women look at professional life and achievement.* Sydney: Hale & Iremonger, 136–53.

—— (1985). '"Sisterhood is powerful": A memoir'. In Marilyn Lake & Farley Kelly (eds). *Double Time: Women in Victoria – 150 Years.* Ringwood: Penguin, 445–53.

—— (1996). 'Women must keep talking'. In Jocelynne Scutt (ed.), *Living Generously: Women mentoring women.* Melbourne: Artemis, 187–98.

Niland, Carmel (1977). 'NEAT and women: The promise and the reality', *Women and Politics Conference 1975*, Vol. 2, Canberra: AGPS: 39–45.

—— (2006). 'Women's policy'. In Troy Bramston (ed) *The Wran Era.* Leichhardt: Federation Press.

NSW Women's Advisory Council to the Premier (1987). *A Decade of Change.* Sydney: NSW Government Printer.

O'Neil, Pam (1989). 'A national women's organisation? Which way?' *Refractory Girl* 33: 29–30.

O'Shane, Pat (1976). 'Is there any relevance in the women's movement for Aboriginal women?' *Refractory Girl,* September: 31–4.

Outshoorn, Joyce & Johanna Kantola (eds) (2007). *Changing State Feminism.* Houndmills: Palgrave McMillan.

Owen, Mary (1980). 'The political participation of women'. *Labor Essays 1980.* Melbourne: Drummond, 132–54.

Paisley, Fiona (1998). 'Federalising the Aborigines? Constitutional reform in the late 1920s.' *Australian Historical Studies* 29 (11): 248–66.

Penrose, Sandra (1976). 'The Women's Electoral Lobby'. In GS Reid (ed.), *The Western Australian Elections – 1974.* Nedlands: Department of Politics, University of Western Australia, 103–5.

Phillips, Susan D. (1994). 'New social movements in Canadian politics: On fighting and starting fires'. In James Bickerton & Alain Gagnon (eds), *Canadian Politics.* Toronto: Broadview, 188–206.

Preddy, Elspeth (1985). *Women's Electoral Lobby: Australia/New Zealand 1972–1985.* Wellington: WEL–Australia and WEL–New Zealand.

—— (2003). *The WEL Herstory: The Women's Electoral Lobby in New Zealand 1975–2002.* Wellington: WEL–New Zealand and Fraser Books.

Reade, Katy (1994). '"Struggling to be heard": Tensions between different voices in the Australian Women's Liberation Movement in the 1970s and 1980s'. In Kate Pritchard Hughes (ed.), *Contemporary Australian Feminism.* Melbourne: Longman Cheshire, 198–222.

—— (1996). 'Limited gestures, white feminists and aboriginal women in the 1970s women's movement.' In Pat Grimshaw & Diane Kirby (eds), *Dealing with Differences: Essays in gender, culture and history.* Melbourne: Network for Research in Women's History, 118–29.

Ramsay, Janet (2007). 'Policy activism on a "wicked issue": The building of Australian feminist policy on domestic violence in the 1970s'. *Australian Feminist Studies* 22 (53): 247–64.

Reid, Elizabeth (1986). 'Creating a policy for women.' In Australian Fabian Society (ed.), *The Whitlam Phenomenon.* Melbourne: McPhee Gribble.

Reynolds, Margaret (2004). 'Changing feminisms – a personal view'. *Hecate* 30 (1): 206–11.

—— (2007). *Living Politics.* St Lucia: University of Queensland Press.

Rhode, Deborah L (1995). 'Media images, feminist issues'. *Signs* 20 (3): 685–710.

Richardson, Pat (1990). *Belle the Bushie*. Rozelle, NSW: Gumleaf Press.
—— (1992). *Belle on a Broomstick*. Rozelle, NSW: Gumleaf Press.
Richmond, Katy (1974). 'Notes on my first year and a half'. *The WEL papers*, 65–70.
Richter, Juliet (1975). 'Women in politics: Reflections on WEL's Third National Conference'. *Refractory Girl* 9: 35–40.
Rischbieth, Bessie (1964). *March of Australian Women: A record of fifty years' struggle for equal citizenship*. Perth: Paterson Brokensha.
Roberts, Jan & Bev Stewart (1999). *We're Not Ladies, We're Women*. Wagga Wagga: Wagga Women's Health Centre.
Ross, Williamina (1952). 'Votes for women in Western Australia', *Western Australian Historical Review* 4 (4): 44–54.
Russell, Lani & Marian Sawer (1999). 'The Rise and fall of the Australian Women's Bureau'. *Australian Journal of Politics and History* 45 (3): 362–75.
Ryan, Edna (1972–75). Autobiographical writing, Papers of Edna Ryan, National Library of Australia, MS 9140, Box 1.
Ryan, Edna & Anne Conlon (1975). *Gentle Invaders: Australian women at work 1788–1974*. Melbourne: Nelson.
Ryan, Lyndall (2004). 'Women's Electoral Lobby celebrates the 30th anniversary of the adult minimum wage'. *Ink–WEL*, April: 2–3.
Ryan, Susan (1999). *Catching the Waves: Life in and out of politics*. Sydney: Harper Collins.
Sawer, Marian (1988). 'Life after Block—EEO in the Australian Public Service.' *Canberra Bulletin of Public Administration* 54: 125–9.
—— (1990). *Sisters in Suits: Women and public policy in Australia*. Sydney: Allen & Unwin.
—— (1996) 'Femocrats and Ecorats: Women's Policy Machinery in Australia, Canada and New Zealand'. UNRISD Occasional Paper. Geneva: UNRISD.
—— (ed.) (1997). *The Removal of the Commonwealth Marriage Bar: A documentary history*. Centre for Research in Public Sector Management, University of Canberra.
—— (1997). '"Shooting the messenger": Australia and CEDAW'. *Proceedings of the Australasian Political Studies Association Conference*. Department of Politics, Flinders University: 897–906.
—— (1998) 'Engendering constitutional debate'. *Alternative Law Journal* 23 (2): 78-81.
—— (2002). 'Governing for the mainstream: Implications for community representation.' *Australian Journal of Public Administration* 61 (1): 39–49.
—— (2002). 'Australia: The mandarin approach to gender budgets'. In Debbie Budlender & Guy Hewitt (eds), *Gender Budgets Make More Cents*. London: Commonwealth Secretariat.
—— (2003). *The Ethical State? Social liberalism in Australia*. Melbourne: Melbourne University Press.
—— (2005). 'Gender Equality in an Era of Governing for the Mainstream', paper to UN Division for the Advancement of Women Expert Group Meeting, Rome, 2004 <http://www.un.org/womenwatch/daw/egm/nationalm2004>
—— (2007). 'Wearing your politics on your sleeve: The role of political colours in social movements.' *Social Movement Studies* 6 (1): 39–56.
Sawer, Marian & Abigail Groves (1994). 'The women's lobby: Networks, coalition building and the women of middle Australia.' *Australian Journal of Political Science* 29 (3): 435–59.
—— (1994). *Working from Inside: Twenty years of the Office of the Status of Women*. Canberra: AGPS.
Sawer, Marian & Barry Hindess (eds) (2004). *Us and Them: Anti-Elitism in Australia*. Perth: API Network.
Sawer, Marian, Jasmina Brankovich & Gail Radford (2006). 'Generations of advocacy'. In Louise Chappell & Deborah Brennan (eds), *No Fit Place for Women? Women in NSW politics*. Kensington: University of NSW Press, 200–24.
Sawer, Marian, Manon Tremblay & Linda Trimble (eds) (2006). *Representing Women in*

Parliament: A comparative study. London and New York: Routledge.

Scalmer, Sean (2002). *Dissent Events: Protest, the media and the political gimmick in Australia*. Sydney: University of NSW Press.

Scutt, Jocelynne (1983). 'Legislating for the right to be equal'. In Cora Baldock & Bettina Cass (eds) (1983; 1988). *Women, Social Welfare and the State*. Sydney: Allen & Unwin, 227–48.

—— (1987). *Different Lives*. Ringwood, Victoria: Penguin.

—— (1993). *Glorious Age*. Melbourne: Artemis.

—— (1996). *Living Generously: Women mentoring women*. Melbourne: Artemis.

Siedlecky, Stefania & Diana Wyndham (1994). 'Women and abortion in Australia'. In Alice Yotopoulos-Marangopolous (ed.) *Women's Rights: Human Rights*. Athens: Hestia.

Sloniec, Elizabeth (ed.) (1993). *WEL: 21 years in South Australia*. Adelaide: WEL SA.

Smith, Julie (2004). *Taxing Popularity: The story of taxation in Australia*. Sydney: Australian Tax Research Foundation.

Stevens, Joyce (1985). *A History of International Women's Day in Words and Images*. Marrickville: IWD Press.

Strachey, Ray (1936). 'Introduction'. In Ray Strachey (ed.) *Our freedom and its results*. London: Hogarth Press.

Summers, Anne (1975). 'Where's the women's movement going to?' In Jan Mercer (ed.), *The Other Half: Women in Australian society*. Ringwood, Vic: Penguin, 405–20.

—— (1975). *Damned Whores and God's Police*. Ringwood, Victoria: Penguin.

—— (1979). 'Women'. In Allan Patience & Brian Head (eds), *From Whitlam to Fraser*. Melbourne: Oxford University Press, 189–200.

—— (1999). *Ducks on the Pond*. Maryborough: Viking.

Szekeres, Viv (2006). 'Out of the limelight: The League of Women Voters at the time of the Great War'. Paper presented to conference on 'The Great War and its Aftermath', Adelaide: History Trust of South Australia.

Taperell, Kathleen, Carol Fox & Margaret Roberts (1975). *Sexism in Public Service* (RCAGA Discussion Paper No. 3). Canberra: AGPS.

Taylor, Anthea (2004). 'Readers writing *The First Stone* media event: Letters to the editor, Australian feminisms and mediated citizenship'. *Journal of Australian Studies* 83: 75–87.

Taylor, Verta (1989). 'Social movement continuity: The women's movement in abeyance.' *American Sociological Review* 54 (5): 761–75.

Teather, Elizabeth (1993). 'The Past and Present Mandate of the Country Women's Association of New South Wales'. Paper for Conference on Interest Groups and Political Lobbying, Politics Department, University of New England.

Tilly, Charles (2004). *Social Movements, 1768–2004*. Boulder, CO: Paradigm Publishers.

Trimble, Linda & Shannon Sampert (2004). 'Who's in the game? The framing of the 2000 election by the *Globe and Mail* and the *National Post*'. *Canadian Journal of Political Science* 37: 51–71.

Van Gelder, Lindsy (1992). 'The truth about bra-burners'. *Ms.* magazine, September: 80–81.

Vickers, Jill, Pauline Rankin & Christine Appelle (1993). *Politics as if Women Mattered*. Toronto: University of Toronto Press.

Wainer, Jo (1997). 'Abortion before the High Court'. *Australian Feminist Law Journal*, 8: 133–38.

Warhurst, John (1998). 'In defence of single-issue interest groups.' In David W. Lovell, Ian McAllister, William Maley & Chandran Kukathas (eds), *The Australian Political System*, 2nd edn. Melbourne: Longman, 389–93.

WEL (1974). *From the Gilded Cage*. Dulwich Hill, NSW: WEL Sydney.

WEL (1974). *The WEL Papers: The national journal of the Women's Electoral Lobby 1973/4*. Mentone, Vic: WEL and Alexander Bros.

WEL (1974). *WEL Reports 1973–74*. Dulwich Hill, NSW: WEL Sydney.

WEL (1980). *The WEL Papers: 1980: A New Era for Women*. Melbourne: WEL–Victoria.

WEL–Sydney (1977). *Working WEL 1977*, 5th Annual WEL Conference, Brisbane.

Whittick, Arnold (1979). *Woman into Citizen*. London: Athenaeum.

Women's Information Service (2003). *Women's Information – Women's Power: A brief history of the Western Australian Women's Information Referral Exchange*. Women's Information Service, Office for Women's Policy, Dept for Community Development.

Wyndham, Diana (1982). 'My doctor gives me pills to put *him* out of my misery'. *New Doctor* 23: 21–5.

—— (1987). 'Ad men, subtract women: Profit without honour'. *Media Information Australia*, August: 52–7.

Theses

Anderson, Peter (1973). 'A description and analysis of aspects of the Women's Electoral Lobby (Victorian branch)'. BA Hons, Politics, La Trobe University.

Asher, Louise (1980). 'The Women's Electoral Lobby: An historical inquiry'. MA, History, University of Melbourne.

Brankovich, Jasmina (2007). 'Burning Down the House: Feminism, politics and women's policy in Western Australia 1972–98'. PhD, School of Humanities, University of Western Australia.

Cockburn, Marjory (1999). 'Towards a Feminine Manifesto: The history of the Women's Electoral Lobby, Cairns'. BA Hons, School of History and Politics, James Cook University.

Cooper, Margaret (1999). 'The Australian Disability Rights Movement: Freeing the power of advocacy'. MA, School of Social Work, University of Melbourne.

Edwards, Daniel (2005). 'The Use of Internet Communications Technologies by Global Social Movements in Australia'. PhD, Political Science, Arts Faculty, Australian National University.

Gorring, Pam (1978). 'The Political Development of the Women's Movement in Queensland'. BA Hons, Government Department, University of Queensland.

Grey, Madeline (2005). 'Second-Wave Feminism and Women's Political Representation in Victoria, 1972–1997'. PhD, History Dept, University of Melbourne.

Hill, Elizabeth (1987). 'Working Within the System: The Women's Electoral Lobby fifteen years on'. BA Hons, Government Department, University of Sydney.

Hooper, Anne (1973). 'The Emergence of Contemporary Feminist Groups in Australia: With special reference to the Women's Liberation Movement and the Women's Electoral Lobby in the ACT.' BA Hons, Political Science, The Faculties, Australian National University.

Martin, Ruth (1981). 'The Women in WEL'. BA Hons, History, Monash University.

Munro, Bev (1982). 'A Survey of Sydney WEL 1972–1982'. Report of a fieldwork placement for a BSocStud, University of Sydney.

Nicholson, Joyce (1991). 'The Women's Electoral Lobby and Women's Employment: Strategies and outcomes'. MA, Women's Studies, History, University of Melbourne.

Pott, Omega (1981). 'WEL as a Social Movement'. BA Hons, History, University of Melbourne.

Richter, Juliet (1974). 'Political Participation and Political Change'. Unfinished MA thesis, Department of Government, University of Sydney.

Szramka, Annabel (1986). 'The Interrelationship between Interest Groups and Social Movement Organisations: The experience of WEL 1972–1983'. BA Hons, Politics, University of Tasmania.

Watson, Louise (1982). 'The Women's Electoral Lobby 1972–1982: Sites of conflict in non-party feminism'. BA Hons, Politics, University of Melbourne.

INDEX